RUSSELL
BRAND &
KATY
PERRY *The Love Story*

RUSSELL BRAND & KATY PERRY
The Love Story

Dave Stone

JOHN BLAKE

Published by John Blake Publishing Ltd,
3 Bramber Court, 2 Bramber Road,
London W14 9PB, England

www.johnblakepublishing.co.uk

First published in paperback in 2010

ISBN: 978 1 84454 991 7

British Library Cataloguing-in-Publication Data:

A catalogue record for this book is available from the British Library.

Design by www.envydesign.co.uk

Printed in Great Britain by CPI Bookmarque, Croydon, CR0 4TD

1 3 5 7 9 10 8 6 4 2

Papers used by John Blake Publishing are natural, recyclable products
made from wood grown in sustainable forests. The manufacturing
processes conform to the environmental regulations of the country
of origin.

Every attempt has been made to contact the relevant copyright-holders,
but some were unobtainable. We would be grateful if the appropriate
people could contact us.

'AS AN INDIVIDUAL, WE'RE ALL JUST BORN AND WE'RE GONNA DIE AND WHATEVER WE ACHIEVE IN THE CONTEXT OF THE UNIVERSE, WHETHER YOU'RE BOBBY MOORE AND YOU'VE WON THE WORLD CUP OR YOU DIE A PENNILESS BUM, THE VIEW FROM JUPITER WOULD REGARD YOU AS INSIGNIFICANT REGARDLESS,'

RUSSELL BRAND

Contents

Contents

INTRODUCTION

Marry Me, Katy

THE NEWS BROKE JUST AFTER NEW YEAR. NEWS THAT A FEW MONTHS EARLIER SIMPLY WOULD NOT HAVE SEEMED POSSIBLE. BUT THE REAL SURPRISE WAS – IT WASN'T EVEN A SURPRISE.

Russell Brand – the flamboyant, wild-haired bad boy of British comedy, the former drug addict, recovering alcoholic and notoriously randy snake-hipped motormouth fop – was engaged to be married to Katy Perry – the candy-coloured, all-American pop star, daughter of evangelical Christian parents, and his girlfriend of not much more than three months.

It happened on New Year's Eve, in the city of Jaipur in India – and elephants were involved. But really, after the events of the preceding 100 days or so, who could possibly be shocked?

Four months earlier they had barely known each other. Their previous encounters had been limited to an awards ceremony and on a film set. Then, a year after meeting at

1

an awards show where Russell was the controversial host, they met again – at the same show where he was again the controversial host. That's when it all started to happen: an extraordinary, intoxicating, breathless, globe-spanning and very passionate love affair.

It began in the hours following the 2009 MTV Video Music Awards in New York. Then it continued on a secret holiday to Thailand, where things got serious. From that point onwards, the romance had bounced between London and Los Angeles, but also managed to include important diversions to Paris, Berlin and the Austrian Alps. And now India.

That incredible, whirlwind few weeks had seen them make out for the first time in New York, while Lady Gaga and her entourage danced nearby. It had seen Russell recite love poetry to Katy in Thailand, and then in recording studios in Los Angeles. And it had seen Katy wear a sexy outfit in honour of Russell's favourite football team in front of millions of TV viewers.

Russell Brand and Katy Perry, two of the biggest and brightest names in showbusiness, had entranced each other – and a watching world, intrigued, astonished but also delighted to see these two very talented and fiercely independent spirits come together.

The proposal itself? It was perhaps the most extraordinary and most romantic moment of all. In India, there really was an elephant, a guru who blessed the couple, fireworks and a big engagement ring – hidden in a bouquet of flowers. Russell had planned everything himself with some precision – and was only prevented from proposing to Katy on the back of the elephant when the poor creature became spooked by the fireworks.

But when the announcement of the engagement came, it really wasn't that unexpected. It was obvious within a few weeks of Russell and Katy getting together that they were completely mad for each other. Less than a month into their relationship, the L word was being regularly used in the papers, magazines and gossip websites. And this was not a manufactured media story – this was completely genuine.

At the beginning of October, less than three weeks after the MTV event, Russell told startled reporters outside his London home, 'I think I'm in love'. A couple of days later, Katy was telling her Twitter followers that she was 'in a love K-hole' and then tweeting lyrics to songs about falling in love in Paris (where she was with Russell).

'She's amazing,' said Russell of Katy in a radio interview a few weeks later. 'I'm having a right laugh. She's a good person to spend time with and it's changed me. It's made me stop doing stuff that I probably shouldn't have been doing.'

Meanwhile Katy was busy tweeting her love for 'Rustyrockets' (Russell's Twitter name) – and displaying it on the back of her frilly knickers at the MTV European Music Awards.

Katy also revealed her feelings in a big magazine interview that came out just as their engagement was announced. 'He could slay anybody with the things he says. He doesn't even need his fists,' she said, before hinting at a different side of Russell Brand. 'I'm excited to find a partner who can just be my teammate... It's easy for me to steamroll guys. I need a man who tells me the party's over.'

But has Russell really changed? There is no getting away from the fact that his romance with Katy and their engagement has been an extraordinary state of affairs. After all, this is Russell Brand we're talking about, and Russell is not your average 34-year-old bloke. He's not even your average Jack-the-Lad who fancies himself as a ladies man. He's Russell Brand, the notorious and incorrigible womaniser who has bedded thousands of women – often several at a time.

This is the man who has regarded it his sworn duty to seduce as many females as possible, for as much of the time as possible. He's the man who has held the *Sun*'s infamous title of Shagger of the Year three years in succession (the tabloid has now renamed it the Russell Brand Shagger of the Year Award in his honour).

Even though his occasionally camp manner has meant he has often (in his less famous days) been mistaken for being gay, Russell is a 6ft 2in sex machine whose rapid-fire gift of the gab, razor-sharp wit and (beneath the scruffy appearance) dark good looks have made him irresistible to countless women. Russell has been wholeheartedly committed to shagging all of them – and his fame and notoriety has only made him more attractive to the female sex.

Russell's conquests have included the famous, the not-so-famous, the attractive and the not-so attractive. He's not been that choosy. Even in professional situations, female journalists and interviewers, young and not so

4

young, have been prey to his attentions. This is a man who has seriously flirted with Vanessa Feltz.

Russell's relentless obsession with bedding as many women as possible had led him to a sex addiction clinic in 2005 – recognition that this might be more than simply the natural urges of a virile young chap, but behaviour verging on the compulsive and self-destructive. Then there were the other issues, well documented down the years – the drugs and the booze that brought him to the brink of disaster.

Russell had escaped a depressing and fairly lonely childhood in Essex to achieve minor fame as young comic and TV presenter. But he had lost almost everything due to his dependencies on heroin, crack and the demon drink. Somehow he had recovered, after which talking about his hopeless addictions provided a lot of very funny material for the resurrection of his career.

Russell had stayed clean but sex became his mantra – and caused him quite a lot of trouble. If it hadn't been for his brief fling with a girl called Georgina Baillie a year or so earlier, he wouldn't have been involved in Sachsgate – one of the biggest controversies ever to hit the BBC. It had ended several careers at the Beeb – including his own and probably that of his big pal, Jonathan Ross.

Since his partial move to the US, due to his increasing activity in Hollywood in films like *Forgetting Sarah Marshall*, *Bedtime Stories* and *Get Him to the Greek*, Russell had been stepping out with more starlet types, while occasionally giving a passing nod to monogamy. But he hadn't really changed. He was the same old Russell.

But then Katy Perry came along. The girl from Santa

Barbara, California, who got her big break in the music industry as a result of singing in church. Whose first album, made when she was a teenager, was a gospel record. Whose parents are not just born again Christians, but evangelical pastors.

It's not hard to see how Russell would be attracted to the beautiful, talented and curvy Katy. Russell had often waxed lyrical about large-breasted girls and Katy proudly boasts of her 32DD cup size. And she has changed a fair bit since her church-singing days too. Sex has also been a major factor in her success.

'I Kissed a Girl' – her big breakthough hit in 2008 – created a sensation when it was released. Its 'les-ploitational' theme – talking about the curiosity of one girl kissing another – brought her fame and notoriety. She was the gospel singer who had become a 'pseudo-lesbian' pop princess.

Katy's look is also distinctively sexy. Her fashion influences are vintage, mostly from the 1950s – tight-cut dresses, skirts and blouses over classic lingerie, stockings and suspenders. But also Katy is also sexy in a wholesome way. She's all-American as Mom's apple pie – and she's still close to her God-fearing parents. How could she have tamed Russell, the debauched sex animal from Essex?

The fact is, the extraordinary events in the last months of 2009 came after an extraordinary journey for both of them. Katy, in the music biz since her mid-teens, had thought about giving up entirely after a series of gut-wrenching setbacks, as different record companies tried to mould her into something she wasn't. But having stuck to her guns and kept control, she finally made the album she wanted to make and in 2008 everything suddenly exploded. Songs like 'I Kissed a Girl', 'Hot N Cold', 'UR So Gay' and 'Waking Up in Vegas' – all from her album *One of the Boys* – had sold in their millions all over the world.

As for Russell, he was nearly all washed-up in the early Noughties – a sad, self-destructive drug and drink casualty before his career had really begun. But by 2006, he had transformed himself and his career. He had become the country's most exciting new stand-up comedian, and one of the most talked-about men in Britain. Three years later, he was a household name in the US as well as the UK, a recognised Hollywood star – and now his fiancée was one of the world's biggest pop stars.

Where did it all go right for Russell Brand? Could it keep going right for Russell Brand? And could he keep that famously rampant libido in check and stay faithful to Katy Perry?

Chapter 1

Citing

Winter was out for the night. A clear, cold night. Russell Brand was out, too. He was in town. Russell – Essex's self-styled Noam Chomsky. Stand-up comedian. Sex god. The man with the delicious dinkle.

TV's favourite funnyman had brought his sold-out *Shame* show to town and the Assembly Hall Theatre was packed with teenagers out for birthday treats, Goths in leather and grey hairs checking what the all fuss was about. Who was this vain dandy in their midst, this 'citing comedy man playing the drab, 1960s' modernist hall?

When Russell walked out on stage – to Morrissey's 'The Last of the Famous International Playboys' – it signalled a dramatic turnaround in the comedian's fortunes. Just a few short months before the start of the nationwide *Shame* tour, Russell had almost no profile. He was familiar only to comedy rats on the live circuit or miniscule

9

audiences tuned in to late afternoon, low-budget shows on satellite and cable channels.

By the end of the tour, if he was not the best stand-up in Britain, Russell could at least claim to be the best-known comic in the country. Suddenly, he was all over television and radio – the BBC, no less – and he was writing his own column for a national newspaper. And he was a tabloid journalist's dream with his outrageous antics, usually sexual. He was regular red-top fodder, the central player in a thousand feverish gossip columns.

And, if Russell's ubiquity didn't get him noticed, his sartorial makeover would. Russell eschewed the comedians' wardrobe staples. There was no corduroy in his closet. Russell's fashion inspiration was Keith Richards and Byron. He hit the Assembly stage, a loquacious gothic vision strapped in skin-tight grey jeans. Stick thin – his thighs were in different postal codes – he was a camp, Kohl-eyed confection, trussed up in a series of belts, black pointy Chelsea boots, skimpy black shirt and loosely-wound silk scarf. It looked as though a bat had backcombed his artfully tousled beehive. He looked dirty and the effect was instant. He was an object of teenage lust for girls and a new rock 'n' roll star for boys.

'Hello, my name's Russell,' he lisped. His only props on stage were a stool – the kind found in bistros and wine bars from the late 1970s – and a small square table draped with a black cloth. 'Hello,' he said again, and the audience shouted back and whooped and screamed. 'We love you Russell!' His delivery was a mannered mix of Kenneth Williams, his comedy hero Peter Cook and Wilfred Bramble – the gurning geezer who played old man Steptoe.

His movements were effete, prancing. He was all high kicks, shimmies and sashaying saunters across the stage. 'You seem to be doing quite well without me,' he joked. 'Am I perceived to be some kind of latecomer?' he asked. He'd been late and there had been panic backstage earlier. Before Russell took the stage, the audience was treated to a half-hour blast of the Dirty Pretty Things album while they hit the bar and loosened up. 'The taxi went the wrong way,' Russell explained. No public transport for Russell. He was famous.

Ordering the house lights up, Russell left the stage to walk among his congregation. As he passed by the massed rows, camera phones clicked, digital cameras snapped and young women swooned. He spied the brown curtains that hung limply over the municipal hall's windows. 'What's behind the curtains?' he asked, camp as a Christmas panto. 'Porn,' someone shouted back. 'Oh,' he cried, a dead ringer for Kenneth Williams in *Carry On Camping*, 'Disgusted of Tunbridge Wells.'

The length of the microphone lead halted Russell's progress as he went walkabout. But a little technical difficulty was not enough to stop this boundary-pushing stand-up at the top of his game. 'See them two little windows,' he said, pointing at the glass panels in the theatre's exit doors. 'I think they look like the door's eyes. The window looks like a face,' he joked. 'Do you sometimes look at the front of a car and think: "That car's got a face"?' he asked. Before any wag in the crowd could reply, he leapt in and put the audience right. 'Well no,' he declared, 'a car is not a cognitive being.' While the punters considered this one, Russell dropped his mic and wandered further into the throng, ad-libbing without amplification as he clambered up into the circle. 'Hello,' he greeted another thrilled member of his fan club. 'Get yer hair cut,' someone shouted.

Russell surveyed his crowd, oiled up after an intermission spent sucking on G&Ts and beer chasers in the theatre bar. His verdict: 'You look like the kind of people you see at a bus stop.' He then clambered back down to the stalls, informing his devotees: 'You know, when I climbed up there I really hurt this nut,' as he gently cupped his testicle, one of his precious ball bags. 'Isn't it interesting,' he added, 'that we're all alive with corresponding genitals?'

He walked back to the stage and stepped on the boards again; back in his natural habitat. 'Leave them lights on a bit 'cos I like looking at everyone,' he instructed. He picked up the local newspaper. This was one of Russell's trademark gags, mining the stories in the town rag for comic effect. 'We'll have a look at the old *Kent and Sussex Courier,*' he told the crowd. 'And work out: is the media a tool designed to keep us stupid and docile and prevent us from thinking, or is it a bit of a laugh?' Then he was off on a roll. The most exciting comedian of his generation had found his groove. 'Toy cigarettes,' he announced, 'that weren't right was it? "Ooh, you're a bit young to actually smoke, but just to get you used to the idea here's some confectionery, which is the next best thing." I mean, it's a big damaging to your health in that it's made of chemicals.'

This is what the audience had come for – Russell in full flow, letting his imagination take him where it would. He balanced his six-foot-two-inch frame – 'what feels like a fragile precipice' – on the stool and twisted his calves around the legs. 'Right, what's this that we're living in now? Sunday isn't it? Here we all are, alive at the same time. 'Citing...'

Swing

Chapter 2

Swine

'Life is basically a series of problems that you have to somehow solve yourself. I had to deal with feeling ordinary, dull, tedious and powerless by trying to subvert those ideas, being anarchic and dangerous. I'm sure that people like Tony Hancock and Peter Cook behaved the way they did for the same reason – to escape the tedium of normal life. You feel this burning need to swim against the natural current of your human misery,'

RUSSELL BRAND

Britain hadn't heard of Russell Brand in the first half of 1975. How could it? He hadn't even been born yet. What Britain did know about was the IRA, bombs, Baader-Meinhof, the National Front and the Cambridge Rapist. It was pretty dark, grim stuff.

Then, on Wednesday, 4 June 1975 a bundle of fun

popped out into this fun-free zone. A comedian was born. His parents, Barbara (Babs for short) and Ron Brand, named him Russell Edward Brand. So, even as the Cold War rumbled on and Liz Taylor and Richard Burton considered another remarriage in their interminable are-they-or-aren't-they relationship, the world got just a little bit brighter.

Russell didn't know this, of course. He was too busy being a baby – a baby born in Grays, Essex, an 'ordinary mundane suburbia' as Russell later described it. Slap bang next to a grey slug of Thames near the Dartford crossing, it's a tantalising few miles down the A13 from the bright lights of London. Grays is a lot of things, but the one thing it isn't is funny.

From the top of the town's multi-storey car park, clinging for dear life on to the staggeringly ugly Grays Shopping Centre, it is possible to glimpse Tilbury docks further down the Thames. In 1588, at West Tilbury, Queen Elizabeth I addressed her troops as the Spanish Armada approached. Purfleet, which featured in Bram Stoker's novel *Dracula*, is also nearby. And that's it – the complete history of Grays. There are no bright lights in Grays. There is a 99p shop, a Wimpy bar and a Blockbuster video store, housed in the former Burton's menswear outfitters. Further out, late Victorian terraces give way to 1930s semis and the tanning shops are replaced by DIY superstores.

Russell lived in a cul-de-sac in Grays – one of many dead-end streets in a dead-end town. Things didn't get off to a good start for baby Russell. Within a few months his father, Ron, 'a bit of a wheeler-dealer', upped and left the family home. 'My mum and dad got divorced when I was a kid. My dad left when I was about six months old... saw him at weekends, normal sort of fun stuff,' said Russell later. 'Saw him sometimes when I was a kid, but sometimes wouldn't see him for a long period of time.'

Brand Sr admitted that he and Babs 'fell out completely' and that he didn't see his infant son again for a long while. 'I don't know how long it was. I remember coming back,' he recalled years later. '[It] would have been about 18 months.' But Ron was adamant that by removing himself from the domestic scene he had given Russell a better start in life. Ron's absence meant that Russell did not have to experience the friction, the battles, the rows and the dread of living in a house with two parents at war with one another. Ron believed that by leaving Grays he gave Russell some 'tranquillity' at home. He explained: 'The option was to grow up in a house with two people consistently bickering and arguing. That's the option. That was the more likely alternative.'

Ron, whose own father died when he was just eight, also recalled that his son would get 'really emotional' about those weekend visits, especially when his father turned up late. 'I didn't realise it was such a big deal,' he said. Russell remembered that when his dad did call for him – as he sat waiting with his mum – his parents would often launch into a series of arguments that got 'quite emotionally volatile'. His father, he recalled, was during these rows 'very forceful and abrupt, [it was] mad and intense stuff.'

Russell has struggled with these issues of abandonment. More than a decade later, during the filming of a TV programme that also featured his father, the comedian admitted that he didn't think his father really cared about him. Russell told Ron: 'I don't think you have ever really given a fuck about me 'cause, ultimately, when I was a baby, when I couldn't defend myself, when I couldn't do nothing, you left. You were more important. It was more important for you to pursue your ambition that to look after me.' Ron denied this. He explained he had left to leave the bickering behind, that he left to avoid the rowing. Russell, then in his late 20s, didn't buy it. 'Bollocks dad,' he exploded, 'that wasn't the fucking reason you left. You left for you, you didn't leave for me, because you didn't want to deal with it. It did my head in.'

There were no brothers and sisters to help Russell through this upheaval. The only other person he could turn to was his mother, but even that wasn't enough for the solitary child. 'You've only got yourself haven't you?' he later mused. 'That's the only thing you can hold on to. For me, I found it hard to motivate myself to keep breathing.'

Despite his absences, Ron remained in some contact with Russell. He took photos of his good-looking son and used them to advertise baby competitions he ran at the photographic shop he managed. But Ron Brand couldn't see that his son would one day come to actively seek the attentions of other cameras. In those days Russell would run away from the limelight. His father noted: 'I used to take Russell to Pontin's holiday camps all over the country, but he wasn't the sort of kid to get on stage and enter the competitions.'

Then, Russell's mother hooked up with another man

and the whole family dynamic changed. 'Yes, I was very unhappy,' he said. 'I didn't get on with my stepdad at all. And I just remember feeling lonely and totally impotent. There was nothing I could do about my situation.' One incident, when he was about five, appeared to sum up Russell's feelings of alienation and isolation. Russell described a birthday party where he was presented with a teddy bear-shaped cake. As everyone sang 'Happy Birthday', the candles ignited the ribbon around the bear's neck. The cake burst into flames and melted before little Russell's appalled eyes. 'It became inflamed,' he recalled. 'Its eyes peering out, all its face melted. The icing dripped down its face, a horrible thing.' Russell fled to the sanctuary of the garden until his dad turned up and helped to make things better.

It seems that Russell had problems at parties. A couple of years later, Russell was accused of ruining a playmate's celebrations when he jumped into the other boy's paddling pool. Russell thought that he was the greatest, that he was bringing some 'joy and life' to the party. But that's not how the other guests saw it and Russell's friend declared that he did not want to see him any more. 'My feeling about my childhood is that it was lonely and difficult,' Russell admitted. 'Mum got on with her job, she was a secretary. But, she also sold everything from clothes to dishwashers to make ends meet.'

Russell's stepdad drove vans for a living. But Russell didn't really take to his substitute parent. He was, according to Russell, 'Good-looking, with all those masculine energies, just sitting around, drinking Tennant's, dominating the sitting room.' His stepdad didn't particularly take to Russell either. 'I felt like he hated me,' the comedian admitted, 'this flouncy kid. I was all "Oooh! Noel Coward"'. Russell's emerging camp persona didn't do anything to hold back his marginalisation. Both his dad and his stepdad were men's men, decent amateur footballers. They didn't wear silk scarves.

Isolated and alone, Russell mooched around Grays. A typical Saturday afternoon might have involved blowing £2.50 at The State, the 1930s-built cinema in the centre of town. Then it might be a trip down to Thameside Library to check out some Kafka and read all about alienation. After that, there really wasn't much to do. Maybe hang around outside Bacons shoe shop and look at the footwear, and then take your place sitting on the wall outside the railway station at the top of the High Street. From this vantage point Russell could watch the trains heading west, where London lay just 30 minutes away. So close.

Ron Brand knew all about London and he sometimes took Russell there, especially to watch football. Russell is soccer mad and it was his old man who got him into it, taking him to Upton Park to watch West Ham play. Ron first took his son to the football when Russell was just seven. That's right: Russell Brand, the camp comedian and prancing dandy, is a Hammers fan. Wonder what the tough guys on the terraces at West Ham's Boleyn Ground think about that?

Formed in 1900 from the old Thames Ironworks club, West Ham was the team that won the World Cup for England in 1966, with Geoff Hurst banging in the goals and captain Bobby Moore – West Ham personified – lifting the trophy at Wembley after seeing off West Germany 4–2 in probably the most memorable World Cup final ever.

'They think it's all over... it is now!' Well, it was for Bobby Moore, who left the Hammers the year before Russell was born. But under manager John Lyall – who was appointed in 1975 – West Ham went on to lift the FA Cup in 1980 and played a cultured style of football that a man of taste like Russell could well appreciate. When Russell began to go to games regularly in the 1980s the Hammers' star man was Trevor Brooking, a midfielder whose silky skills and effortless creativity surely left its mark in the aspiring young comedian's imagination. He also admired Frank McAvennie and hard man defender Julian Dicks, a shaven-headed, eye-bulging no-nonsense stopper who didn't mind winding up the crowd and getting in his opponents' faces.

West Ham was a good team for Russell to support. They weren't really his local club – that was Grays Athletic. But who supports Grays? West Ham was close enough to Essex for locals to support, plus, for Russell, it had the added bonus of being in London. Also, the Hammers weren't too flashy, not like some other London clubs. They were reliable, dependable, solid – but with a bit of flair, too. Russell has argued: 'There aren't that many clubs like West Ham in Premiership football now – perhaps Portsmouth, perhaps Newcastle – where there is a sense that the club is, to a degree, owned by the fans.' Russell also values tradition and West Ham is one of the clubs where tradition is important, too. It's no surprise that he supported the fans' Stand Up, Sit Down campaign when all-seater grounds were introduced to football. Ever the free spirit – but one who liked a bit of tradition thrown in – Russell, like his fellow West Ham fans, felt that if you wanted to stand you should be able to stand and that if you wanted to sit down you should be able to sit down. That's what Russell was, a good, old-fashioned anarchist.

One of Russell's first memories of going to West Ham was watching the exodus of fans from the ground to nearby Green Street. He asked Ron: 'Is that all the people in the world, Dad?' Russell liked the sense of belonging football gave him. 'When feeling that sense of inclusion, that sense of shared humanity in the enhanced context of a crowd of 34,000 as one sometimes does at football matches, it is a sensation approaching the Utopian,' he enthused. 'When I stop thinking and watch the football and chant, I'm taken out of myself, the individual submerged into the whole and that, I suspect, is football's primal forces, this mystical ability to unite.'

Russell's first World Cup was Mexico 1986, when he was ten years old. He only half-remembered the tournament in Spain four years before when Italy, helped by top scorer Paulo Rossi, overcame Germany 3–1 in the final. He witnessed extraordinary players like Brazil's Zico and Socrates and the French maestro Michel Platini, but admitted that his overriding memory of this World Cup was the mascot: a strange orange with legs.

He was ready for Mexico, with Gary Lineker, John Barnes, Ray Wilkins, Peter Shilton and Peter Beardsley in the England team, as they skipped past Paraguay 3–0 in the first round of the knock-out stage. Russell recalled, 'In

'86 I still felt part of the World Cup, enthralled by the Mexican Wave and the partnership of Gary Lineker and Peter Beardsley... I wheezed and stumbled after a plastic ball on the rec with Topsy, my dog, guesting as Paraguay.'

Unfortunately, that year Argentina's captain Diego Maradona was in his prime and England came up against him in the quarter-final. He'd already scored five goals in the tournament, yet he saved his most majestic performance for the England game. He scored both Argentina's goals as his team beat Lineker and co 2–1.

His first effort was the notorious Hand of God goal. The whole world – except the referee – saw the pint-sized genius blatantly punch the ball into the net past a flailing Peter Shilton. In his post-match interview Maradona, making light of his cheating, claimed that the goal was scored, 'a bit with the head of Maradona and another bit with the hand of God'.

But if his first goal was hand made, his second was created from pure genius. Often rated as the best goal ever scored, Maradona picked up the ball on the halfway line, dribbled past what seemed like the entire England team – some of them more than once – and poked the ball into the net as the goalkeeper rushed out to meet him. Like many Englishmen, Russell's opinion of Maradona is coloured more by that devious first goal than the sublime second. 'At the time the confusion and indignation were unmanageable,' he mused many years later 'I thought, "He can't do that, can he?" The second goal was irrelevant. He cheated, that's not allowed.' Russell also recalled that the toughest kid at his school, Jamie Dawkins, assured him that the game was going to be replayed. 'I believed him,' recalled Russell. 'Not just because questioning his word was punishable by death, but because it seemed right.'

But despite his love of the beautiful game, Russell was – and still is – useless at football. He can't kick a ball for toffee. He has described his attempts as a humiliating experience. 'I was crap at football,' he confessed. 'A shameful admission for any man, amplified by the fact that both my dad and stepdad were, at different times, favourably eyed by West Ham scouts.' In typically eloquent – and offbeat – form he added: 'Pre-pubescently, an inability to kick a ball was akin to having a My Little Pony in lieu of testicles. I immediately lose all grace and posture when in pursuit of a ball. I adopt the air of a citizen of Pamplona fleeing a bull in that lethal festival they persist in having.'

He last played football in 2001, when he was still smoking grass. The kick-about with a few mates turned into a full-blooded and brutal game after a bunch of ne'er-do-wells joined in. Russell recalled his horror at colliding with his 'brutish' opponents. His only thought at the time was to get rid of the ball as soon as possible, lest he find himself on the receiving end of an aggressive boot from the other team.

Russell still endures a 'bilious dread' when a park football game is in progress and a wayward ball flies towards him. He always hopes someone else will get it, maybe his old man, who will dazzle the watching players with his soccer skills before floating it back and nonchalantly strolling off. Failing that, Russell will ignore the cries to return the ball and pretend to be otherwise occupied. On the rare times when he has kicked a football the results have been disastrous. He says: 'On the occasions when I've obliged, I've always hoofed it skyward or spooned it in a lake or a pensioner's lap.'

But, when it comes to being a football fan, Russell can claim he is no Johnny-come-lately. He is not some celebrity drawn to the game by the money, the beautiful birds and the fast cars. He's been there all along – the bonus now is that he gets to enjoy it even more. Now that he's well-known, Russell gets to hang out in the West Ham players' lounge after games. There, he can swoon like a love-struck teenager as he tries to catch the eye of Anton Ferdinand and company. Yet he still prefers to watch the games from the Doc Marten stand like all the other fans. He may not be there week in, week out, nor will you find him making the long treks up to Middlesbrough or Newcastle like some, but he's definitely a familiar face at the ground. Has been for years.

He was even there in the dark days, when West Ham weren't much cop and the most notable thing about them was the evil reputation enjoyed by some of their most extreme fans. A lot of clubs had a hooligan element back in the 1980s, but few had mobs like West Ham's ICF, the notorious Inter-City Firm. These trainers-and-track suit-clad casuals got their name from their mode of transport to away games. With a Stanley knife tucked into the back of their Lois cords, they would take on their rivals – Chelsea's Headhunters or Millwall's Bushwhackers – and, thoughtfully, leave a calling card on the mangled bodies of their victims. 'Congratulations,' it would say, 'you've just met the ICF.'

It was obvious why some West Ham fans had so much

pent-up rage. West Ham, until recently at least, was a classic yo-yo club, up and down the leagues like a whore's drawers. 'The mood among my friends who are West Ham followers is one of glum acceptance,' Russell admitted. But 'acceptance' is the key word. Fans like Russell stick with their teams, come what may. Especially a team like West Ham. 'The notion that there's something magical about West Ham is somehow easy to indulge. There's something innately romantic about the Hammers,' he says.

CHAPTER 3

It's Moreish

RUSSELL'S SCHOOLDAYS WERE AT THE GRAYS SCHOOL. GO UP
HATHAWAY ROAD, LEFT AT GRAYS BAPTIST CHURCH ON ORSETT
ROAD, PAST THE ROWS OF PRE-WAR SEMIS, OVER RUSSELL ROAD
(RUSSELL WOULD HAVE LIKED THAT TOUCH), SWING BY THE LOCAL
REC FOR IMPROMPTU FOOTBALL AND DOG WALKING, AND THE
COMPREHENSIVE IS HUNKERED DOWN ON THE RIGHT.

Built in 1932, the mixed school has about 900 pupils.
From the mid 1980s Russell was one of them, roaming
the low-rise school buildings arranged around a large
quadrangle with two blocks tacked on just before
Russell was born, housing social sciences, English, art
and food technology. There's also a gym, sports hall and
playing fields.

Walking up to school in his black blazer and blue tie,
while the lollipop lady helped the kids cross the road by the
parade – where highlights included second-hand shops like
Second Andys – Russell would have cut a cute figure at 11.

Cute, but not happy. From early adolescence Russell was suspected of being bipolar and hypermanic. He was certainly treated for depression and started binge eating and vomiting. 'I have a lust for life,' he says. 'I love people and I get excited by things, but I can be miserable as fuck. When I was younger, I had difficulties with mental illness, and I was on medication for mood balancing and what-not. You don't want be around when the laughter stops, dear.'

From about the ages of 12 to 16 Russell was a fat little kid, a bit of a porker. Fatty Russell. And when he decided he wanted to lose weight, Russell's solution was typically unusual. Rejecting the possibilities afforded by exercise or dieting, the mentally fragile Russell proceeded straight to all-out bulimia. 'It went on for three years,' he said. 'I would make myself sick on a daily basis, binge and purge. It was really unusual in boys, quite embarrassing. But I found it euphoric.' It was inconvenient, too. The only comment his eating disorder provoked at home was his stepdad asking Russell to stop puking up in the sink because it kept blocking the drain.

Politically, the young Russell was naturally left-leaning. In the days, when there was still left and right in politics, Russell took the Labour-supporting *Daily Mirror*. 'I used to get the *Mirror* and my stepdad used to read the *Mail*. I think I got the *Mirror* because I liked the cartoons and the gossipy stuff,' he said. 'I had an unspoken and un-nurtured sense that the *Mail* might have been trying to make me racist. I've been very fortunate not to have been lured into a lifetime of small-mindedness.'

Looking back, Russell can muster some sympathy for his teenage self. 'Of course I've been through lots of therapy,' he says, 'but I do feel a sense of "You poor little sod". I loved my mum madly, but I had a lot of prohibiting, inhibiting things around.' Life at home was made doubly difficult because his mum was ill. Babs had battled with cancer several times before Russell had reached his 16th birthday. Russell was and still is close to his mum, even through the tough times. 'I never felt secure,' he said. 'I always had this feeling that she might not be around much longer and then what would I be left with?' He went on to add: 'My mum was ill a lot, so I'm very solipsistic and introspective and most of my relationships were with television.'

Bulimia, depression, loneliness, weight problems – these were the real-world ingredients that left Russell with an abiding sense of nihilism during his teenage years. As if that wasn't enough, he also started cutting himself. 'I had problems with food and self-harming,' he revealed. 'I've always had these compulsive traits looking for an outlet.' Russell still bears the scars of his anxious, lonely childhood on the inside of his forearm, a visible sign of his obsessive personality. TV, however, offered him an escape from his unhappiness. His favourite shows as a kid were all comedies: *Blackadder*, *Fawlty Towers* and *Only Fools and Horses*. Later, he'd even incorporate the theme tune from David Jason's Peckham-set classic into his act.

He also cited the then-radical Ben Elton (long before *We Will Rock You*) and Harry Enfield among his favourite comics at that time. Russell loved to analyse the shows he watched and criticise the action. 'Really watching them and trying to understand how they put together the language, obsessively,' he explained. Russell's detailed studies of language, syntax and grammar would stand him in good stead for his chosen career as a word-loving, prose-proud, verbally dextrous comedian.

It was just as well that Russell was learning something from what he watched on TV, because he wasn't learning too much at school – he was too busy bunking off. 'I was barmy by the time I was 14,' he says, 'so I didn't go to school that much.' Russell instead found inspiration and excitement in music, especially The Smiths, and in books. His chosen authors were outsiders like himself, those who wrote about the margins of society. 'If you're lonely – and my main sense of growing up was being alone, isolated – if you find things like the music of The Smiths or the writing of Oscar Wilde or Alan Bennett then you start to think, "Ah, there's other people",' he explained.

Then, when he was 15, Russell found his vocation. The Grays School was casting for a production of *Bugsy Malone*. The portly Russell went up for the part of Fat Sam – and got it. He found that he loved being on stage. When others forgot their lines he leapt in and ad-libbed to cover their tracks. 'Things started going horribly wrong,' he recalled, 'and I had to improvise my way out of it. And people laughed and I felt this sudden rush of adrenaline surging through me. It was like a drug.'

Russell loved everything about the experience. He loved the lights and the attention – it was certainly more attention than he got from his stepdad at home. Russell felt that this was a turning point and that he'd found his calling. He described it as 'a blissful epiphany,' adding: 'I got this holy sense of "Oh, my God, I've got this thing now: me showing off and people laughing." From then on I didn't want to do anything else.'

Actor Colin Hill, who directed Russell in the production at Grays School, doesn't have quite the same recollection, but he does remember a dedicated fledgling actor. 'Russell wasn't the best thing in it by any means, but he was determined,' said Hill. 'He is the sort of person who would run at a wall until the wall falls over. At that age, he certainly had the gift of the gab and he liked to join in and express himself. He was articulate. I think as time went by, he realised that he could employ his natural enthusiasm by using it in the theatrical sense.'

His transformation on stage coincided with the teenager finding a new identity to go with his new-found vocation. Russell lost weight and acquired a thin, stripped-down look. 'At about 16, I suddenly became slimmer,' he remembers. 'It took a while, that bulimia, but once it took hold it was truly was a blessing.'

This change in Russell is echoed in how some of his old classmates remember him. Some recall a 'quiet, sensitive lad', while others say he could be quite boisterous.

One pupil noticed another thing about Russell at school. He liked girls. 'He had a very specific type,' she said. 'He loved tall, voluptuous girls and didn't go with just anyone. They were always good-looking with big boobs.'

Academically, Russell did okay at The Grays School, but he was no scholar. No one could call him a brain box. But he was no dummy either, not in the artsy subjects anyway. He struggled in Maths but picked up good grades in English Language, English Literature, Drama and History. Russell expounded: 'I failed the rest... I wasn't very good at sitting around and doing exams.'

What he was good at doing was drugs. He would regularly bunk off school to smoke weed with some classmates. It started there and soon escalated. 'I grew up in Grays, and if you're from a small town drugs can be very useful,' he explains. After his experiences with bulimia, drugs seemed a logical next step. 'The baton of self-harm was handed directly from eating disorder to narcotics abuse in a single graceful movement,' is how Russell describes it. After the weed he swiftly moved to speed, then LSD, which he described as 'wonderful and enlightening'. Ecstasy was next, followed by coke, which he found 'titillating' for a while. Then, of course, it was heroin. 'I started at 16 smoking stuff and drinking a lot,' he says. 'I started with loads of grass and hash, then took loads of amphetamines, then loads of acid, loads of ecstasy and loads of coke, till in the end I took loads of crack and heroin.'

He first bought heroin at 19. He did it on a whim, buying it at Hackney Central, waiting for a train on the North London line. He saw a group of Turkish kids on the station platform, smoking what looked like a joint. It turned out to be heroin. Russell got himself a cap, went home, fired up and smoked smack for the first time. This was the way Russell says he always consumed the class A drug – smoking it, not injecting. Usually, when heroin is smoked it is placed on a piece of foil or very thin piece of metal. A lighter or flame is held below the foil, heating the drug, which gives off smoke. The user will then use a tube, usually made of foil, to chase the fumes. The one main advantage for heroin smokers is that it eliminates the risk of acquiring syringe-borne diseases such as HIV or hepatitis.

Russell was instantly converted to the joys of heroin. He had found what he was looking for – the perfect drug that blocked out the pain and replaced it with an intense feeling of well being and relief from stress. 'Finding heroin, it's like God, home, a lover,' enthused Russell on the joy of smack. 'Just this feeling of being engulfed by warmth, everything moving away, your life, everything, and withdrawing into this beautiful sanctuary.'

Heroin also relieves physical pains and many users demonstrate an increase in self-confidence, an empathy with people around them and even increased creativity. On paper, it is the perfect drug for a comedian-cum-TV presenter. 'I went home and smoked it and suddenly felt enveloped in this womb of comfort,' he recalled. Russell describes heroin as the only drug that has ever delivered to him what it promised. For him, heroin was the zenith of his drug-using career. 'It never goes away because it seems so comforting in an absolute way,' Russell said. '[No other drug] really stopped the pain or reached out to my consciousness in the way that heroin did. It's a very nihilistic drug because you think, "Who cares about anything? Why does any of this matter?"'

Russell also tried crack but was less enamoured by it. 'It makes you feel like you're breathing through plastic,' he stated. He described his descent into multiple drug-taking as an 'innate tendency towards addiction'. This may well be true. Drug-taking was never a recreational activity for Russell. There was no dabbling or, as he put it, 'a Timothy Leary exploration'. No way. Russell was full on, 100 per cent, 24/7. 'The reason you take drugs is to prevent yourself from confronting what you actually are. In my case, in my childhood I had no power and I felt insignificant, impotent and small so I did things to abate those feelings,' he said. 'There was never a point where it was gleeful decadence. Well, there was a pose of bohemian excess, but really it was always medication to assuage pain and doubt.'

To 'anaesthetise the pain' – that's why he took drugs. 'I always felt desperately unhappy,' he revealed. 'When I first started taking drugs I thought, "Oh thank God, something that makes you feel less miserable." The first time I performed, that was my life from then on. The first time I took drugs, I took drugs every day until I stopped 11 years later.' As the drugs poured in, the fat poured out. Skinny again, Russell knocked the bulimia on the head, but didn't hold back from his chemical intake. 'I was really thin by the time I was 17, but I stopped [the bulimia] because by that time I was a drug addict and had other self-destructive behaviour to be getting on with.'

With school a drag and Russell's weed intake growing, things suddenly got even weirder. During the last few months at Grays, Russell's father Ron proposed a unique bonding experience for father and son – a whoring holiday in Thailand.

They stayed at the Mandarin Palace Hotel and, after touching down in Bangkok, immediately hooked up with the nearest hookers. Russell's memories of his excursion into sex tourism are of brothels, the clickety-clack of prostitutes' spiked heels on marble floors and of half empty glasses of champagne. The experience brought father and son closer together. 'We got on better since I've been an adult, since we went on holiday to Thailand,' he said.

Boosted by his small success in the school production of *Bugsy Malone*, Russell left school and enrolled with an extras agency. He also landed a place at the famed Italia Conti stage school in Clapham, south London. Founded in 1911, Italia Conti was the alma mater of Noel Coward, Leslie Philips and Charles Hawtrey. Russell's contemporaries at the school were of a slightly different order, including *EastEnders* star Martine McCutcheon and the singer and proto footballer's wife Louise Nurding (who went on to marry former Spurs and Liverpool midfielder Jamie Redknapp, whose father, Harry, was once manager of Russell's beloved West Ham).

Moving to London, Russell briefly stayed in Romford with his old man. But that arrangement didn't last long and Russell was soon crashing at his gran's and openly smoking weed in front of her. She'd seen *Kilroy* on the TV, with its endless parade of drug-addled losers and victims, and told Russell that he should be careful: she warned his dope smoking could lead to much worse. Russell called this his nan's Kilroy warning. 'Of course, I scoffed at her for falling for such obvious media scare tactics,' he said, 'and then promptly descended the helter-skelter, through amphetamine, ecstasy and LSD to crack cocaine and heroin.'

Amazingly, Russell landed some bit parts on TV, in cop show *The Bill* and in a BBC kids' programme. But they didn't lead anywhere, and by this time Russell's spell at Italia Conti was running out. His drug-taking and a growing interest in the opposite sex were proving to be too much of a distraction. After cutting classes and generally making a nuisance of himself, Russell was expelled, later claiming it was for 'smashing things up, crying and cutting myself, breaking down in tears all the time'. However, his personality and antics at least got him noticed. 'When the headmistress informed me of my expulsion,' Russell recalled, 'I remember her saying, "He's always in the corridors with girls, wearing that ridiculous cape of love." That was a successful bit of branding. I had this long black coat which I called my ridiculous cape of love, and in a way I was quite proud that this had not escaped her notice.'

Russell's brief enrolment at Italia Conti was followed by an equally short-lived stint at the Camden Drama Centre. His self-destructive urges were at the time just too difficult to suppress. He explains: 'I've had this thing in me, a bacchanalian impulse. The thing that says, "There's only this, there's only now, there's nothing else, so fuck everything." I have to say to myself, "Remember you've got all these things to do, don't ruin it just for the moment."'

Nevertheless, this behaviour was also the first sign of his precocious talent for self-publicity. 'He had only been gone a few months when I saw a piece in the local paper in which Russell was almost saying he had already "arrived",' recalled Colin Hill. 'The truth is, it took him another 15 years – he just announced it earlier than everyone else.'

After his brush with drama, Russell moved in with some friends in Bermondsey, south London. This was when he properly dedicated himself to addiction. The drugs were working, but Russell wasn't. He settled into the druggie's lifestyle taking on a series of dead-end McJobs in bars and restaurants to support his habit. He even had a short stint at the Post Office. But even this didn't go smoothly. When he was 18 Russell got some work as scab labour covering for striking postmen over the Christmas period. He claimed he was unaware at the time that there was a postal strike, plausible enough given his drug-addled state. 'I thought they just needed a bit of help with the Christmas cards,' Russell said. 'I only learned of union action whilst on my rounds one bitter December morning.'

Part way through his letter deliveries he stopped to eat a sandwich and watch a football match taking place in a park. 'Right bawdy they were, the players, very physical and vocal,' he recalled. Then the ball went out for a throw-in and rolled towards Russell. His guts churned. He would have to kick the ball back. He did, but sliced it badly. Then, one of the players noticed the postbag. He asked Russell if he was enjoying the game. Russell said he was and the player replied, 'Well you should be posting those letters not watching the game you fucking scab!' Some of the other players, whom Russell then realised were all striking postmen, loomed over him menacingly. 'Dirty scab,' they shouted, not unreasonably. 'Come on, it's Christmas!' pleaded Russell, before beating a hasty retreat. 'That cold Christmas morning, I learned a hard lesson about worker solidarity,' he later remembered.

CHAPTER 4

Katy's Early Days

KATY PERRY STARTED LIFE AS KATHERYN ELIZABETH HUDSON, ON 25 OCTOBER 1984, IN SANTA BARBARA, CALIFORNIA – ABOUT 70 MILES UP THE PACIFIC COAST FROM LOS ANGELES. THAT'S A LONG WAY FROM GRAYS IN ESSEX, WHERE RUSSELL BRAND GREW UP – AND KATY HAD A VERY DIFFERENT UPBRINGING TO RUSSELL.

She's the daughter of Keith and Mary Hudson – both born-again Christian pastors running their own Pentecostal-style ministry. Katy was the second of three kids – younger than sister Angela but older than brother David – and a natural blonde. As children the Hudson kids naturally became members of their parents' church. In fact, although Katy went to a regular school, she also regularly attended Christian schools and camps – and went to church several times a week – throughout her childhood.

She also showed an early talent for singing. 'I was at that point in my childhood where I was copycatting my sister and everything she did,' she has explained. Her sister practised with cassette tapes, so Katy took the tapes when her sister was not around, rehearsed the songs and performed them to her parents. She was so impressive that they suggested she should take voice lessons.

Her desire to perform, show off and basically draw attention to herself was thus established and encouraged at an early age – something Katy has put down to 'middle child syndrome'. 'I was just getting whatever attention was left over,' she has said, 'and I loved people's reactions, the looks on their faces.'

She was nine years old when she started taking singing lessons – and got her start as a public performer. Like many American pop, soul and R&B performers through the years, that meant singing in church – which just happened to be her parents' church. But at that point she was not allowed to listen to anything other than gospel music. '[Non-religious] music wasn't allowed in the house because it's the Devil's work [according to her parents],' Katy told *Blender* magazine. 'And if I brought home friends, my mom wanted to know if they were Christians.'

Katy has also described it as 'kind of an island. We spoke in tongues. We knew there was this one way, and all the other ways were wrong.' But the seeds of her individuality were soon emerging. 'I was always into dressing up, even when I was a little girl,' she recalls. 'My mom says I would wear a different outfit for breakfast, lunch and dinner. It was my way of saying I wanted to *arrive*.'

According to Katy, she was something of a black sheep of the family, bucking against the strict ways of her parents. This wasn't expressed by outrageous acts of rebellion but rather by words. 'It was my kind of dark sense of humour and my thick layer of sarcasm, which is slapped on everything. Even though I've had a strict Christian upbringing, they've always known that about me.'

She did have outlets into a freer, less buttoned-up world, however – most notably through her family's Hollywood connection. Katy's uncle, Frank Perry, was a Hollywood producer and director – most notably for *Mommie Dearest* – while her aunt, Eleanor Perry, was a top screenwriter whose credits included the Oscar-nominated comedy *Diary of a Mad Housewife*.

As a child Katy visited Frank Perry in New York with her family several times. Uncle Frank's film *Mommie Dearest* had attained cult status for its depiction of Hollywood legend Joan Crawford as a monstrous child-beater, and it was loved by the drag queens who frequented Frank's colourful neighbourhood in Manhattan. They made a big impression on Katy, who to this day, says her favourite movie is *Paris Is Burning*, a film about Harlem drag queens made in the late 1980s.

When she reached her teens, Katy started sneaking out of the house to go drinking. She also started to develop a reputation for attention-seeking behaviour and a tomboyish streak. A scar on her ankle is evidence of having accepted a dare to jump off a roof at a pool party. 'I like a nice dare from a boy,' she has said. 'It's fun. It makes me say, "Ha! You didn't think I would do that."'

When she was confronted about her behaviour, she discovered that her parents' histories were not as squeaky clean as she had supposed. In fact, they were quite the opposite. 'I started spending Sunday mornings crying and hung over,' she told *Blender*. 'Because crying is what you *do* when you're hung over. So my dad started telling me about when he was my age.' It turned out that back in the 1960s her father Keith had been involved with a strong form of LSD called Strawberry Fields. He would often hang out with Timothy Leary, the guru of the original hippie generation who coined the phrase 'tune in, turn on and drop out'. He had been a prime candidate to become an early acid casualty if he hadn't been born again.

Meanwhile, her mother Mary had been a privileged Southern Californian debutante who, in the spirit of the times, became a hippie chick and rebellious free spirit. She ran off to see the world, had a tempestuous first marriage in Africa and enjoyed a brief fling with Jimi Hendrix in Spain.

Becoming born-again Christians was the way that Katy's parents found to stop themselves from going completely off the rails. 'They found God at a time when they really needed to, and I believe in the God they found,' Katy said to Katie Couric's *All Access Grammy Special*. 'My dad would have died from one tab of Strawberry Fields too many if he hadn't found God.'

Katy would not drop out or become a drug casualty. She accepted her parents' strong Christian faith – she still does – but she was also trying to be a normal teenager. When a skate park opened in her neighbourhood she became an avid skateboarder – a girl who was 'one of the boys', as well as being fascinated by fashion. 'I can still do a mean half-pipe,' she has declared.

As for her music, that was still almost entirely based around the church. But ironically it would also provide her with a route into the wider world. Katy left high school in Santa Barbara after taking her GED – the American equivalent of GCSE exams – to study music full time. She enrolled in the Music Academy of the West in Santa Barbara and even studied opera for a short while. But she wasn't destined to stay at music school for very long: her recording career was already taking off.

By the time she was 15, Katy's singing in her parents' church had attracted the attention of a group of music producers from Nashville, the home of country music and the Christian music industry. America is a very devout Christian nation – particularly in the southern 'Bible Belt' – and Christian music is an important part of the music industry in the USA, and big business.

Katy was signed to Christian music label Red Hill and invited to come to Nashville to work on a debut album. But even the producers were probably surprised that she knew virtually nothing about the mainstream music scene, having grown up on a diet of gospel music at home.

'When the producer I was doing my demos was with was like, "OK, so who would you want to work with if you could work with anybody?" I was like, "I really have no idea,"' she recalls. Slightly mortified at her lack of knowledge, she rushed back to her hotel with her mother, turned on the music channel VH1 and saw the top producer Glen Ballard talking about working with Alanis Morissette on her smash hit album *Jagged Little Pill.*

'I thought, "You know what? I want to work with him – that's who I'm gonna work with." So the next day I came into the studio, and I said, "I want to work with this guy Glen Ballard." He [the producer] is like,

"OK, well, I can pull all the strings I have and make that happen."'

In fact, Katy would work with Glen Ballard – but not right away. Before that she would make an album in Nashville, called simply *Katy Hudson*, which was released in 2001. It was an album filled with songs – written or co-written by Katy – with titles like 'Faith Won't Fail' and 'Trust in Me'. It was not, however, an album of hymn-like spirituals but a fairly angst-ridden Christian pop-rock album from a teenage girl who was perfectly aware of sin, temptation and all those things that good Christian girls need to avoid at all costs. Musically she had already become strongly influenced by Alanis Morissette.

On its release the album gained some respectable reviews from music critics, but as Red Hill was a small independent record label there was no huge budget to promote the record. It didn't sell. Red Hill folded and the album sank completely.

After that, Katy would edge away from Christian pop-rock. The intense and earnest blonde Katy Hudson would transform herself into the sassy, sexy and smart brunette Katy Perry. But it would be a long and difficult journey. There was no easy path to success and fame (or notoriety) – and Katy would experience painful setbacks and crushing disappointments along the way.

CHAPTER 5

Saucy

MEANWHILE, RUSSELL WASN'T GETTING ANYWHERE. WHERE NEXT FOR AN ANARCHIC CHANCER? THEN THE ANSWER CAME: COMEDY. RUSSELL THOUGHT ABOUT HIS COMEDY HEROES, A RUM BUNCH TAKING IN LENNY BRUCE, BILL HICKS, BILLY CONNOLLY AND RICHARD PRYOR. THE THING THEY ALL HAD IN COMMON WAS THAT THEY ALL TOLD THE TRUTH ABOUT THEMSELVES, NO MATTER HOW REVEALING, UNPLEASANT OR EMBARRASSING. THEY WERE BRUTALLY HONEST. BUT THEN THERE WERE RUSSELL'S OTHER ICONS – VIC REEVES, BOB MORTIMER, EDDIE IZZARD AND PETER COOK – SURREALIST LUNATICS AND FLAMBOYANT WORDSMITHS. IF RUSSELL COULD FIND A WAY TO MARRY THOSE TWO COMEDY TRADITIONS TOGETHER, WHO KNEW WHERE IT MIGHT LEAD?

So, in 1996, Russell started doing stand up. It was nothing fancy at first, just a few gigs in pubs and bars like 93 Feet East in Hoxton. It was certainly not enough to earn a living, so Russell was forced to sign on, which he did for 'years and years... to get disability and housing benefits'.

Russell still wasn't getting anywhere fast, But he at least knew what he wanted to do. He wanted to get up on stage and make people laugh. But it wasn't only that. He wanted to be honest and lay himself bare. In his opinion, 'I think the truth is the only thing that's worth joking about... artificiality has no value to me.'

Russsell's way with words was obviously a big help. He put all that time spent watching *Only Fools and Horses* to good use. He discovered that he could tell a tale, think on his feet and turn a phrase or two. He could take a subject – any subject – and make it funny. The key to it all was his vocabulary, his strange articulations. It is his belief that, 'I've become articulate because I always felt misunderstood. I'm still littered with reminders of my anxious childhood. I was a miserable little weirdo for ages. I'm still weird.'

But it was his lonely childhood and his depression that gave him plenty of material to mine for his act – which in turn offered him a kind of therapy. 'Look at how Peter Cook is someone who was dead depressed and his response to that is to be hilariously funny,' he argues, 'like someone who lived on an island would become a dead good swimmer.' Comedy, for Russell, is simply him reacting against his early life. 'Some would say that the personality is a reaction to your problems, the personality in itself is a series of malfunctions, a series of ways of redressing what you are,' he explained.

Russell also believes it is a fair trade-off to experience depression and then be allowed to explode into life on stage. 'I think the same thing that makes me sad and self-obsessed and awkward is the same thing that gives me drive, to be extreme, compelled and propelled by this sense of yearning for extremity and a fear of mediocrity,' he says.

The stage, telling jokes and spinning yarns, is where Russell feels alive. He's much happier up there than doing something mundane. It's where he feels relief. 'I feel more relaxed on stage when I'm performing, when it's going well, than anything else,' he says. 'I'm more happy doing that than buying a loaf of bread. [On stage] I'm engaged with something else, something that's bigger than me and I feel... at one.'

Russell reckons that it's only when he's not on stage that things don't run so smoothly for him. He doesn't feel right. When he's off-stage, he says, 'I'm irritated or self-conscious or thinking "God, I need the toilet" or nervous and worried by trivia and minutiae.'

He also claims to be a very different person outside of performing. 'I'm shy, awkward, nervous, gauche,' he says. 'My confidence is for what I know that I'm good at. I've been sculpted by failure and by time. You see me doing my job. You know, obviously I am different when I am chatting to my mum or playing with my cat.'

On stage, entertaining, working, Russell believes he reaches a higher ground. 'Through performance,' he continues, 'I attain something beyond me as an individual. Some people would call that truth and others would call it God, accessing something that is intransient – and life is about transience – and through performance and rituals you can access something bigger and for me it's that.' On tour, doing gigs, making people laugh, Russell feels like he has 'electric tendrils of information that are hanging everywhere'. With the help of these 'tendrils' he claims that he can be brilliant and funny.

But, in the early days Russell had some tough times scraping by on the comedy circuit. He later revealed that: 'I've had a few lucky things, but then I have had the momentum of years of toil, pain, agony and humiliation, which I have endured and single-mindedly continued when all about me were telling me I was insane.'

Then, in 2000, after all the crap gigs and nights of no laughs at sad little pubs, something incredible happened for the 25-year-old comic. Russell got his first big break when he made the finals of the New Act of the Year competition at the Hackney Empire in east London. Suddenly, he was on his way. Hot from the Hackney Empire finals Russell, accompanied by Mark Felgate and Shappi Khorsandi, sped up to Edinburgh to play the Gilded Balloon at the Tailors' Hall – a fringe slot booked and organised by Russell himself. Their three-man set was called *Pablo Diablo: Cryptic Triptych*. There was very little to link the three artists and some suggested the evening would have benefited from a compere to tie the whole performance together. Mark Felgate went on stage first and his act was as a ventriloquist who appears as his own dummy. He had a nice line in self-deprecation and some well-honed running gags. He mixed anecdotes of his family with unexpected applications of ventriloquism, his raconteur style punctuated by the odd foray into the front rows. But he found the audience reaction was frosty. It was a tough crowd.

Shappi Khorsandi went next. Sassy, yet disarmingly self-critical, she made some headway with the audience.

Many of her gags revolved around her London Iranian background and her problems finding a boyfriend. She also had some acute observations on her fellow females and their names – all women named Sally were kooks, and all bitches are named Flora. After Felgate's slow start, Khorsandi got things nicely warmed up.

With the room nicely cooking Russell, the third part of the triptych, went on. 'Tall and swoonsome,' according to David Belcher in the *Herald Review*, 'Russell Brand looks like a male model or the great-great-great grandson of romantic seducer Heathcliff.' *Time Out*'s Anna Adams had Brand looking more like a 'Spanish pin-up'. Tossing his long locks, Russell strode on stage and cut loose. The audience hung on his every word as Brand launched into a fast-paced whirlwind of contemporary observations. His topics that night included a *News of the World* campaign against paedophiles, which he dissected with improbable humour. Having spotted signs for the Samaritans on Edinburgh's North Bridge on his way to the gig, Brand also tossed in some dark stuff about suicide.

Belcher could hardly contain himself. He panted: 'Russell's got loads of brains and lots of education, all of which he puts to good use in ruminating wordily about a wide range of singular preoccupations.' Although Belcher did rate Brand as 'pretty jolly funny', he did venture that the novice comedian would be even funnier if he developed some stage craft and stopped being eager to please. 'His mockney tones could grate,' he warned.

The Scotsman also reviewed *Pablo Diablo*. It reported: 'Playing to a slightly bemused audience who have been tempted in by free tickets is often the lot of the shiny new stand up-hoping to make waves at the Fringe, but anyone finding themselves in the audience at the *Cryptic Triptych* can count themselves lucky to discover three such promising acts on the one bill.' However, of the three comedians in the show there was one clear talent. *The Scotsman*'s reviewer, Jane-Ann Purdy, had no doubt who would make it big. She wrote: 'While each of the three newcomers acquitted themselves admirably, it is Brand who has "Star of the future" tattooed beneath his Calvin Kleins.'

While he was up in Edinburgh, Russell met someone who would be an important part of his life – Trevor Lock. Cocky Locky.

Trevor Hugh William Lock is a couple of years older than Russell. He was born on 2 September 1973 and studied philosophy at University College, London. A comedian and playwright, he is also a keen cricketer and has represented his home county, Lincolnshire. Russell met him when he auditioned for a play written by Lock.

Lock's comedy is less in your face than Russell's. It's slow, more surreal. He is a good foil for Russell's fast, excited jabber and often punctuates Russell's ego with a well-observed jibe. In the late 1990s, Lock cropped up on Stewart Lee and Richard Herring's BBC TV show, *This Morning With Richard Not Judy*, where he was often the butt of Lee's mockery, being told not to speak because that would mean having to pay him more. Lock also appeared as a medic in Al Murray's Sky One sitcom *Time Gentleman Please*, so, unlike Russell, he had a bit more experience behind him.

He'd visited the Edinburgh fringe since 1998 and

performed at the 1999 event in the *Number One Show* alongside Daniel Kitson and Andrew Maxwell. He performed his first solo Edinburgh Fringe show, called *When I Was a Little Girl: The Very Best of Trevor Lock*, in 2006. But it was back in 2000 when his and Russell's paths crossed for the first time. Russell explained, 'I went to audition for his play. I had to go in there, a man of my gifts, and sit before that absolute lunatic and be judged by him.' But, Russell must have impressed Lock. The playwright gave Russell the part of his best friend in his play.

Russell claimed that Lock was a Greta Garbo-type character, secretive and mysterious and gave little away. 'He was very mysterious,' reported Russell. 'He was this person you never used to know anything about, you never used to know quite what was going on with Trevor Lock because he never used to tell you anything. [He was] always into mysticism, stuff like that. But he was lovely to me.' Russell also admired Lock's talents as a playwright. Although the pair didn't associate off-stage much during the play's run, Russell recognised that they had chemistry on stage. About his friend he said: 'So I immediately knew Trevor was dead special, lovely person, but in them days the relationship only existed on-stage not like nowadays, when I have to put up with him for real.'

CHAPTER 6

Telly

CRITICS WEREN'T THE ONLY PEOPLE IN THE AUDIENCES WATCHING RUSSELL DURING HIS PERFORMANCES IN EDINBURGH. TALENT SPOTTERS WERE ALSO IN TOWN LOOKING FOR THE NEXT GOBBY DJ, THE NEXT MOUTHY PRESENTER – THE NEXT BIG THING. UNSURPRISINGLY, IT DIDN'T TAKE THEM LONG TO SPOT RUSSELL AND HE WAS WHISKED BACK TO LONDON WHERE MTV WANTED TO AUDITION HIM AS A PRESENTER.

After that, things moved fast. Russell was a hit with MTV and he found that he had his foot on the ladder. He was asked to present MTV UK's *Dance Floor Chart* and also became a frequent host on MTV Select.

One of the high points of his time at MTV was meeting Matt Morgan, who would become a close friend, collaborator, co-conspirator and writing partner. Russell was still a relative novice to the showbiz game and, in his own words, was 'just becoming a bit of a junkie. I was on heroin by then, maybe crack'. Russell's work colleagues at

MTV weren't his cup of tea. But he hit it off with Matt, who was working as an intern at the music station. 'I liked him straight away. We have similar backgrounds: he comes from Dartford, I come from Grays. We're both unusual little fellas,' said Russell. 'There were some people I liked at MTV then, but there was no one else I really got on with. So Matt was only an intern at MTV, but I didn't want to work with other people. He was my muse back then, that boy, I looked over at him and I knew everything would be all right. And we've stayed friends ever since that beautiful day.'

Matt was not immediately smitten. He was initially unimpressed with the MTV presenter. Morgan recalled: 'When I went for my interview at MTV the man interviewing me said, "We've got this brilliant presenter", and he quoted a few things he'd said. And I thought: "That's not funny."' The interviewer, of course, was talking about Russell. Things didn't improve when Morgan saw Russell for the first time, 'all loud and tanned. He was like some Latin lover.' This only amplified his antipathy. 'I thought, "I hate that man." He was a right old show off and he was all tanned and sort of a pretty boy.'

According to Morgan, the pair eventually bonded on a flight after an administrative cock-up saw Russell bounced from business class to economy. Morgan explained: 'We were stuck on an aeroplane. He was meant to be in business class, but they'd booked him back in economy with me. I had to sit next to him and we talked about comedy and stuff and I thought, "No, he's all right actually".' Later, Russell and Morgan dined together in

54

Dublin and the meal cemented their friendship. However, there was one more obstacle to overcome – Russell's chosen threads for the dinner for two were a vest and a tiny pair of shorts. Morgan joked, 'Everyone thought we were a gay couple.'

The pair learned their craft together. Morgan recalled that Brand had a lot of learning to do, especially as he had no quality control and thought that almost anything he came across was worth filming. Russell believed that inane was good, that boring could be brilliant. Morgan claimed Russell would tell him: 'Put a camera on me and that's telly. I just went to the toilet and spoke to that bloke – and it was brilliant, and that's telly. Just film me.' Morgan told him there needed to be a format, a structure, but Russell simply thought that whatever he said and did would make great TV, no matter what.

Russell and Morgan worked together on *Dance Floor Chart*. Russell's image at the time was nothing special, just the usual club garb of blue jeans, T-shirt and long, straggly hair. Typical music-presenter uniform. The programme's brief was to get the lowdown on clubs, which ones were in, who went there, who were the good DJs and what were they playing. It wasn't supposed to be a vehicle for Russell's wit, but that's what it became. Morgan recalled that because the programme was run on a shoestring he was sometimes drafted in as a cameraman and told to accompany Russell to clubs. 'Normally it was in the dark,' he said, 'and he'd sort of talk rubbish to people and amazingly, he'd get some good jokes and good comebacks... it was totally improvised.' Morgan would sometimes prompt his presenter by providing him with a visual image to stimulate his train of thought, such as telling Russell to think of a horse pulling him through a medieval town. 'I'd say a load of things to him, fill his head with nonsense, then he'd go over to someone and it would come out. It was amazing actually, because fully formed jokes came out.'

But while Russell was coping with everything that his job threw at him, his use of narcotics didn't exactly help. After getting his job at MTV Russell increased his drug intake significantly. Now that he was earning more money he could afford to buy his drug of choice, heroin. Soon, he was involved in a serious relationship with the substance, spending around £100 a day on his habit. He would take it throughout the day, from the moment he got up to the minute he crashed out in bed. Each day was spent in a heroin haze, but it was a view of the world that he preferred. It protected him and numbed the pain. 'It just seemed to make life more manageable,' he admitted.

Russell described his addiction as like being 'wrapped in a duvet of heroin'. He added: 'It reached so far back, people didn't know because I was always drinking, smoking loads of grass, doing coke and pills and it got worse and worse.' Significantly, for such a ladies' man, Russell must have been aware of heroin's potentially disastrous effect on the libido. In smaller doses, heroin – like many drugs – can stimulate sexual appetite and may also increase sensuality. And, although orgasm is generally more difficult to achieve, it will prolong the sexual act. Premature ejaculation isn't a problem for an H user. However, regular users of smack often suffer from a suppressed sexual drive and can find it impossible to orgasm.

Not content with street drugs, Russell also dabbled with prescription medicine. He took Ritalin, or Methylphenidate (MPH) as doctors call it. Ritalin is an amphetamine-like prescription stimulant commonly used to treat Attention Deficit Hyperactivity Disorder (ADHD) mostly in children. It is also one of the primary drugs used to treat symptoms of traumatic brain injury and the daytime drowsiness symptoms of narcolepsy and chronic fatigue syndrome. It is claimed to have a calming effect, reducing impulsive behaviour and can help adult users to focus on tasks and organise their lives. Although Russell hasn't publicly revealed how he ingested Ritalin, abusers often crush the tablets and snort them. The resultant high is similar to snorting coke or speed.

Russell was running quite a few risks by dumping Ritalin down his neck. Side effects include sleep problems, loss of appetite, depression, irritability, nervousness, stomach aches, headaches, dry mouth, blurry vision, nausea, large pupils, dizziness, drowsiness, motor tics or tremors, hypersensitivity, anorexia, palpitations, blood pressure and pulse changes, cardiac arrhythmia, anaemia, hair loss, toxic psychosis, abnormal liver function, and disturbing hallucinations often involving worms, snakes or insects. Oh yeah, and death.

Russell escaped the hair loss, but he really did live on the edge by taking the cocktail of chemicals he did.

Russell's father was worried about the effects the drugs were having. He viewed his son's descent into drugs and addiction with horror. 'I did worry,' he says. 'But, I knew it was important to keep talking to him.' His father's frustration at Russell's self-destructive nature often boiled over, though. At one comedy gig, Russell flopped. He had more coke than jokes. 'I lost my temper with him a couple of times,' said Ron. 'We had one furious row after a gig where he was all over the place. He died a death on stage. He told me that he'd had an ounce of cocaine and no material. It was awful. I shouted at him: "What are you doing? Get a grip."' The pair didn't speak for weeks.

Despite his drug intake, Russell did well at MTV and they liked him. He interviewed pop stars by day and dossed down in crack houses by night. He even introduced Kylie Minogue to his drug dealer, Gritty.

Morgan said: 'He'd swing from massive self-belief to drugged, darkness and madness.' He recalled one incident when Russell was openly smoking heroin. 'The producers were trying to sort out cabs and came to us and Russell was smoking heroin and said: "You're meant to be a producer, all you're doing is producing problems. Go and get us a taxi for God's sake. You're so unprofessional."'

Brand would think nothing of trying to film while high and the drugs began to test his friendship with Morgan. One day, when he was pencilled in to present a programme, the drugs caught up with him. Russell had been due to take the helm of *Select*, an afternoon kids show. But when the time came to shoot Russell was nowhere to be seen. He hadn't called in sick or left a note so no one knew where he was. Aware that he was a friend of Russell's, an MTV factotum approached Morgan and asked if he knew where the comedian was. He said: 'Look, we know Russell has been on heroin. Is that why he is late?' The MTV flunky was only guessing about Russell's heroin use, but when Morgan confirmed that it was the reason for his friend's absence, he went wild. 'What? He's on heroin?' the flunky cried. Morgan attempted to backtrack, but it was too late. He'd dropped Russell in it. But, even fucked up, Russell knew he was spinning out of control. He said: 'Earning more money than I could cope with I metamorphosed overnight from a grateful, cap-doffing Essex boy into a crack-smoking, smack-addicted, fake-tanned slab of unreasonable demands.'

And he hated that fucking dance music, couldn't stand his ears being filled with tinny beats. And he didn't much like the people who came along with it. Throughout most of that year he says he just talked surreal rubbish to pilled-up people. He said: 'People used to say: "You're taking the piss out of clubbers on pills." But, I'd been smoking crack. I was on crack. I didn't know what was going on.'

It was a strange life. He took heroin every hour of the day and the more cash he got the more drugs he bought. His addiction worsened. 'When I was addicted to heroin, I'd wake up, use and do it every hour or so throughout the day,' he said. 'So even when I was doing kids' TV people used to think I was eccentric, which I am, but also I was off my head all the time.'

It was remarkable that he could hold it all down, juggling a heavy workload and an even heavier heroin addiction. 'I was functioning,' he recalled, 'and the reason I was able to function was because I was a child and then I was a drug addict, so there was never a point where I had to cope, like, "Oh God, I feel different from usual." It was constant. I was used to it and I'd just incorporate it into my life.'

This thinking extended into all areas of Russell's life at the time. He would even perform the most mundane tasks while high and elegantly wasted. His thinking was also fucked up, but strangely logical. 'I remember when I started doing driving lessons I thought, "I'll make sure I do driving lessons high because when I'm driving I'll always be high anyway."'

CHAPTER 7

Music and Mayhem

NOTHING LASTS FOR EVER, AS RUSSELL FOUND OUT THE HARD WAY AT MTV. THE DAY AFTER 9/11 THE PRESENTER OVERSTEPPED THE MARK WITH THE BROADCASTER'S MANAGEMENT. ON 12 SEPTEMBER 2001, WITH THE TWIN TOWERS IN NEW YORK STILL SMOULDERING AND WITH THOUSANDS OF LIVES LOST, RUSSELL TURNED UP FOR WORK AT THE MUSIC STATION DRESSED AS OSAMA BIN LADEN. AS A JOKE, IT BACKFIRED BADLY. THE ONLY PERSON WHO FOUND IT FUNNY WAS RUSSELL HIMSELF. HE SAYS: 'BACK THEN I WAS VERY ANARCHIC IN A VERY UNEDUCATED WAY. I THOUGHT, "GOOD, I'M GLAD SOCIETY IS CRUMBLING, I'M GLAD EVERYONE IS AFRAID." WHEN A CATASTROPHE HAPPENS IT'S LIKE I FEEL THAT WAY ALL THE TIME; EVERYTHING'S ALWAYS A CATASTROPHE. SO STUFF LIKE THAT LEVELS THE PLAYING FIELD, I THINK.'

Russell's bosses didn't see it that way and he was sacked. His had not been an auspicious start to a career – he'd only been in the job about a year. However, he soon found work elsewhere, when he was taken on at London's indie radio station, Xfm.

This seemed like an ideal move for Russell. Working on a radio station wasn't too much like hard work, just spinning a few discs and spinning a few lines on top of that. It was right up Russell's street. Plus, it was Xfm. It played indie, the kind of music that Russell liked. He could indulge his love of The Smiths and Morrissey to his heart's content.

The Smiths had been the band that Russell grew up on. He was only seven when they released their first single, 'Hand in Glove', nine when 'How Soon is Now?' came out. For Russell, Morrissey songs such as 'Sheila Take a Bow' and 'Panic' 'surmises being a teen and having dreams.' Russell even named his pet cat after the Stretford singer.

Morrissey's lyrics, with their tales of ordinary, dreary lives strongly appealed to Russell's sense of being an outsider. He confessed: 'For me, Morrissey is the poet of alienation and isolation; he beautifies the mundane. Sometimes I feel, "Oh I'm not good enough, I'm all weak and vulnerable, I'm not like the bigger boys."' Morrissey, however, is able to take Russell and put him in another place. 'He defies being gauche and an outsider and makes it seem beautiful and poetic and humorous. The reason I like Morrissey so much is because he's the pope of the damned and awkward. It makes you want to kick a door in and get your bum out.' The song that Russell wants played at his funeral is 'Asleep' by The Smiths.

However, Russell's musical tastes do not begin and end with Morrissey. His tastes are catholic and he isn't swayed by fashion. What he liked when he was a kid, a teenager smoking weed, he still likes. And he likes a bit of oomph with his music. It's got to have passion, energy and some bite – plus lyrics that say something and mean it.

Of course, he likes the outsiders. Pink Floyd's Syd Barrett is one of Russell's favourites, a man whose childlike sense of wonder is, for Russell, 'a necessity when it comes to the trials of modern living'. First thing in the morning, Russell will often play Barrett's 'Dominoes' or 'Wouldn't You Miss Me' and Barrett's *The Madcap Laughs* is one of Russell's most cherished CDs. According to the comedian, Syd takes the 'imaginative insanity of children and turns it into beautifully phrased, perfect melodies and funny and delightful lyrics. He transports you to a place called home.'

Nick Drake also gets two thumbs up from Russell, who has described the singer-songwriter as 'insular, isolated, socially incapable and, of course, dead. Committed to him 100 per cent.' Rapper Snoop Dogg's album *Doggy Style* also gets a look in.

Dead and miserable isn't Russell's only bent. Too much black can weary a man and Russell, who clearly has a flamboyant side to his personality, occasionally needs to cut loose and enjoy the sheer glitz of showbusiness. Russell has a soft spot for pop stars who ooze glamour. He includes Elvis and Michael Jackson in this category, and is prepared to forgive them almost all of their sins in return for their making great music. 'I'm almost inclined to let Michael Jackson do what he wants,' he has said.

The cheesy sounds of Lionel Richie have also given Russell comfort in the past. His hoary standard 'Three Times A Lady' was often unsheathed and given a whirl on the decks when his flatmates – at the time, all hard house fanatics – left Russell alone. Embarrassingly, he was once having a moment alone with Richie when they returned and caught him listening to it.

But even Richie isn't romantic enough for Russell. If love is in the air, Russell will flick through his record collection until he emerges with the Ink Spots classic 'If I Didn't Care'. He also likes Arcade Fire and ex-Blur guitarist and 'King of Camden' Graham Coxon, whose album *Happiness in Magazines* Russell believes is 'Near perfect: humorous, English, stunning and intense'. Editors, purveyors of gloomy, Joy Division-esque tunes like 'Munich' and 'All Sparks', and the more jaunty Zutons, are also Russell favourites.

Even indie chuckle merchants Half Man Half Biscuit, who number tunes like 'I Hate Nerys Hughes' and '99% of Gargoyles Look Like Bob Todd' among their repertoire, get a look in with Russell.

The dance misfit Tricky also holds some interest for the former dance show host. Although, he prefers his early work, such as *Maxinquaye*, which was released when Russell was still a teenager and reminds him of dope-fuelled days. 'When it came out... I was taking far too many drugs, but I was also getting comfortable around girls. I was cuddling with pants on, listening to Tricky,' he said. 'I used to smoke soft drugs to soft music while sitting on soft furnishing.' As for dance music, forget it. Russell hates the stuff.

But country and western music does do something for the comedian. He may not dig the rhinestone-and-stetson look, but there's something about the music that gets

Russell's juices flowing. It must be the loneliness and despair – just like it is with Morrissey. Russell has cited the Loretta Lynn track 'Portland Oregon' as a favourite, especially as it features Jack White of the White Stripes. 'It helps me to bridge that gap with country,' he confesses. 'I feel safer getting there if I know Jack is with me.' On the sad side of town, Billie Holiday's 'Love Me or Leave Me', has also been a Russell staple on karaoke nights. 'If the karaoke machine didn't have it, I would march out the pub in disgust,' he said.

Prior to walking out on stage Russell has relied in the past on Jeff Buckley's 'Lilac Wine' to put him in the right frame of mind for whipping back the curtain to be confronted by thousands of faces demanding to be entertained. But when Russell's not in the mood for Jeff Buckley he turns to the more forceful sounds of rapper Xzibit to give him some pre-performance energy.

But, undoubtedly, one of Russell's favourite acts of recent years has been Dirty Pretty Things, run by his mate Carl Barat, former partner of Pete Doherty in The Libertines. He was a fan of that band, too. Russell saw Carl and Pete, who would stage guerrilla comedy shows in squats or their East End flat – the so-called Albion Rooms – as London's punk laureates. 'Much of their music sounds like the capital, distilled into sound, and their relationship with this city, particularly the East End early in their career, is legendary,' Russell enthused. 'The spontaneous gigs have stitched the band into the tapestry of London's musical heritage.' Indeed, The Libertines' 'sexy, raw, beautiful' album *Up The Bracket* has been spun on Russell's hi-fi countless times. If he wants to get a party started, he will always slip on something by The Libertines, preferably the 'beautiful poetry' of 'Tell the King' or 'The Delaney'.

Russell was an early champion of Dirty Pretty Things. He has played their songs at his comedy shows – the entire *Waterloo to Anywhere* album during the 2006-07 *Shame* tour – and acted as compere – complete with dandyish silver-topped cane – at Dirty Pretty Things' gigs, including the band's acoustic appearance at the charity fundraiser *For Pity's Sake* at Koko in November 2006.

Russell says that meeting Barat was one of the turning points of his life. He first met the singer at a gig in Camden's Underworld. Russell was hosting a benefit for suicidal young men and Barat was playing. Barat arrived with the Queens of Noize, who were also appearing. Russell's impression of his friend, who that night was clad entirely in black, was of an 'impossibly dashing' man. Barat, Russell also noted, was wearing a hat, which would have looked sadly out of place on lesser men, but which gave the 'troubadour assassin' an appropriate sartorial flourish.

Russell was intrigued at Barat's sense of humour, 'his mumbled witticisms and twinkling self-awareness'. But what also surprised the comedian was the singer's voice. 'He speaks like Harry H Corbett and his personality is richly comedic. Indeed, I think The Libertines were as much influenced by Hancock and Sellers as they were by The Jam and The Clash, and like [Peter] Cook, Carl is a quintessential Englishman: eccentric, romantic, charming, and noble.' At times, Russell worries that he overdoes his fan worship of Barat and his group. 'I've not seen him for a while and I'm worried that I've driven him away with excessive adulation,' he said in May 2006.

Strangely, for a raving hetero Russell confesses to a record collection largely devoid of female stars. Apart from Holiday, he can't muster much enthusiasm for any other divas. Debbie Harry of Blondie, perhaps. 'Because I'm heterosexual, I think I transfer whatever latent and unexplored homosexuality I have into the adoration of male pop stars,' is how Russell explains it.

However, landing a job at Xfm – for all its obvious advantages – was a double-edged sword. Russell was still in a cycle of addiction – and here was Xfm giving him even more money to keep that cycle going. When he got his deal with Xfm, Russell admitted, 'That was it. I was fucked.'

And he was. Fucked up at Xfm, and then fucked by Xfm. For all its alternative, indie credentials, Xfm was then part of the broadcasting giant Capital Radio Group (later, after merging with GWR, media conglomerate GCap). When Russell read out live on air pornographic letters from the *Sunday Sport* his time was up. He was canned. This smut was too much for the indie kids, deemed the station's bosses. They were also reportedly underwhelmed by their Sunday afternoon presenter when he brought a homeless man, James, into the studio while midway through filming a programme for a cable channel.

At the same time, Russell's stand-up career went into freefall. He recalled: 'It reached the point where I wouldn't have any material, so I'd just turn up at gigs and rant. They were invariably dismal failures. There were fights and injuries.' But Russell's failure – or lack of ambition – to capitalise on his MTV and Xfm gigs and land himself a steady job as a DJ or teen presenter did not stop him from getting noticed. He had a real talent for that.

In 2001, while still at MTV, Russell got himself some real exposure, literally. He stripped and ran naked around Eros in Piccadilly Circus during the May Day protests.

Russell claimed that the first riot he was involved in was a Reclaim the Streets protest in April 1997. The direct action group was originally formed in London in 1991 around the dawn of the anti-roads movement. However, its brief widened over the decade and on 12 April 1997, it organised a march in support of some recently sacked Liverpool dockers, workers at Hillingdon Hospital and strikers at the kitchen group Magnet. The group invited trade unionists, the unemployed, pensioners, the disabled, the homeless, refugees, asylum seekers and environmentalists to support the protest. Basically, anyone with a grudge against society was welcome.

But what about those without a grudge? People like Russell? Like many of his stunts, Russell's involvement in the Reclaim the Streets riot was not planned. In fact, it was spur of the moment stuff. A whim.

Travelling on the underground that day, Russell's tube carriage was taken over by the anarchist group Black Bloc at a central London stop. These anti-capitalist hooded urban guerrillas fascinated Russell. 'I became, at once, enchanted by the rebellious energy of these masked rascals,' he claimed. When the anarchists surged off the train at Embankment, Russell followed. They made their way up to Charing Cross Road, which was heaving with an incendiary mix of sacked dockers, their mates, demonstrators and troublemakers, all chanting and waving banners and placards.

The angry mob was faced with an impassive wall of riot police. Russell says the air crackled 'with insurgent danger' and that he was 'immediately, giddily intoxicated with the thought that people protesting can change the world'. Unfortunately, since it was Russell's first riot he was unfamiliar with the protocols of protest. While anarchy and chaos reigned about him, Russell typically managed to make a fool of himself.

Spying a woman engaged in a sit-down protest and being manhandled by the cops, Russell intervened. However, he misread the situation miserably. Russell failed to realise the woman was making a sit-down protest. As the cops grappled with her the comedian sidled up to the police and commanded them to 'at least let her stand up first'. He then leaned into the woman's ear and whispered: 'On your feet soldier.' She was indignant, telling Russell: 'It's a sit-down protest. I don't want to stand, that's the point.' What a *faux pas*. Poor Russell. The demo error, he admitted, had him blushing 'as red as the flags and banners' that fluttered about his head.

However, failing to observe the etiquette of insurrection was not the only experience Russell took from the protest. In the midst of all the mayhem he claimed that he felt 'a sense of socialist euphoria and gleeful solidarity'.

Thus, when the anti-capitalist May Day demonstrations rolled around in 2001 Russell was ready. He thought that the protests would be a good subject for a TV project. 'We grabbed our camera and kit and made our way through the throng to Piccadilly Circus where thousands of people were engaged in a sit-down.' he explained. This time he didn't help any of them to their feet – he joined in. But instead of sitting down he began to prance about and rail against the establishment. One of his first actions was to attack a stationary police van with a giant rubber phallus.

Then, moving towards the statue of Eros and surrounded by hordes of protesters and cops, Russell began to strip off his clothes in support of socialism. In his defence, Russell also admits that, at the time 'I was addicted to crack and heroin and was a bit of a liability in public.'

Russell got down to his Y-fronts before several unimpressed coppers pounced. Despite his pleas of suffering from epilepsy, Russell was frog-marched to a theatre doorway and read the riot act. 'The police folded in around me like dough and dragged me off. I pretended I was epileptic,' he confessed. Morgan, who was with Russell at the time, also recalled the incident. He claimed, even as the police were trying to control the comedian, there were journalists and TV crews shoving cameras and microphones in his face while Russell cried: 'Power to the people!' Russell later dismissed the whole incident as the outcome of too many drugs, too much time and too much ego. 'I was on the old Persian rugs in them days. A bit daft I was. I used to get all exhilarated and excited and I went to the statue of Eros and stripped. Just senseless showing off.'

The police eventually let Russell go, but he wasn't done – not by a long way. Later that afternoon he was arrested for indecent exposure in nearby Wardour Street. 'High on the fervour of the day's revolutionary spirit and opiates', Russell had clambered on to the top of a satellite communication van and stripped again – this time in solidarity with a sex workers' parade. 'While I stood there all naked, my tiny dinkle flapping in the breeze, I thought to myself, "I'm free", he said, adding that his strip must have seemed 'gratuitous and arriviste' to the sex workers.

About his penis, Russell has said that it is 'lovely and delicious' and 'a gorgeous size'. On the same subject he has also opined: 'It does vary though in size, I will say that. It's just the proportions are like... mine is in different areas. I have more in the shaft.' However, few people that May Day would have seen Russell's Johnson in its full glory. The nip in the air did nothing for his drooping dinkle. 'It was chilly that spring and Class A narcotics are no friend of the penis. No one so naked ever revealed so little,' he joked.

Later, Russell confessed the prank had less to do with socialism than showing off and sulphates. 'It was ridiculous – I was always getting up on top of vans and pulling my pants down,' he admitted.

The public nakedness might have been embarrassing, and it might have confirmed what many thought – that Russell wasn't endowed with a weapon of any description during his riotous activity – but the episode did provide him with a seam of comedy that he would use extensively in his stand-up shows.

CHAPTER 8

Hudson to Perry

KATY LOST HER VIRGINITY IN NASHVILLE, TENNESSEE. SHE ALSO LOST HER NAME.

Teenager Katy changed her professional name to Katy Perry – her mother's maiden name – in 2002 because her real name was just too close to that of Hollywood actress Kate Hudson. It is a plausible reason, but there is no denying that it was also a useful way of cutting herself loose from her hit-and-miss stab at Christian rock.

In fact, Katy Perry is also very similar to the name of the Australian clothes designer Katie Perry. When she became famous, Katy's lawyers asked the designer to withdraw her trademark. The designer refused, and the matter hasn't been taken any further.

Katy's first album had failed to storm the charts – even the Christian music charts. From that point she would move away from her roots and recreate herself as Katy Perry – sassy, sexy and smart, and a mainstream pop-rock performer. She did not immediately reject her evangelical parents' strict values, but being away from home – and in a place as colourful as Nashville – she definitely broadened her horizons.

'It was a gradual thing, not like a super "OK, done with that, next!" kind of thing,' Katy has since explained. 'The things that I thought when I was 15 and 16 didn't make sense when I was 21 and 22, just because my perspective had changed. I'd seen more of the world. I'd lived more life and met more different types of people.

'When I started out in gospel music my perspective then was a bit enclosed and very strict. Everything I had in my life at that time was very church-related. I didn't know there was another world that existed beyond that. So when I left home and saw all of that, it was like, "Omigosh, I fell down the rabbit hole and there's this whole Alice in Wonderland right there!" My motto from then on was to live life to the fullest, because at the end you're dead.'

Katy in Wonderland – or Nashville – inevitably meant meeting young men, and just as inevitably this beautiful girl with a delightful figure discovered sex. 'I lost my virginity listening to that *Grace* record [by Jeff Buckley] in Nashville,' she has revealed. 'The good ol' days. We were going to get married. I'm so glad we didn't.'

A new Katy was beginning to emerge: the kooky, wisecracking, colourful glamour queen. Maybe it was hanging out in Nashville – the home of the rhinestone, after all – but Katy had started to develop her own individual and distinctive style, based on retro glamour – very heavy on colour, sequins, makeup and heels. 'Two degrees from a drag queen!' she has joked.

In fact a major influence was a dance class she had begun taking back home in California, where she learned some of the classic old-time dances of the 1930s, '40s and '50s. 'I started [learning] swing dancing, lindy hop and jitterbug,' she has explained. 'I would go to the Santa Barbara rec hall and I would learn how to dance there. I was taught by some of the more seasoned dancers who were actually very involved in the scene.

'These girls would get out of their old vintage Cadillacs with their pencil skirts and their tight little cardigans and their bullet bras. I thought it was so unique and different than what was going on in the 2000s.'

This became the basis of Katy's new look, to which she then added other ideas. 'I think it's grown a lot – it's changed. I love details. I love different colours. I love funny things. I have this one shirt that's got smiley faces as shoulders – so it's really cute and quite humorous. I love a good sense of humour in clothes.' Back in California, she would sneak into Universal Studios in LA, posing as a clothes stylist. 'I'd try on all the clothes, all these vintage gowns, and hope nobody would bust me. I was a glamour ninja!'

While she was developing her own personal style, she was also developing as a musician and songwriter. Apart from giving her a wider perspective on life, these were the other important things that Nashville – with its thriving industry of musicians, singers, songwriters and producers – would give her: a much broader knowledge of pop and rock music, and how to craft her songwriting.

From the age of 17, Katy was writing songs, making demo recordings and meeting record producers. It was the same hard road that thousands of other singers and songwriters have travelled down, and inevitably she faced numerous knockbacks. She would become used to rejection, and that would become important later on when she faced some bitterly disappointing moments but came bouncing back each time. But all the time she had some other very important attributes: self-confidence, self-belief and ambition. She had a burning desire to succeed.

And she did get a big break. When she had arrived in Nashville to make her first album, her record label had asked her who she wanted to work with. She'd had no idea, having had hardly any exposure to non-religious music at home. But watching a documentary on VH1 that night about Alanis Morissette's hugely successful album *Jagged Little Pill* she discovered Glen Ballard, who had produced the album, as well as writing and producing several other mega-selling hit records – for Wilson Philips, Curtis Stigers and Michael Jackson, to name but a few. She decided she wanted to work with this man and told her producer so.

'He got me a meeting with Glen in Los Angeles, and I had my dad drive me up to LA,' Katy recalls. 'I said, "Dad, stay in the car. I'm just gonna go in, play a song for this guy and come back out." And I did, and I guess it went well, because I got the call the next day.'

As a result of that meeting Katy would work with Glen Ballard on songs for her new album – the first Katy Perry album – for the next three years. It was not straightforward. It would take a long time, and there would be some gut-wrenching setbacks. On three separate occasions the album projects she was working on collapsed. Katy even reached the point where she was considering quitting the music business completely.

At first, things looked very exciting indeed. In 2003 – the year she turned 19 and about the time she hooked up with Glen Ballard – she signed a record deal with a major record label – Island Def Jam. It was a massive breakthrough for the new artist called Katy Perry. What's more, around the same time, her singing talents were spotted by The Matrix – Scott Spock, Lauren Christy and Graham Edwards – who were responsible for writing and producing hits for Avril Lavigne, Shakira, Britney Spears, Hilary Duff, Korn, Busted, McFly and many others. Along with unknown British singer Adam Longlands, Katy was asked to be one of two vocalists on the trio's own debut album.

So by 2004, Katy was working on two albums – one for The Matrix, and her own solo record with Glen Ballard. She had also shed her good girl image. 'I'm completely outrageous and I'll do anything for attention!' she declared in an interview in the October 2004 issue of American music magazine *Blender*, in which they named Katy as 'The Next Big Thing'. It was a few weeks before The Matrix album was due for release. 'At first, I thought, "Crap! There goes my credibility!"' she said in the interview. 'They've worked with some brilliant people, but also people who are hardly artists at all. But if people buy the record, that's all the credibility I need.'

The fact that The Matrix were working with a couple of 'nobodies' on vocals – but who had also contributed music and lyrics to the record – created a bit of a buzz about the album. The first single was 'Broken', and The

Matrix shot a video for it that featured both Katy and Adam performing – Katy bursting with personality in a 1950s-influenced outfit of tight-fitting Western-style red shirt, pencil skirt and stilettos.

But people never got the chance to buy the song. Suddenly, just weeks before it was due for release, The Matrix shelved the whole album indefinitely. In the next couple of years a few of its songs would turn up elsewhere, recorded by other artists – but the album did not see the light of day until after Katy had become a star in her own right in early 2009.

It was a huge blow, but Katy was still working on her own album with Glen Ballard. And she had said in the *Blender* interview that it would be different from the bubblegum-pop approach of The Matrix. 'My album will be more rock, which is probably why my parents think I'm going to hell!' she said.

The interviewer may have thought she was kidding, but she was probably only half-joking at best about her parents' views – although clearly she was not backward about coming forward with her wisecracking. When asked whether she had talent to burn she said, 'No, I've just got really big boobs. And my sweater gets tighter every week...'

Katy was now living in LA and despite the setback with The Matrix, she was certainly making an impact in the music scene in the city, the hub of American music industry. But greater disappointment would follow. Despite working with a producer as highly regarded as Glen Ballard, Island Def Jam dropped her from the label a year after signing her. She then signed to another major label, Columbia – and things got even worse.

Katy and Glen now worked together for more than two years on another album, subsequently titled *(A) Katy Perry*, of 11 songs, each one co-written by Katy. Videos were made for several tracks, with some finding their way onto YouTube. One song, 'Simple', was placed on the soundtrack of the movie *The Sisterhood of the Travelling Pants*. But Columbia would not release this album either.

'Nobody at those labels got what she was about,' says Glen Ballard. 'She had talent, personality, humor, a sense of fashion. They didn't know what to do with it.'

Still Katy would not be deterred. She began writing new songs and recording demos – the start of album that would become *One of the Boys*. But at that point Columbia Records applied the brakes. According to Katy's manager Bradford Cobb, the label did not want Katy to have control over the direction of her music, believing that she should be put with a writing and production outfit like The Matrix.

'Columbia was never really willing to embrace Katy's vision,' Cobb has said. 'Here was this ambitious young woman with a clear picture of who she was and the willingness to work hard, and Columbia just wouldn't put her in the driver's seat. Eighty per cent of the record was done, and Columbia decided not to finish it and dropped her. We got the masters back and then started looking for a new home.'

'It was super-discouraging,' Katy admits. 'I got so close on records that I would bring a copy of it and the artwork and I would show it to my friends and say, "Can you believe it? It's finally happening!" And two weeks later I'd get the call that it wasn't happening.

'You've got to have alligator skin,' she adds, recalling a disconcerting experience when she signed for Island Def Jam in 2003. 'The first time I got signed, they brought me in a room with three other girls they signed at the same time. They sat us down and said, "Maybe *one* of you will ever make a record. One of you will actually take a swing. The other three can go back to middle America and pop out babies."'

Part of the problem was that Katy was different. She wasn't plastic pop but she wasn't a rocker either. She was beautiful – but she also played guitar and wrote her own songs. She did not fit into an easily identifiable category for her record company and they did not know how to deal with that. So they dropped her.

She admits that at that point she did think about packing it all in – but she was still only in her early twenties. 'What else was I gonna do? I'd just turn into a depressed, pill-popping disaster of a housewife.'

At the end of 2006, Katy was an unsigned pop singer and songwriter once again. She was working at an independent A&R company called Taxi Music in Los Angeles, and turning up in videos for POD, Carbon Leaf – and for Gym Class Heroes' 'Cupid's Chokehold', as the love interest of lead singer Travis McCoy – a role she was also playing in real life, with mixed results.

But the outlook was about to improve considerably for Katy.

CHAPTER 9

Wanky Wanky

RUSSELL'S NEXT CAREER MOVE WAS A MASTERSTROKE. WITH HIS CV ALREADY BLIGHTED BY THE MTV AND XFM SACKINGS, UK PLAY, THE MUSIC AND COMEDY SATELLITE CHANNEL, TOOK A RISK AND HIRED HIM.

Russell was given a series of programmes called *Re:Brand*, which arguably had the biggest effect in moving him from being a presenter to becoming a personality and a real TV force.

Critically, Russell was given carte blanche. The subjects he picked for *Re:Brand* were purely those he was interested in. Consequently, the programmes turned out to be idiosyncratic and irreverent. They weren't shows designed by committee and made for the masses.

Some of the things Russell attempted on *Re:Brand*, which he made with Morgan and which aired on UK Play in 2002, were genuinely ground-breaking. The programmes were not particularly amusing. but they were different. It was not the sort of stuff your common or garden TV presenter would like to attempt, and this is what Russell traded on. It became his USP.

On *Re:Brand* he could do anything he wanted as long as it didn't get him killed. 'Most people wouldn't be able to do what I've done, wouldn't be prepared to do what I did,' Russell said. Right there. Alan Titchmarsh standing up to a right-wing fanatic? Vernon Kay fighting his old man? It wouldn't happen. Unless Russell did it.

During the filming of *Re:Brand* Russell wore his hair long and lank, with long sideburns. He looked like Neil Young with big mutton chops – a Crazy Horse who was crazy on horse. Some of the stunts for *Re:Brand* were out there. They were almost social experiments rather than comedy sketches. Each one was based on a premise raised by Russell. One that was not screened because it was deemed too wild for public tastes was based on Russell's thesis that no one could have sex with a prostitute if they got to know the hooker and 'respected her as a person'.

Russell knew a bit about hookers. He had indulged in a little light sex tourism in Thailand with his dad and had used them in Soho. He hadn't wanted them for anything unusual or kinky. Sometimes, he just wanted to have quick, meaningless sex. Hookers were ideal. It was unnecessary to chat them up. No need to wine them and dine them or linger for a conversation after the act. Russell explained: 'For me it was: "I just wanna have sex, I can't be bothered to talk to anybody." Which is terrible, but that's how I was.' However, he did go on to qualify this statement: 'I was mentally ill at the time. And I could never do it again. It was unique.'

Although his underlying thesis for the prostitute programme ignored the fact that many men who are regular users of prostitutes do know the prostitutes they have sex with, it was an inspired idea for a TV show. It was certainly better than *Location, Location, Location* or *Strictly Come Dancing*.

Russell found a willing prostitute and went to stay with her for a week. When he moved in he found that she lived with her husband and her husband's brother, who both pimped her. As a bonus, they were all junkies so Russell fit right in. They would sit around by day and get out of their heads together. Then, the hooker's husband and his brother would rustle up some business. Russell would listen in while his friendly prostitute entertained her clients. He explained: 'They would be out trying to drum up business and scoring drugs and she'd go upstairs with a punter. You could hear them fucking upstairs and we'd be looking after their daughter, their little girl. It was mental.'

After a week of this, Russell wanted to test his thesis and rigorously interrogate his loopy idea. He took the hooker and her husband to the Norfolk Broads.

Out on a boat in the middle of the canals, Russell fished out £50. 'Let's fuck,' he said to the prostitute. The husband was appalled. 'This withered, pinched junkie of a man just cried and cried,' remembered Russell. The guy thought Russell was his friend. In the event, Russell didn't fuck the prostitute – but did that prove his thesis? Who knows.

The programme was never screened, but it did demonstrate Russell's inventive imagination. This wasn't mainstream programming or reality TV. It was something else; it was tricky, challenging and difficult – for its subjects, for the audience and for Russell.

Demonstrating that his living with a prostitute idea wasn't a one-off, Russell set out to test his sexuality. Or, as he put it, 'try and understand homosexuality'. Russell set aside the easy route, the daytime TV, Oprah option of gathering together a few gay men and asking them what they got up to with each other. Russell decided that he had to do what gay men did in order to understand them. He wanted to measure his heterosexuality by engaging in a homosexual act. His solution was to seek out a homosexual man and masturbate him. He would, he felt, only learn about being gay by jerking off another man.

The programme opened with Russell being driven in the back of a black cab to London's Soho. He told the viewers: 'See, I'm not actually gay. People always come up to me and say: "You are gay you are." I say, "No I'm not gay, I've got a really nice hairdo."' He pressed on: 'There is nothing wrong with being gay, it's just that I'm not. Don't mean there is anything wrong with it. So what I wanted to do is wonder why I'm not gay. I wondered if it's social conditioning or if there really is a gay gene. So, what I'm going to do is meet my mate, who is gay, look at his sexuality and see if I can overcome mine. I'll see if I can overcome any heterosexual prejudices and get a man's winkle, a stiff cock, in my hand and wank it until it orgasms. Wank a man's cock into orgasm. See if that makes me gay!'

This programme was called *Wanky Wanky* and Russell expanded on his thesis as the cab drove on. 'I don't know if I turned out heterosexual just because of how I grew up, where I grew up, or whether it is because of glistening, soft orb-like breasts, nipples brushing against my lips, the slow glow of a vagina lowering itself on your cock. Could be that or it might be social conditioning.' Offering a unique insight into his theory of sexuality, Russell went on to confess that he liked 'having stuff stuck up my arse'. He added that he only enjoyed the act if it was performed by a woman. 'It is only gay to have a man stick things up your arse,' he informed the viewers.

After a quick trip around a sex shop, looking at butt plugs and various other toys, Russell performed fellatio on a hotdog. As shoppers and tourists ambled through Covent Garden's Seven Dials, Russell deep-throated a sausage. He then moved on to the market and unsuccessfully attempted to ask out a few gay men. He then tried his luck in a gay pub, where he met Gary. After Russell explained the nature of his experiment, Gary readily agreed to join Russell in the toilets for the TV presenter to offer him hand relief.

As the time to perform his sex act neared, Russell's mood shifted from cocky – 'all right, Gary, get in there my son. I'm gonna toss you right off, you cunt' – to trepidation: 'I'm scared. It's only a physical act though, isn't it? Helping out a friend.'

Eventually, Russell and Gary went into the pub's toilets. The camera tactfully stayed outside while Russell toyed with his new friend's winkle. 'I can never again say I've never wanked off a man in a toilet,' Russell acknowledged, once he had successfully brought Gary to orgasm. 'I just wanked off a man in a toilet. I can't fucking believe I just did that. That crossed the line.'

While ostentatiously washing the hand he had used to jerk off his new friend, Russell confessed that he found the task 'a bit upsetting'. He added: 'It was harder than I thought.' Although he didn't make it clear if he meant the task or the man's cock.

Russell also complained that his hand was now batting for the other side. Fortunately, Gary did not take offence at this or of being the subject of an experiment, which Russell also claimed had 'fucked my head up'. Gary, instead, offered his own counselling: 'Just see it as an experience. You've done a brave thing for yourself. What you've done, the challenge was for you, not me.' He then gave Russell his assessment of his handiwork. 'It was very nice. You were a bit rough.'

Although, Russell revealed that he had had no previous homosexual experiences – he told Gary that he 'didn't jerk off my mates at my school' – there was precious little debate about genetics versus socialisation. If social conditioning had turned Russell heterosexual, it wasn't explored in the programme.

The remaining part of the show saw Russell being chauffeured around Piccadilly in the back of a stretch limo. Champagne in hand, he explained that he needed a woman to set him back on the heterosexual track. 'I want to put my hand in a pussy,' he said, and fortuitously picked up two young ladies who seemed happy to oblige.

Possibly realising that some of his comments might be judged homophobic, Russell screened a rough edit of the show to two gay friends. There was a brief discussion among them about gay sex in public places and then his programme was cleared. Neither of them deemed it offensive to the gay community.

Again, the question that Russell set out to answer at the top of the programme – Why was he not gay? – was never addressed. And, despite suggesting that he was going to 'learn' about gayness, there was also no real insight into the behaviour of gay men.

However, the programme worked brilliantly as an exercise. Put simply, it asked if Russell Brand had the balls to wank off another man – and the answer was yes. And because of that the programme succeeded. He may have overstated the programme's aims and ambitions, but *Wanky Wanky* did answer some questions. Plus, it was entertaining. *Wanky Wanky* demonstrated that Russell Brand wasn't like other TV presenters. He'd have a go. He'd get in there where others wouldn't. He was more than prepared to test himself and his theories, no matter how fucked up they were.

In another piece of inspired journalism for the series, Russell travelled up to Leeds to spend time with Mark Collett. At the time, Collett was leader of the youth wing of the odious British National Party. 'Mark Collett has taken up the sabre of British nationalism,' suggested Russell in his introduction. Russell explained that he had become interested in the student's passionate idealism and wanted to understand what drove it. 'He is quite an idealistic young man. He's got a strong belief system,' Russell said, before adding, 'I don't think I know any fascists.'

Collett was a student at Leeds University, reading business and economics. Russell conducted his interviews with Collett against the backdrop of the 2002 World Cup. England playing football always provides an opportunity for an outpouring of unfettered nationalism so the timing was perfect for Russell: Fascism v Football. It was a good match.

At first glance, Collett appeared like any other young student, albeit one with a metal security gate on the front door of his rundown digs and right-wing memorabilia plastered over his walls. He was slight and articulate. Sensitive even. He wasn't an archetypal ranting skinhead, but his personality did exude a worrying mix of insecurity and intolerance. The young politician did concede that he wasn't universally liked. 'Certain lefties don't like me,' he told Russell, 'but, I'm not really bothered if those greasy freaks don't like me.'

At first, Collett and Russell bantered, sounding each other out. Collett tossed out some paranoid thinking for Russell to digest, a few naïve and misguided arguments. He claimed that the radical left and the media were simply tools of the government. He claimed that Ian Stewart, lead singer with fascist rock group Skrewdriver who had died in in a car crash in 1993, had actually been assassinated because he was becoming too powerful for the establishment. Nuts. Despite this, Collett and Russell initially enjoyed a good rapport and good humoured argument. It was never obvious that Russell had left school with just four GCSEs, while Collett was the product of a privileged education. At no time did Russell look like he was struggling with a rigorous intellectual debate.

In fact, their conversations largely gave politics a wide berth and concentrated on the BNP's social and cultural programme. The pair joked about the sartorial appearance of most right-wing marchers. 'Got to keep the wardrobe white and the ethnic policy white,' quipped Russell. Both initially appeared to relish the cut and thrust and the gentle sparring, which was enlivened when Russell spotted Collett's kick-boxing equipment. 'We thought if we couldn't talk you out of fascism we would just thrash it out of you,' he told Collett.

However, the tensions soon became apparent. It was inevitable that they would. When a camp, left-leaning liberal and self-confessed drug addict rubs up against a member of the BNP, differences are bound to spill out. How Russell dealt with those differences demonstrated that his wilfully destructive and facile behaviour often masks acute journalistic skills. It also showed that he has balls.

The pair went to Leeds–Bradford Airport. Collett was waiting for a friend to arrive from Germany. As Collett and Russell stood in the arrivals area they began to bicker. The whole thing was sparked off when Russell slipped on a pair of sunglasses. Not a crime. No need to call the fashion police. But it plainly upset Collett, who castigated his interviewer for donning sunglasses on an overcast day. Collett claimed that it had taken the presenter's coolness 'down a peg or two'. Russell's response was typical of his quick wit and totally obliterated Collett's pointless badgering. 'I would rather wear these sunglasses than your blinkers.'

What followed then set the tone for the shift in power between the two men and appeared to signify that Russell was tiring of the BNP apologist. When Collett told Russell he was 'not a violent man', the presenter sarcastically imitated him and then replied: 'You are not a man.' It wasn't great insight, but it had the desired effect. Collett, sniffily eyeing Russell, who he had obviously judged as soft and effete, jumped right in. 'Well,' he stammered, 'I think I am a little bit more of a man than you.' Whereas lesser presenters might have let that go, Russell instinctively rose to the challenge. 'Do you?' he spat. 'Based on what?' His verbal attack put Collett on the defensive, and the BNP man was only able to offer: 'Well, based on many things.'

Russell challenged him. 'Such as?'

'Well, I take myself as more of a bloke, more of a man than you.'

Again, Russell pressed the right-wing student. 'Based on what?'

Collett dismissively flicked at Russell's lank barnet and lamely offered: 'Girly hair.'

'You are a princess.'

It was like a panto. 'No, that's you.'

Russell cradled Collett's face and spat, 'You're a little princess, a little frightened rabbit of a boy.'

The effect of fondling Collett's face while simultaneously slagging him off totally disconcerted the BNP activist. It also vividly demonstrated who was winning the ideological battle.

The conflict was continued later in The Original Oak pub, where England supporters had gathered to watch a grudge match between England and Argentina in the group stages of the World Cup. It was a match that England would eventually win 1–0, courtesy of David Beckham.

Collett's political views were again given short shrift by Russell, who used both charm and skill to get the BNP man to reveal his true feelings about homosexuals. Cosying up next to Collett, pint in hand, Russell got the student to confess that he wouldn't sit so close to Russell if he was an 'AIDS monkey'. Although Russell obviously knew what Collett meant, he asked him to amplify. 'A bum bandit, a faggot,' elaborated Collett. When Russell quizzed him further on this, Collett replied: 'It's a pretty sickening thought, having another bloke's dick shoved up your arse.'

Collett's relentless political views began to play on Russell's patience. He had watched the BNP supporters hug and kiss after David Beckham's goal against Argentina. The fact that England, at the time, relied on the talents of several key black players, including Ashley Cole, Rio Ferdinand and Sol Campbell, didn't seem to compute with the right-wingers. 'I recall the jarringly homoerotic views they shared, which sat uncomfortably with their ill-informed views about gays,' said Russell. He admitted to the student that his views were 'making it hard for me to love you'.

Collett's views grated. But, at least he seemed committed. However, this passion soon dissipated. Collett's eagerness to express his views was totally blown apart when he and Russell walked outside the pub and fell into a conversation with two locals, a couple of ordinary working-class lads. Collett and his crew thought that the two boys would be willing recruitment fodder, but they weren't. Like the vast majority of the country, they were appalled at Collett's political stance and they told him so.

Fearing that he'd been set up by Russell – or, more

likely, realising his opinions were only shared by morons – Collett retreated like a sulky teenager. He sought solace with his fellow boneheads. Pathetically, he clung on to the group of like-minded right-wingers and refused to speak to or co-operate with the presenter and the programme any further. Again – and to his credit – Russell didn't concede defeat. He didn't bow to Collett's mood or try to get back in his good books. Instead, he went back on the offensive and challenged Collett and his views. He told the racist: 'Two blokes walked over and what do you know? They think it is wrong to be racist. Sorry about that Mark. That's the world you are living in.' Russell lectured the student further: 'What you believe is fundamentally wrong. You're gonna come up against opposition. That's gonna happen. If you want to believe in that stuff, mate, be prepared for the people around you to reject you. You might have got a bit of local celebrity out of it and congratulations. But let me tell you, this is the end of the road because what you believe is wrong.'

Having the debating skills of a pack of seals didn't help Collett's mates when they attempted to argue that Russell was guilty of making a biased documentary. An even-handed look at fascism is what they wanted, but they didn't get it and the presenter told them why: 'I can't be neutral... It's too important. I can't let you destroy my fucking planet. I love people.'

The resulting 30-minute programme did not critically wound the UK's right-wing movement, but Russell's approach was brave and passionate. And, in showing up the pathetic arguments that sustain bigotry, he revealed Collett and his cronies as marginal characters, as the outsiders and losers that they were. As an outsider himself – and a drug addict to boot – Russell knew what he was talking about. He demonstrated it was possible to be an outsider and not be a loser.

Russell's other programmes in the *Re:Brand* series also showed another rarely seen side to the comedian. One episode was called *Dadfight* and attempted to explore relationships between fathers and sons. More specifically, it dealt with the relationship between Russell and his father, Ron.

The Ron and Russell show, which also set out to identify what it meant to be masculine, pitched the Brands against each other in a boxing match. Russell did this in the full knowledge that his father was much tougher than he was. 'You are aware,' Russell told his old man, 'in Greek mythology and all that kind of stuff to become a man you have to at some point overcome your father or you will be trapped for ever in a place of childhood. And that's not a place that I would like to see myself trapped for too long.' By choosing to pick a fight with his own father, Russell was attempting to move on from his own troubled childhood. He was going to become a pugilist for a day, he said, 'because there are unresolved issues, because I don't think I've crossed that final threshold to become a man.'

The pair went into training for their three-round thriller in an East End boxing gym, with Russell all the while keeping up a running commentary on how he viewed his relationship with his father. At one point, he visited his mother to tell her about the forthcoming bout. She thought the whole thing would be humiliating. Russell told her he thought it would be bonding. He also revealed an unhealthy degree of self-loathing, saying that 'I hate myself. I hate being alive,' and accused his dad of being ambivalent about his future.

Viewers would have discovered very little about the bonds between fathers and sons in general, but were treated to a warts-and-all portrayal of Russell and his dad's fraught relationship. His father's absence during his formative years had taken its toll on Russell, and his low self-esteem was an obvious symptom. Russell was also still bitter that his father had abandoned him as an infant.

The boxing element of the film proved little, apart from the fact that neither man was a natural born slugger. For the record, Russell won the bout. However, the film was successful in the respect that it allowed Russell to undergo successful therapy – on air – in order to realise that the 'problems are in my head, not my family'. It also demonstrated that a less than perfect childhood does not necessarily lead to broken relationships. Russell's bond with his father throughout the programme appeared far stronger and natural than that of many kids raised by a 24-hour, seven-days-a-week dad.

One of Russell's other *Re:Brand* programmes featured the 1980s stunt motorbike rider amd Levi jeans model Eddie Kidd, who Russell hero-worshipped when he was a child. Kidd had been seriously injured in a motorcycle accident some years before and Russell visited the wheelchair-bound and speech-impaired rider at his suburban home in Aylesbury. It was a surprisingly moving film with Russell again demonstrating that he was a sensitive and intelligent interviewer. In one memorable segment, the crew took Kidd out to a disused airstrip and, kitted out in his old Vivienne Westwood-designed jumpsuit, the stunt man climbed on a quad bike and rode off. Kidd beamed as he slowly revved up the machine and recaptured some of the pleasure he used to get from thrashing around on two wheels. Russell was visibly moved.

In another episode, Russell invited a homeless man called James to live with him for a couple of days. The purpose of this programme was to examine how the experience would affect them both.

But, according to Morgan, it was also a testament to Russell's idealism and spirit. 'Russell was ultra-liberal and really believed in human goodness,' he said. Again, it was a case of Russell putting himself at the centre of things – but not for the sake of his ego. It was all for the sake of the programme. Few TV presenters would agree to have anyone, let alone a homeless man, stay at their house as an experiment.

James slept rough on Oxford Street, would shower once a fortnight and could pick up around £50 begging on a good day. But he was depressed by his lifestyle. He felt like a misfit and was sick of being ignored – or worse – on the street. All he wanted was to work. Russell asked James if he felt out of place because he lived on the street, or did he think that he lived on the street because he'd always felt out of place. James told Russell that his life would be improved immeasurably if people gave him – and others like him – some of their time, instead of simply blanking the homeless on the streets as if they didn't even exist.

James and Russell spent some time together, including a visit to Xfm, where the presenter worked at the time. James also spent two nights at Russell's East End flat. Ironically, the experiment petered out when James found that he actually missed the street and his friends on it. 'I couldn't hack it, had to come back,' he said. He returned to his doorway lodging. 'Let's get you homeless,' Russell joked.

Russell admitted that he was surprised, but he also revealed that he was in some way relieved because he wanted his privacy back. 'It totally lets me off the hook that you don't want to be here,' Russell told James. 'This whole experience has left me feeling very strange. Definitely weirder than I thought it would be. I thought I'd coast through it.'

The homeless programme was probably the least successful of the *Re:Brand* series for UK Play, because neither Russell or James had their lives changed dramatically – or for long enough. However, it again illustrated that Russell was prepared to shake up his own life and endure some discomfort for the sake of creating a new angle on a programme about homelessness.

Another programme in the *Re:Brand* series also didn't pan out as Russell expected. But it ably demonstrated Russell's skills as a presenter and instigator because, despite not following the script he had planned, Russell was still able to make an interesting and sometimes moving film.

My Old Tart had a simple premise. Russell would romance an old dear, a pensioner. It was his way of looking at old age and the barriers between different generations. He said: 'What better way to examine the process of getting older and what it's like to be old in the modern world than by me dating an old tart.'

Accompanying Russell on his 'dirty weekend' in Eastbourne was 73-year old Wendy. Russell wanted to see how people reacted when they saw the pair act as though they were in a sexual relationship. The success of the programme relied on the relationship between Russell and Wendy being genuine – or as genuine as the time they spent together allowed. Russell and his crew, therefore, did not plump for some septugenarian freak who was prepared to jump straight into bed with him and who would add little to the discussion.

Instead, they choose Wendy, who had been married and had two grown-up daughters and four grandchildren. The last time Wendy had been on a dirty weekend, she admitted, was when she was in her 40s.

The pair checked into their south-coast hotel as Mr and Mrs Smith, with Russell asking if the room had a porn channel. The staff didn't react at all. Much to Russell's chagrin, none of the other seaside town's residents or guests had much of a reaction to his and Wendy's relationship either. There were no hostile comments or aggressive baiting. No name calling either, just good wishes.

Russell's solution was to push things a bit further, but his ambitions were thwarted when Wendy revealed that she had absolutely no interest in sex. She couldn't give a fig for Russell's dinkle. On that bombshell, it seemed that the central point of the film had been removed. Russell's whole plan had been to seduce Wendy 'because other people think it is weird and unusual [and that] makes me want to do it.' But with Wendy not wanting to play ball Russell had to call it a day – on that front anyway.

What emerged instead was a warm, entertaining and

often frank film that again showed a caring and loving side to Russell. He didn't try to bully Wendy. He simply adapted to the situation to create another style of show. Russell thought that he learned something from the process. 'In the end we did prove something,' he concluded. 'You can have relationships across the generations. Sexual ones probably aren't a good idea. But friendships – it's not a problem at all.'

In 2002, Russell landed a role alongside Steve Coogan and Rob Brydon in a one-off comedy for BBC2, *Cruise of the Gods*.

The 90-minute film united the twin comedic talents of Coogan and Brydon for the first time. Brydon played Andy Van Allen, a washed-up actor. The character had once enjoyed celebrity as the star of a TV science-fiction series. But, in *Cruise of the Gods*, he is down on his luck and working as a hotel porter. Desperate to rescue his self-esteem and conceal his failure, Van Allen embarks on a Mediterranean cruise for die-hard fans of his old show. This on-the-waves convention was organised by the ultra-nerdish Jeff Monks, played by future *Little Britain* star David Walliams. To compound Van Allen's humiliation, his one-time co-star, Nick Lee, played by Coogan, also gatecrashed the cruise. The twist was that Lee had in the meantime become a Hollywood big shot thanks to his starring role in the detective vehicle *Sherlock Holmes in Miami*.

Unfortunately, Russell's role in the Aegean farce didn't make it to the final cut as he was fired after the first week of shooting. Reports had the comic dangling drunkenly from the side of the ship in an attempt to impress a female passenger. He was also said to have been involved in a brawl in an Athenian lap-dancing club, and in a fight in an Istanbul brothel. After he was sent packing, Russell was typically philosophical about the experience. 'The producer told me I was being sent home for a week's shore leave because they feared my reaction to being sacked. I was delivered to the airport like a vet-bound hound who believes he's en route to a sumptuous country run,' he revealed.

However, the ill-fated adventure did have a silver lining. Russell met Walliams on set and although they didn't have much to do with each other at the time they went on to become firm buddies. Walliams confessed on Russell's 2006 TV programme, *The Russell Brand Show*, that he had been repulsed by the comedian's behaviour on board the cruise liner and that it had taken him a while to warm to the comic.

Meanwhile, Russell was still performing in standup – not always with success. In fact, it was in 2002 that he performed what he described as his worst ever comedy gig. It was a show that left him in stitches – literally.

Ever since his first foray to the Edinburgh Fringe as one third of *Pablo Diablo: Cryptic Triptych*, Russell had been regularly returning to the festival. One of his lowest points at Edinburgh came when the comedian, fuelled by drugs and hooch, dragged what he thought was a heckler from the audience to castigate him on stage. It turned out that the supposed offender was in fact mentally ill and had been mumbling incoherently throughout Russell's performance.

On another occasion, Brand managed to get himself

banned from Edinburgh's Gilded Balloon, one of the Fringe's most revered spaces that has played host to every comedian worth their salt, including Frank Skinner and Eddie Izzard. Russell's offence was to have caused a near-riot with his rabble-rousing act and his simulated self-harming on stage, complete with concealed packets of fake blood.

A misguided attempt to spread the Brand brand also backfired on Russell when he employed a rabble of local street urchins to distribute his flyers. According to the comedian, they 'ran amok in the venue, spitting at theatregoers and stealing prophylactics from the production office.'

These, Russell conceded, were 'all humiliating affairs that blighted the Fringe at the beginning of the millennium as I, blanched with booze and weary with narcotics, stretched the term comedian membrane-thin.'

However, the nadir of his early stand-up career came in August 2002. Russell was the compere for a show called *The Best of So You Think You're Funny?* Instead of playing an avuncular host, a charming guide through the evening's entertainment, Russell came out to face the audience loaded on booze and drugs. In a crazy piece of abstract theatre, Russell attempted to educate the audience in social culpability in relation to crime and criminals – namely, how murderers grow amongst us. Unfortunately, Russell picked as an example the Soham murderer Ian Huntley and his former girlfriend Maxine Carr. Both had been arrested – and would later be sentenced – for the murders of ten-year-olds Jessica Chapman and Holly Wells.

His mind awash in a sea of hooch and narcotics,

Russell found that his argument ran aground. He said: 'If memory serves correctly, I climaxed by bawling accusations at several individuals in the front row, damning them for these faraway atrocities.' When Russell introduced the next act, the comedian, Rob Rouse, he left the stage with the audience seething with resentment. Rouse did his best to lighten the atmosphere, telling the crowd that, 'Russell's comedy is terrific, if you watch whilst high on heroin.'

When Russell returned to the arena after Rouse's act he proved that he wasn't finished yet and began to goad the crowd further. He does not have a clear memory of what happened next, but he believes that he bared his genitals and then hurled a bottle. He also knocked the mic to the floor before climbing into the front row of the audience, where he got into a fight. At this point, the Gilded Balloon's security men piled in.

The revue's erstwhile compere was forcibly ejected from the arena – and in the process was thrown through a glass door. That evening Russell found himself in Edinburgh Royal Infirmary, where he was given stitches to a badly lacerated leg and told he was lucky he didn't lose the limb. He was also charged with criminal damage to the venue's door. Not a bad night's work.

Of this period, including his stints at MTV and Xfm, his series for UK Play was the work Russell felt most pride in. 'I examined taboos: hanging out with Nazis, wanking off a man, having a bath with a tramp. The show was essentially me having a mental breakdown. But I think it's one of the few worthwhile things I've done,' he commented.

CHAPTER 10

Straight Man

FUELLED BY DRUGS AND ALCOHOL, RUSSELL WAS CREATING MORE COLOSSAL FAILURES THAN SUCCESSES. HE'D BEEN SACKED BY MTV, KICKED OUT OF XFM AND PHYSICALLY EJECTED FROM THE FRINGE. BY HIS MID 20S, RUSSELL HAD A £100-A-DAY DRUG HABIT THAT WAS TAKING OVER HIS LIFE. HE HAD BEGUN TO LOSE HIS BEARINGS AND THINGS HAD TO CHANGE. SO THEY DID.

In late 2002 Russell's manager John Noel insisted that he sort himself out and go into rehab. He told Russell that his behaviour was a turn off for commissioning editors, comedy bookers and his fellow performers. He would soon be unemployable.

Russell agreed. He said: 'I've learned that grand principles and ideas are meaningless if in your daily behaviour you're an arsehole.' He booked himself into Focus 12, a drug-addiction rehabilitation organisation based in Bury St Edmunds. After months of therapy the comedian re-entered the world, drug and alcohol free.

Clean. The Russell that emerged from Focus 12 was a different proposition from the one who went in. He was conscientious, not contentious; professional, not prattish; composed, not chaotic.

More important, he was off smack. He knew he'd never make it shackled to a habit. 'The thing about being an addict is that you retreat into your own little world,' he said. 'Whether you're an alcoholic *Big Issue* seller or high-flying executive coke head, the thing you share is that you are not really there. Addicts are not part of the real world, they are governed by their own agenda. They are glazed.'

When Russell got clean, his old man was impressed. His son had turned his life around and Ron praised him. 'I am so proud. He doesn't even drink coffee these days,' he said. 'He's obsessive about yoga and Buddhism and all those good things. Not many people wean themselves off drugs like that, but he's very strong, like a lion.'

Russell was such as success at Focus 12 that he became a patron of the organisation. He also discovered a surprising and welcome by-product of a life without heroin, crack, alcohol, cigarettes and coffee: Russell got his mojo back. He got his winkle working again. High doses of drugs, out-of-control stress levels, bad diet and generally poor physical health all contribute to lowering libido in addicts. But the sex drive often returns – with a vengeance – following withdrawal. Many former users also find that sex helps to relieve tension during withdrawal.

In Russell's case he swapped one obsession (heroin) for another (sex). He became a fully fledged sex addict. Although he conceded that everyone is motivated by sex to some degree, he claimed he was diagnosed as a sex addict in his first week at Focus 12. 'At this point my behaviour with women was identified as compulsive and dangerous,' he said. 'Deprived of narcotics and banished to rehab in wildest Bury St Edmunds, my predatory nature and promiscuity became ever more apparent. I hounded the market town's shop girls and waitresses with insatiable lust and a fortunate degree of metropolitan aplomb that meant my desperate endeavours weren't entirely fruitless.'

Russell elaborated that in the same way he had become addicted to heroin – he used drugs 'until the tick-tock of constant self-awareness recedes into a cosy brown silence' – he had become addicted to sex.

And it was no joke. He had heard the reports of Hollywood star Michael Douglas admitting to sex addiction. For a pre-diagnosed Russell, it all sounded a bit ridiculous. 'When Douglas was reported to be a sufferer I remember thinking, "Oh, how awful it must be. Be strong, Michael,"' he said. But, at Focus 12, Russell learned that the subject of addiction becomes almost irrelevant; it's the condition itself that's the real difficulty. With sex, Russell claimed, 'I love the act itself but that's natural – I am a biological machine designed to enjoy sex. The problem is that, unless I'm careful, I will try to seduce any woman at any time, regardless of cost or consequence.'

Russell believed that people like himself who have already had one addiction are predisposed to pick up other obsessions. It might be chocolate or collecting model train sets. But Russell picked sex. It was more interesting.

Russell was keen to expand. He explained that whereas many people have a type – like black men or girls with big

105

tits – he has no type. 'My sole criteria is, "Will she sleep with me?" There are no other factors because it's not about them, it's about me – it's about escape, a few hours of being out of my head,' he said.

And there are risks involved. According to Russell, his mission to achieve fulfilment has put him in many compromising and sometimes dangerous positions. His pursuit of coitus has resulted in tricky – and sticky – scenarios, such as sleeping with the sisters of friends. He's diced with death by banging partners of relatives. He's risked life and limb with prostitutes. 'Eschewing the safety of any long-term relationship, I've got myself into dangerous scenarios to impress and seduce women in brothels in Istanbul, lap-dancing clubs in Athens, bordellos in Havana and discos in Basildon,' he said. 'All to get high, to anaesthetise the ever-nagging mind but, like all fixes, it's short term, a brief holiday from your head and, when you get back, you find no one's fed the cat, you left the gas on and someone's nicked your washing.'

Since leaving the clinic, Russell has said it has been harder to give up his sex addiction than his drug addiction. But he tries. Oh yeah, he tries and he tries. Yet the odds are stacked against him. The world is a harsh place and it always puts temptation in his path. 'I try, try to behave with control and dignity around women – it's harder than giving up smack,' Russell explains. 'We live in a culture that uses our sexuality to control us. Every commercial you watch, movie you see, or chat you have with your mates endorses the idea of sex. In this context, settling down and not chasing women while not feeling like a manacled eunuch is a staunch challenge.'

But it's better than chasing the dragon, of that he is sure. In fact, Russell believes that sex – in addition to his therapy at Focus 12 – is what saved him. It gave him another way to express himself and was a diversion from smack. It was also less harmful, careerwise, healthwise – everything-wise. 'I realise that if I take drugs again, it will quickly destroy my life,' he said. It's inconvenient being a drug addict. The problem is that being high makes you feel so good. 'I had a big appetite for them,' Russell says of drugs. 'Crack is very good; heroin is wonderful. But, I can't do it all again or I won't get all the things that I want.'

He isn't Reckless Russell any more. He won't do drugs again as he now knows where that leads. No longer reliant on pints of Tanqueray and ounces of smack, Russell found comedy again. 'Now, I always have material and remember that it's my job to entertain,' he said. So that's what he set about doing. At the start of 2004, Russell's return to the big time was being plotted assiduously by his agent, John Noel.

One of the first projects to see Russell return from the wilderness and back onto television was a 30-minute sketch- and stand-up show, *The Russell Brand*, on Channel 4.

Produced by So Television and Vanity Projects, the latter Russell's own production company, the show aired as part of the TV station's experimental series *Comedy Lab*. Noel was credited as executive producer.

Screened on Tuesday, 17 February 2004 at 11.05 p.m. the show, written by Russell and his former MTV colleague, friend and collaborator Matt Morgan, featured

Russell orchestrating the sort of miscellaneous mayhem that has subsequently made his name. Acting as a cross between a circus ringmaster and a glam, gothic MC, Russell introduced guests, rapped a mix of surreal gibberish – sometimes funny, sometimes not – and confronted the public. Alongside all that there were sketches. They were hit and miss admittedly, but inventive and outlandish nonetheless. Russell's high energy levels and wit compensated for the relatively small production budget that had obviously been allocated to the project. The show blended several ideas and comedy genres and some of the humour got lost in the mix. But the embryonic sketch ideas that Russell put together were something Russell was to pursue in later TV shows.

However, as a showcase for Russell's presenting skills *The Russell Brand* couldn't have come at a better time. It put him out there and within weeks he would be picked up by Channel 4 to host the show that would make his name.

In the meantime, he also found that he had a renewed appetite for comedy. Whereas in the past he had sometimes arrived at gigs with a paucity of material, he now put together a new, joke-filled show. As a dig at his former self, he called it *Better Now*. He took it to Edinburgh in August 2004 and treated it as a test of his rehabilitation. It would be his trial by critics. His last visit to the Fringe had seen Russell had been thrown out of the Gilded Balloon for abusive behaviour, so this really was some test. Russell passed – with flying colours. The 2004 shows at the Pleasance Courtyard went well. Very well.

The new material was a chronicle of Russell's odyssey

through a twilight world of whores, heroin and hairdos. Russell described the show as a snapshot of his life on drugs and everything that went wrong with his life because of that. He said, 'It's about the last couple of years of getting sacked from all my jobs and coming off heroin.'

Oddly, after many years of gigging in Edinburgh high on H, he found the experience of being straight – and not in hospital or in the cells – just as strange. His previous experiences of Scotland's capital had taken place purely through cocaine eyes. 'It's weird being here and not drinking and taking drugs,' he commented.

Clean Russell did well. The critics had tired of old, druggy Russell, but they also knew that talent lurked in his fucked-up shadow. The reviews for his gigs were good. Brian Logan wrote in the *Guardian*: 'After this new show, you'd rather hug him that hit him. What works so well is the combination of deceptively sharp wit and Tigger-ish physical enthusiasm... this is still an accomplished comeback for a comic with a flair for language.'

By September, Russell was at London's Soho Theatre, where critic Bruce Dessau described the comic's show as 'funny, frank and frequently jaw dropping'. Dessau thought the highlight was Russell's video footage of his Y-fronted exploits at the May Day protests.

CHAPTER 11

Big Mouth

THE IMPACT OF *BIG BROTHER* ON BRITISH TELEVISION AND CULTURE HAS BEEN IMMEASURABLE. THE REALITY TV SERIES, NAMED AFTER GEORGE ORWELL'S ALL-SEEING, ALL-HEARING LEADER IN HIS 1949 NOVEL *1984*, FEATURES A NUMBER OF CONTESTANTS WHO LIVE IN A SECURE HOUSE, CUT OFF FROM OUTSIDE LIFE.

They are filmed and recorded 24/7 by myriad hidden cameras sited inside the house and are set regular tasks by a remote voice, Big Brother. These vary from short jobs to challenges running over several days. Success in these tasks is rewarded with gifts such as cigarettes or increased weekly shopping baskets; failure results in strict penalties designed to rack up the tension in the house.

Housemates are often called into a diary room to record their progress, air grievances or accept tasks. The contestants nominate their least popular house-mates for eviction and the public decides who should go each week.

The aim of the show is to be the last remaining contestant in the house – and pick up a large cash prize.

Since the first series hit the screens in 2000, it has been a consistent ratings winner for Channel 4. The final of *Big Brother 3* on 27 July 2002 had an audience of 10 million viewers, the highest-ever rating on the channel for non-movie programming. And *Big Brother 7*, screened over the summer of 2006, averaged 4.7 million viewers, with more than 8 million watching the finale.

In addition to the main show, there have been a number of spin-off programmes, the most popular being *Celebrity Big Brother*, in which a number of low-rent personalities are incarcerated together. The public watch as they bitch and bellow about not being famous any more – or not being very famous in the first place.

The first *Celebrity Big Brother* aired in 2001 and a fifth series was lined up to kick off the start of 2007. The show has thrown up some unlikely stars in its time. Left-wing firebrand George Galloway famously paraded around the Big Brother house in an unflattering skin-tight leotard and pretended to be a cat, lapping milk from fellow housemate Rula Lenska's hands. Other controversial participants include US basketball star Dennis Rodman, glamour model Jodie Marsh, 1980s singer Pete Burns and disgraced TV presenter Michael Barrymore.

The show's presenter is Davina McCall, coincidentally also a patron of Russell's drug organisation, Focus 12.

The programme's success led Channel 4 to air several related shows. The first of these, which aired in 2001, was *Big Brother's Little Brother*, presented by Dermot O'Leary. *BBLB* was essentially a magazine-style show, featuring interviews with fans of the show or relatives and friends of the contestants, as well as clips from the programme.

Then, in 2004, Channel 4 and its sister channel E4 launched the show that would find fame as *Big Brother's Big Mouth* with Russell Brand – now clean and sober – at the helm. The show was designed to be a much edgier take on *BBLB*, with a couple of guests and a small studio audience dissecting each day's events in the house. With Russell acting as master of ceremonies, *Big Brother's Big Mouth* was always going to be more hardcore than *BBLB*, especially as it went out live. 'Live television is much better,' Russell said. 'I do get really nervous, but that nervous energy facilitates an excitement. That's just your body getting you ready to have a right laugh.'

Russell's impact on *Big Brother's Big Mouth* was immense and his anarchic approach – often working on the principle of fighting fire with fire and meeting every gobby comment from the audience with a more extreme gobby comment – was ideal for the show's format. The series was a hit almost from the off.

Russell took the success in his stride. 'I'm happy it's done well,' he said. 'I didn't have any expectations, except that it would be a laugh and be good and it's got better.' He was pleased that the *Big Brother's Big Mouth* series on E4 during the run of *Celebrity Big Brother* in 2006 achieved better audience figures than the show on Channel 4. 'You can't argue with statistics. I think it's because it's a show that gives a voice to everyone who wants to talk about *Big Brother*, whether at home or in the studio,' he said.

The shows were totally unscripted and highly interactive. Russell joked that he plied the audience with jelly beans 'lacquered' with alcohol solution to get the party started. 'I delight in seeing people vulnerable,' he joked. He also suggested that the more anarchic things got on the show, the more he enjoyed it. 'I like it when things go mad. That's when I feel at home, whether it's someone getting up and walking out of the studio or someone starts going mental, that makes me excited,' he claimed.

And the success of the sometimes volatile and unpredictable show relied almost entirely on Russell's quick wit and presenting style to control an impassioned, opinionated and often obsessive mob.

He also liked the *Big Brother* inmates. 'A glorious concoction of oddballs!' he said. 'I would watch people and think: "Your behaviour's absurd". But you'd meet them after and they'd be hard to dislike. They're just people going through life and trying their hardest.' He saved his highest praise for the 'astonishing' George Galloway, but also admired Rodman's way with words. 'I truly delighted in Dennis Rodman's colloquial use of the word "motherfucker" instead of "folks". When he was talking... he'd say: "You have to be careful when you talk to thcm people as them motherfuckers will get upset." And he didn't mean it in a pejorative way.'

Indeed, Russell claimed not to have met a 'horrible, spiteful, selfish bastard' connected to the show. He also has no fear of the obsessive fan. 'I like them. I like people. I think everyone's lovely... except perhaps for me. And even I'm all right, really.'

However, the programmes did follow some sort of pattern. There was a format. Each show started with a joke, where Russell picked out a magic moment from the house. Another segment was a caption competition for viewers, who can participate in the show through phone calls, e-mail, text polls or by leaving a message on the 24-hour 'mouthpiece'.

Russell wasn't slow in pushing his own style, which gradually came to define the series. *Big Brother's Big Mouth* eventually became Russell. A whole bunch of Russell-inspired characters and catchphrases developed over the course of the series. Some of these characters have included The Whale, an anthropomorphic cetacean (catchphrase: 'You shithouse') who spoke with a Scouse accent and showed little interest in *Big Brother*. There was also Rosebud the Horse, who Russell suggested shared his home and whom he claimed he forced to engage in perverted sex. Little Jon Connell became another regular, normally appearing in a scientist's lab coat to conduct a variety of experiments and scientific research.

One of Russell's favourite characters was Little Paul Scholes, a small doll with ginger hair, a nasal voice and snub nose based on the Manchester United midfielder Paul Scholes.

A lot of the material on the show was definitely not for children. There was a lot of swearing and Russell was also not afraid to regularly big-up his fabled 'ballbags', the Brand scrotum. It was given regular airings on the show, and Russell claimed that his man-sac was divided between a 'younger, shyer bag' and the 'older, more confident bag'.

At heart, Russell recognised that *Big Brother's Big Mouth* was nothing more – but, also, nothing less – than 'talking to people about people'. He added: 'I think that's good, that is in keeping with what I believe. I don't feel at all compromised by doing *Big Mouth*. It's just people talking about humanity and people's behaviour towards each other.'

Also demonstrating a depth not usually associated with *Big Brother* or its analysis, Russell surprisingly referenced Desmond Morris. He said that the anthropologist argued that a visitor to an indigenous tribe would usually find out they were not talking about God or mythology or some higher culture, but would be engaged in exactly the same sort of behaviour found on *Big Brother's Big Mouth* – gossiping about who is doing what in the next village. He elaborated on this theme using an analogy that few at *Big Brother*'s production company, Endemol, or the programme's critics had probably considered. 'We are so atomised in society now,' he explained, 'and *Big Brother* gives us common next door neighbours. While it is on, we all live next door to that house.'

Russell even accepted the criticism that *Big Brother*, which he claimed to watch for no more than an hour a day, can sometimes be exploitative, sensational and salacious. In his opinion, it is worth the pain. 'What has amazed me about [*Big Brother*] is that humanity always emerges,' he explained.

However, his show has steered close to disaster. Russell revealed that *Big Brother's Big Mouth* has teetered on the brink on more than one occasion. There was a technical cock-up during the 2006 series when a producer's comments and directions to Russell's earpiece were transmitted live on air. He explained, 'Michael Barrymore heard "25 seconds to the competition" and looked all confused, so I had to say, "Don't worry Michael, we all heard that voice."'

Remarkably, Russell's stint as host of *Big Brother's Big Mouth* has resulted in his longest period of employment stability. 'I've never done anything for that long. I was probably never even at school for that long. It's a miracle that it's gone on as long as this. I don't want to get fired from this job,' he revealed.

And although *Big Brother* and *Celebrity Big Brother* took up about four months of his annual schedule, Russell wasn't tempted to jack in the standup. He was more than happy doing both.

After the previous year's sell-out show, *Better Now*, Russell returned to the Edinburgh Fringe in the summer of 2005. This time he had a show called *Eroticised Humour.*

The *Big Brother's Big Mouth* presenter knew what audiences wanted. They wanted confessional. They wanted to live vicariously. They wanted Russell to take them on that journey. Russell didn't disappoint and addressed the usual topics that prey on his mind: sex, death and the manufacture of consent.

Critics argued he was simply replaying his life, but so what? He did it in an interesting way. Unlike most middle-class commentators who droned on about Volvos, vulvas, diets and their dreary little lives in the Sunday supplements, he'd done some interesting things that really were worth talking about.

Russell retold his experiences in what rapidly became a defining style. He delivered his sentences in a mannered way, elongating his vowels and playing with the language. He deliberately selected quirky, offbeat, anachronistic words to describe quite simple things. Sentences would begin with words such as 'thusly', as in:

'Thusly, the story begins...' Russell had developed his own idiom, inventing new words and catchphrases ('eat my fudge', 'piping aside a duck', 'the swine', ''citing', 'a cuddle') and was becoming ever more colloquial in his speech – often lapsing into complete nonsense.

But, most importantly, what he said – and how he said it – was funny. In developing his own very personal style Russell was doing much more than entertaining people or making them laugh; he was inviting them to join his gang, to learn his catchphrases and way of speaking, to become part of the Russell Club.

Russell insisted that his shift in style was a natural progression and not a clever career move. 'I didn't emerge from the womb with this ludicrous haircut wearing pointy boots, talking all Victorian,' he insisted. 'But, neither did I sit plotting in an attic and thinking, "Ooh, it would be good if I suddenly spoke like that, if I mangled grammar a bit and started to wear tight clothes." These things are accumulative, like anybody's identity is accumulative.'

CHAPTER 12

Battling Bob

2006 WAS RUSSELL'S YEAR, DEFINITELY, DEFIANTLY. HE STARTED IT ON THE UP. HE WAS BACK ON TV. OK, NOT MAINSTREAM STUFF, BUT HE HAD A COUPLE OF *BIG BROTHER'S BIG MOUTHS* UNDER HIS BELT. HIS STANDUP WAS NOW WELL RECEIVED AND HE'D BEEN THE TOAST OF THE EDINBURGH FRINGE A COUPLE OF YEARS RUNNING.

But even Russell could not have predicted how ubiquitous he would become over 12 short months. And what he found was that ubiquity brings its own set of problems and rewards. For every person who claimed to love Russell there was another one who hated him. He would end 2006 at the top of a variety of lists: as personality of the year, and as most annoying personality of the year, too.

The year kicked off much as it would continue – on a high. Russell was named *Time Out*'s comedian of the year in February 2006. He was in good company: previous winners of the award included Eddie Izzard, Jimmy Carr and Bill Bailey. Russell had been shortlisted with Chris Addison and Andrew Maxwell in the best stand-up section and ran off with the gong after gaining most votes from the weekly guide's readers. The listings magazine wrote: 'Russell Brand is probably the most exciting stand-up of his generation. Challenging, often provocative and always likely to take you off on the comic equivalent of a roller-coaster ride.'

The magazine mentioned his chequered CV, including his 'riotous history as a TV and radio presenter', but praised his standup. It added, 'Brand's fierce intelligence and perfectly controlled performing skills make for a powerful combination. His two highly impressive full-length shows, *Better Now* and *Eroticised Humour*, could be just the first steps in a glittering career.'

However, just days after winning the award Russell experienced the downside of his new-found celebrity. It would prove to be the shape of things to come that year – for every good thing that happened, there would invariably be an accompanying disaster.

It began with a little row. A small spat that flared up after the weekly music magazine *NME* asked Russell to present its awards show. This took place at the Hammersmith Palais in London on 23 February. Press-related award dos are notoriously boisterous and this one was no different.

Russell was dressed in his best rock 'n' roll attire. He thought he cut quite a dash in his black leather gloves, white silk scarf and pointy boots. He was prepared – and a little flattered just to be there. He admitted: 'If you're me – and I am – and you sort of grew up thinking you was a little bit fat and awkward about himself and embarrassed. Then you get older and you're asked to host the *NME* Awards, right, and you think, "Oh that's good because the *NME* Awards is cool." The person who hosts the *NME* Awards is cool; I'm hosting the *NME* Awards, ergo I'm cool, right?'

Things got off to a mixed start. There was a bit of slapstick with his new friend, Dirty Pretty Things leader Carl Barat, but some of Russell's jokes didn't quite come off and got lost somewhere in the cavernous atmosphere of the Hammersmith Palais. There was a wobble when the Arctic Monkeys mocked the comedian for some comments he'd made about the north-south divide. In addition to the Sheffield-based Monkeys, there were a lot of northerners – mostly Mancunians – in the room. When the group took Russell to task for indulging in stereotypical presentations of northerners they got a big roar of approval from the crowd.

But it was all light-hearted stuff. Nothing too serious. It was a noisy, boisterous place and it was never going to be a night for refined wit.

Awards were dished out in the usual ramshackle way. New Order bassist Peter Hook presented the award for best live band to Franz Ferdinand, the Buzzcocks' Pete Shelley, celebrating his group's 30 years in the business, handed over the John Peel-themed innovation prize to Happy Mondays' Shaun Ryder, and former Stone Rose Ian Brown picked up a lifetime achievement award.

When Russell revealed that Franz Ferdinand couldn't collect their award in person, Hooky redirected the best live band honour to the Kaiser Chiefs instead. Russell's response to this was to ask in a schoolmasterly fashion, 'Do you think that's fair?' The Kaisers then offered the award to another band, The Cribs, which was the cue for singer Ryan Jarman to launch himself on the Leeds band's table. Unfortunately, he got skewered in the process, cutting himself on the Kaiser's myriad wine glasses and bottles. Jarman was dispatched to hospital to get stitched up.

Then it was the turn of Bob Geldof to pick up a prize. The former Boomtown Rat, who since organising Live Aid in 1985 had reinvented himself as a media mogul and passionate campaigner for Africa, had been voted Hero of the Year by the *NME*'s readers. That was some achievement. To collect the award, Geldof had beaten off competition from Caral Barat, Pete Doherty, Liam Gallagher and Alex Turner of the Arctic Monkeys. The veteran pop star was riding high at the time. In the summer of 2005 he had organised the Live 8 concert to highlight the continuing plight of many starving Africans. The event was a huge success, not least because Pink Floyd re-formed specially to play the gig. More importantly, immediately following the concert in Hyde Park Geldof and fellow crusader, U2's Bono, lobbied a G8 summit meeting of world leaders to tackle poverty and disease in Africa. They were subsequently promised a package of $50 billion more aid per year by 2010 and improved AIDS care.

The Hero of the Year looked almost dapper in a dark grey suit and striped, open necked shirt as he strode on the stage. However, no one was prepared for the elder statesman's opening remark as he accepted the award. 'Russell Brand,' he announced, 'what a cunt.'

The first thing that flashed through Russell's mind was that his mum would be watching. The next thought was of who had said it. 'The thing is, right, when Bob Geldof calls you a cunt, in my experience, it's a difficult night because Bob Geldof comes with a lot of cultural baggage, right?' It was the sort of childish and witless dig expected from a young, drunken band member on the first rung of the ladder to fame and trying to blag some media coverage. Coming from a 54-year-old man who had courted world leaders, the comment played badly. It was pathetic.

Russell was momentarily shocked. What had he done to deserve this? He had no idea what he'd done to elicit Geldof's disapproval. It was like he'd been given the finger by Santa. Perhaps it had come about after he'd introduced a video of Bono with the line: 'Here's Bono live from a satellite orbiting his own ego.' Geldof and Bono are good friends, so Russell concluded that might have upset the Hero of the Year. But a little joke like that did not deserve such an insult, did it?

But if Russell was down, he was not out yet. Earlier that day he'd prepared the perfect riposte in case the notoriously prickly Geldof gave him any trouble. He and Matt Morgan had written the ceremony's links in the afternoon before the awards and for Geldof the first thing they came up with was: 'Here's Sir Bobby Gandalf.' It was not exactly *Seinfeld* but it was something. However, they decided in the end not to use it as they thought it might offend Sir Bob. Russell admitted: 'I was worried about it. Matt's going, "Don't worry." And just as we were debating it, it came to me – the perfect line. Sometimes as a comedian a line will come to you that is so beautiful, so perfect, that you think: "I did not create this line. This line belongs to all of us. Surely this is a line of God."'

He road-tested the quip on Morgan. He said, 'Matt, what about this?' and he shot out the line: 'Bob Geldof, no wonder he's such an expert on famine, he's been dining out on "I Don't Like Mondays" for 30 years.' It was a cracker. A nice putdown for the back pocket if Geldof gave him any grief. Russell remarked: 'It's a good line. It's got it all. It's funny, it's clever, it's succinct. It's true. It's all a good line needs.'

But Russell didn't actually plan on using it. He didn't want to stir up any unnecessary trouble or antagonise anyone. Why would he? What would Geldof say to him that would be that awful?

But then Sir Bob struck. The man who sang about 'lookin' after number one' waltzed up on stage, shook Russell's hand and then called him a cunt in front of everyone. As soon as he recovered his composure, Russell reached for his emergency line. He felt like an assassin. Russell pondered all the 'magnificent' things Geldof had done. He thought about Geldof's charity efforts, all he had done for famine relief. That was all on the plus side; but on the minus side was the fact that Geldof had called Russell a cunt.

Russell ran the debate over in his head. He thought of the pros (his mum was watching) and the cons (making an enemy of Geldof) of using his rehearsed line. In the end he concluded that: 'You've got to do something when someone says something like that to you. You have to respond.'

Russell looked over at Morgan standing in the wings. Matt nodded and Russell made up his mid. OK Bob, he thought, stuff this in your Band Aid. Changing the script slightly, he responded: 'I actually think Geldof's the best person to speak about famine, seeing as he's been dining out on "I Don't Like Mondays" for 30 years.'

It had the necessary caustic effect. Geldof, who had nothing funnier to offer than 'what a cunt', shuffled off stage.

The unpleasant exchange immediately became the most talked-about incident of the night. It also announced Russell's arrival as a bona fide celebrity. Suddenly, everyone had an opinion about him. If the world-saving Sir Bob Geldof called him a cunt surely that meant something, right? Surely that made him someone?

No matter how unpleasant the spat was at the time it had a twofold benefit for Russell. It massively increased his profile, and it went straight into his stand-up routine as a priceless anecdote that he could spin for comedy gold.

The press wouldn't let it lie either. The red tops wanted to know who Geldof was calling a cunt. Russell told them. He said it was akin to getting a slagging from Santa. Russell claimed he'd always admired the singer, who first had a hit record when the comedian was still in nappies. Russell argued: 'It was an abominable thing to say. I was mentally ill. I was a drug addict. I nearly died. I don't see how that's befitting of that word.'

Russell seemed unable or unwilling to let the dust settle over his run-in with Geldof. Six months after the event he told the red tops that Sir Bob had still not apologised for his insulting behaviour. But by this time Russell's star was in the ascendancy and few people probably even remembered who had picked up the *NME*'s Hero of the Year award. Russell said he 'admired [Geldof] before and to a degree I still do.'

Russell's evening as host of the *NME* Awards caused him further agonising when he realised a jokey introduction he had written for Jo Whiley might backfire. He'd planned to introduce the DJ with the link: 'Jo Whiley is a woman who insists on breast feeding her children – curiously she considers all homeless people to be her children. Earlier today she had to be physically prevented from putting her boobie into Shaun Ryder's mouth.' Russell then had second thoughts when he witnessed Ryder, a fellow drug casualty, shambling up to the stage to collect an award for the Gorillaz. He realised that the link might be in bad taste and he didn't want to needlessly offend Ryder.

He explained: 'You can't say anything bad to Shaun Ryder – Bob Geldof's already called me a cunt. I'm too late to write another joke... For this joke to work we have to replace that name. We have to find someone, someone in this room, who we don't mind offending, who looks like they might be homeless – Bob Geldof.'

Russell had already compered several comedy events, with varying degrees of success. But the *NME* gig was his first move into the lucrative world of award hosting. Russell had joined the ranks of comedians and presenters such as Jonathan Ross and Jimmy Carr, who are regularly called upon to provide the funnies while dishing out gongs.

He later claimed that he had enjoyed the experience, with just one reservation. 'I did enjoy working the *NME* Awards, don't get me wrong. It was a fantastic evening. A lovely evening, magnificent event. Exciting. Thrilling. Oh, what an honour to 'ost the *NME* Awards,' he said. 'I had a magnificent time – really enjoyed it. Brilliant. Fantastic evening right up until the point where Bob Geldof called me a cunt.'

Reactions to Russell's hosting skills at the *NME* bash and the resulting clash with Geldof were, unsurprisingly, mixed. Like many critics of his comedy, his performance as a host seemed to generate polarised responses.

No one posting on the NME.com site after the event, for example, sat on the fence. One contributor, wrote, '[Russell] was being rude to everyone winning awards. If they're winning they can't be that shite, surely?' Another suggested that Russell was like the 'fat bully at school' who slags everyone off to feel better about himself. Another visitor to the music magazine site asked whether there is 'a more shit host on the planet? They may as well have had a retarded vegetable presenting the awards.'

However, one obvious Russell fan slammed these posters and succinctly summed up the night's spat: 'Russell Brand is very witty, his Geldof comments were mint.' Writing on the same site, another anti-Geldof poster left the message: 'Geldof, if you're so talented, go make a record, release it and put all the proceeds to the starving millions. He is a wank. Talentless arsehole. No one would know who he was on the back of his pitiful pop career.'

But at least the night held one decent memory for Russell, when he met Pete Doherty for the first time. They bonded over 'doleful English humour and home-grown guitar groups'. Then they went for a piss together. 'Well,' Russell explained, 'I went for a wee and he went to the toilet because he's a drug addict.'

CHAPTER 13

Peyps in a Disco

RUSSELL'S ASCENT UP THE CAREER LADDER CONTINUED IN 2006 WHEN BBC 6 MUSIC APPROACHED HIM TO HOST A RADIO SLOT ON THE DIGITAL CHANNEL. HIS PREVIOUS FORAYS INTO RADIO HADN'T EXACTLY WORKED OUT, BUT RUSSELL WAS A NEW MAN NOW. PLUS, IT WAS NO LESS AN ORGANISATION THAN THE BBC ITSELF THAT WANTED HIM. HE MUST HAVE BEEN DOING SOMETHING RIGHT.

BBC 6 Music, as a digital station, didn't attract a massive audience but it was national. It would give Russell a regular platform and an outlet for his comedy. It was a shop window for his talent.

Russell's show hit the airwaves in March, running from 10.00 a.m. until 1.00 p.m. on Sundays. In the old, drugged-up days Russell would never have made it to work at that hour in the morning. But the new, sober, professional Russell didn't have a problem with early rising.

It was originally planned that Russell would co-host with Karl Pilkington, the hapless sidekick from Ricky

Gervais and Stephen Merchant's Xfm shows. However, that didn't pan out. Instead Russell roped in his mates Matt Morgan and Trevor Lock. 'Hey,' the BBC trumpeted, 'Join ole' Russ, Matt Morgan and Trevor "Cocky" Locky on Sundays for three hours of hilarity and chaos.' There was a real and genuine bond between the three men, who took the piss out of each other relentlessly. Russell loved his cohorts, claming that: 'We are inclusive, open, loving, liberal people. We are dead open-minded people, trusting and naive. So say what you will about us, say we are unprofessional, say we are drunk on air... but we are inclusive and don't give a monkey's about nothing.'

Russell once joked that if faced with a scenario where he could only escape a dangerous situation if he killed one co-presenter, he would sacrifice Lock. 'I'd kill Trev and have it off with Matt,' joked Russell, 'because it would humiliate Matt to be had it off with, and Trevor would enjoy it.' In response, Morgan joked that Russell often went too far with his surreal routines. '[He is an] absurd character from the pores out – absurdity seeps from him,' he explained. Morgan himself has jokingly threatened to kill Russell after one joke too far at his expense or one misfired prank too many, but it never got much further than handbags.

Well, not always never. Morgan and Russell used to go to kickboxing sessions together and Russell wasn't half bad at the martial art. According to Morgan, he and Russell did almost come to blows once. 'We did nearly have a fight in a car,' he said. 'I pulled his hair and then we went over a bump, and as we went over the bump I pulled his hair much harder than I would have liked. He just turned around and spat at me. I can't remember if we actually sort of fought verbally after that – I think we did.'

Morgan also suggested that Russell had told him that if they did fight, he should avoid punching him in the face. The comedian told him that his face was his livelihood and that it was 'beautiful'. If it ever came down to fisticuffs, Morgan was in no doubt that Russell would come off worst.

On one occasion, a Radio 6 listener asked the three presenters how they would describe themselves in a personal ad. The result was an interesting insight into how the three men perceived themselves. Lock, living up to his early rep as a mysterious character, suggested he would write the anodyne and info-lite: 'Do you want an adventure? I'm an explorer – let's go up the Amazon!' Morgan's entry was slightly more racy, although his fictional reply was still a long way short of supplying any accurate personal data normally associated with personal ads. His said: 'Is this a sex thing, or a dating thing? Get in touch and we'll find out.'

Whereas Lock and Morgan had provided no clues to their identities, Russell was not as reticent. He got straight to the point, attaching part of his resumé to the fictitious ad and ensuring that no reader of the personal columns could be in any doubt as to who had placed it. He wrote: 'Thirty-one-year-old male, long hair, four dreadlocks, AWSOH (Award winning sense of humour!). I've got awards for a lot of different things but I'm actually deeply unhappy and alone.... Lots of Love Russell. PS. You might know me from such shows as *Dancefloor Chart* and *Big Brothers Big Mouth*, BYE! Love Ooo!'

Similarly, another programme listener asked if any of the radio hosts would describe themselves as dangerous. Lock confessed he was a dangerous driver, but that's about as hot as he got. Although he also admitted to sometimes leaving the gas on. Morgan upped the ante by suggesting he had the capability of killing a man, but didn't specify who.

Just one death wasn't enough for Russell. He believed he could bring down civilisation: 'I'm dangerous because of my thought-provoking philosophies,' he boasted. 'I could probably crumble down society with some of my ideas.'

The subjects on offer for discussion those Sunday mornings varied enormously. Music would often take a back seat to the banter – sometimes less than a dozen track records would be played over the three hours – and Russell's rambling anecdotes and a series of shambolic competitions.

Morgan would often be called upon to deliver a 'cultural review'. Of course, there was usually little of cultural merit and Morgan would simply recount the goings on at an event he had attended during the previous week. One typical review centred on his experiences at a swingers' party. Trevor, in the meantime, was often the butt of Russell's baiting. He was referred to by the nickname Trevor 'Cocky' Locky, mainly because the ex-philosophy student was anything but cocky.

At various times Russell accused Lock of cruelty to animals, of lying and wearing ridiculous – even inappropriate – outfits. Lock's wardrobe choices, best described as geography-teacher chic, were a rich source of comedy for Russell. Lock was also constantly on the receiving end of one of Russell's catchphrases, 'Eat your fudge.'

It was obvious that Russell was the star of the show. Lock was reminded of his place when he recalled that on their comedy tour of the UK in autumn 2006 the pair drove back to London from Bristol. When they arrived in the capital, Russell was anxious to get home and wouldn't make a detour to drop his friend off at his own house. Lock was forced to walk the rest of the way.

The format of the show wasn't radical and the content was not particularly challenging. Often, the style of the programmes resembled the banter of three mates in a pub. The humour, driven mostly by Russell, was sometimes hit and miss and, for someone renowned for stoking up notoriety, there was also very little controversy generated by the shows. Remarkably, no one at the BBC wanted to sack Russell.

However, Russell did fall foul of his BBC masters over his 13 August radio show. Russell used this programme to discuss what he saw as the poor treatment meted out to his friend Ade Adepitan, whom he accompanied to West Ham games. Adepitan is a TV presenter, who won a bronze medal playing basketball at the Athens Paralympics. He also appeared – in his wheelchair – in the popular corporate idents between BBC TV programmes.

Adepitan had sought Russell's advice after he had been refused admittance to a fancy London club. According to Adepitan's version of events, he had been barred on the grounds that he wasn't a member. Adepitan said he had been allowed inside on previous occasions. After remonstrating with a club doorman for a few fruitless minutes, Adepitan left. But, he alleged, as he wheeled off one of the security staff employed on the door shouted after him. Adepitan claimed the bouncer said: 'Yeah, that's right, fuck off you fucking cripple.' A heated exchanged then followed between Adepitan and the doormen. During this the disabled actor claimed that the bouncer repeatedly abused him. The nightclub refuted Adepitan's version of events.

Outraged at the treatment meted out to his friend, Russell invited Adepitan on to his Sunday show to discuss the incident. Russell said, 'I host a radio show on the BBC's 6 Music and realised that this would be a good forum for Ade to chat about what had happened. When he asked me if he should "just leave it", I said he had an obligation to act.' Russell rightly surmised that nightclub doormen the nation over would continue to abuse disabled people unless men like Adepitan raised the issue. It was a brave decision. 'Ade was in a position to turn this horrible experience into a positive one by ensuring the doorman was sacked and his licence revoked,' said Russell.

The BBC weren't as brave as Adepitan. The broadcaster told Russell that the show contravened legal guidelines because the club, which strenuously denied Adepitan's version of events, had not been able to put its case on the radio show. The BBC, therefore, refused to include Russell's discussion with his friend in the show's regular podcast for downloading. Russell argued that without including Adepitan's contribution the podcast would not be a true record of his show and he asked for the whole show to be withdrawn. He added: 'I understand the BBC's position; it must observe its internal code – but so must

I, and so ought we all. It's my belief that we share a responsibility to banish such repulsive behaviour from our society.'

On 26 October the radio audience measuring service Radio Joint Audio Research Limited (RAJAR) published its quarterly figures on every BBC and commercial station operating in the UK. BBC 6 Music's figures made interesting reading for Russell that morning. A 40 per cent hike in ratings for the station saw the number of listeners reach a record 400,000 for the period June to September – up from 285,000 in the same three months the previous year. The audience had only been 354,000 in the previous quarter.

The best part of this was that the BBC credited Russell with the upswing. It was an easy call; no one else was pulling in audiences in the same numbers and the popularity of Russell's show was also obvious by the number of podcast downloads it generated – 140,000 in September, making it the only programme from a digital station to appear in the BBC's Top Ten podcasts.

Radio 2 and 6 Music controller Lesley Douglas, well known for spotting and grooming talent, was quick to praise her new broadcaster. 'It has been good for digital radio to have a star like Russell presenting on 6 Music. He really is at the top of his form,' said Douglas.

The ratings were irrefutable, proof that Russell was good at his job. These were hard, positive facts and not just positive reviews from subjective critics. It was confirmation, if any was needed, that Russell was really very popular. Funny too.

Just days later – on 2 November – the corporation's

bosses had a rethink. They decided to reward their star asset by promoting him to a slot on Radio 2, the UK's most popular station with almost 13 million listeners.

The BBC gave Russell his own Saturday late-night show. Two hours of maverick messing about taking place between 9 p.m. and 11 p.m. Russell was unleashed from the digital world of radio to a wide audience. It was a shrewd move by the Beeb, an obvious attempt by the station to woo younger listeners and to shake up the grey, jowly, profile of those tuning into what was once Radio Snooze.

So, how would Russell fare on the same station as its team of veteran DJs, typified by old stalwarts like Terry Wogan and Ken Bruce? Although the easy-listening station had spent the previous decade overhauling its image by attracting presenters such as Jonathan Ross and Chris Evans, who had swerved close to the edge in their younger days, it was still boresville central for anyone under 20. Surely Russell would have been more at home with fellow motormouth and breakfast show host Chris Moyles on Radio 1?

Not so, reckoned Russell. The man dubbed the most exciting comedian of his generation was all fired up to continue his radio career broadcasting over the easy listening airwaves. Russell laid out his reasons. 'I had a brilliant time on 6 Music and I now can't wait for the challenge of Radio 2,' he said. 'I am honoured to serve an apprenticeship under the tutelage of broadcast wisdom such as Ross, Wogan and Evans. It is the Hogwarts of radio. I just hope I can keep my wand up.'

But he did register some concern that a move out of his digital world might fetter his fun. He had told BBC presenter Jeremy Vine at an audience festival in October that 'I'm at a stage where I don't want to compromise – I don't want to feel controlled or restricted.' When Vine asked Russell if he worried that a controller – concerned that the presenter may push the boundaries of his show too far – might have their ear to the wall, Russell had a quip on hand and joked that, 'If they've got their ear to the wall, Jeremy, then they've obviously missed the whole ethos of radio.'

Russell, in fact, was bullish about the switch from 6 to 2. He rebuffed any suggestions that he would tone down his material for fear of being blamed for a series of heart attacks amongst more mature listeners. 'Radio 2 has a broad appeal,' he said, 'my transfer is indicative of the direction that the station is taking. All I can do is do what I think is funny.'

Lesley Douglas also waded in with her own view of what Russell would bring to the station. 'I'm sure Russell's new show will become a "must listen" for Saturday nights. Russell established himself as a genuine radio talent on 6 Music and has done a brilliant job there. Radio 2 gives him a fresh challenge and a new audience.'

The BBC promised that highlights of Russell's new show would be made available for download and podcast each week and that he would also write a weekly blog for the network.

However, reactions to the move from the station's army of aged listeners wasn't exactly warm. In fact, it was pretty damned cold. The Radio 2 message boards fairly hummed with vitriol as the station's audience pondered and pontificated over its latest hiring. Few thought that

Russell was up to the job. A typical message board posting read: 'Just what we need on R2.... NOT !!!!' Another listener wrote: 'For me, despite all the criticism of Evans, I think he's far and away a better Radio 2 presenter than Russell Brand. Although not to everyone's taste, he has got a long history of radio work and seems to becoming a more mature presenter. But Brand? Radio 1 surely? I don't see how anyone can think he's for Radio 2: 90 per cent of his fans are teenage girls!'

Another posting said: 'If it's true Russell Brand is coming to Radio 2, isn't it about time somebody confronted Lesley Douglas and her ridiculous illusions as to what the R2 listener wants? Well, Sir Tel?' Another depressed listener slammed Russell for being 'horribly juvenile'. Russell's good news day would have been deflated further if he'd read what another listener thought of his style. This one claimed: 'He is a comedian not a radio DJ! What is he doing on Radio 2? He should have stayed on 6 Music or Radio 1! He is more suited to Radio 1 and where most of his fans probably listen, too!'

It looked as though Russell was entering the dragon's den. However, the professional critics were more forgiving – at least, some of them were. The veteran radio critic of the *Daily Telegraph*, Gillian Reynolds, compared the reaction to Russell's arrival with that experienced by Evans when he joined Radio 2 in 2005. He had been shunned initially, but eventually the station's audience grew to like him. 'This is a very shrewd move by Radio 2,' said Reynolds. '[They] seem to be moving into what you would think of as Radio 1 territory. [Russell] has been very successful on radio and could transfer many 20-something listeners with him.'

Russell went out of 6 Music with a bang. He hosted his final programme on the station on Guy Fawkes Night, 5 November. And his last broadcast had all the fireworks of a broadcaster at the top of his game. The Smiths kicked off the programme, followed by a discussion about the fate of former Iraq dictator Saddam Hussein. Russell then mulled over the best bits of his BBC broadcasting career. He decided they included Katie Melua's appearance in the studio and also a slot by the Puppini Sisters. At the same time, he must also have read some of the less-than-welcoming comments from Radio 2 listeners and at the back of his mind he would have had some trepidation over whether his new station would be a suitable place for his anarchic stunts.

After all, he couldn't expect Radio 2's newscasters to incorporate silly words into their bulletins, as 6 Music's Catherine Cracknell had at Russell's instigation. He voiced his reservations in this way: 'When we are on Radio 2, [we] won't be able to do childish things like "Eat your fudge, Trev". We'll be wearing suits. Reithian broadcasting ideals will be observed. We want to elevate and educate. Lord Reith says it is the duty of broadcasters to elevate the listener or viewer.'

Russell played out of 6 Music with 'Boys Don't Cry' by The Cure and bid adieu to his loyal listeners. 'Thank you for listening to us on 6 Music. We have had a lovely time being on this radio station. I've enjoyed it enormously,' he told them.

Russell's first broadcast on Radio 2 was transmitted on 18 November. In a blog dated the same day, Russell wrote on the BBC Radio 2 website: 'Do not be alarmed. I will respect your radio station, promise! Nah, don't worry, it's all going to be a right proper lovely old laugh. Think of me as the new substitute teacher, but don't be tempted to be horrible and victimise me, give me a chance – and for gawd's sake, look after me!'

The first broadcast took class as its theme. Russell was again joined on the late-night show by his 6 Music co-presenters, Morgan and Lock. The first show kicked off with Lou Reed's 'Vicious' and featured input from *Little Britain* stars Matt Lucas and David Walliams, the journalist and broadcaster Jon Ronson and Noel Gallagher, who had become a regular phone-in guest on Russell's 6 Music shows.

Russell needn't have worried about getting the newsreader to incorporate funny words into the news. She graciously allowed Russell's suggestion of 'shenighans' into her report. But Noel Gallagher, for one, noticed that the pace seemed to have slowed. The Oasis guitarist commented: 'It's a lot less boisterous. [You've] turned into whispering Russell Brand. It's like you're all doing it by candlelight. Listening to it Saturday night is like being in the war.'

Elizabeth Mahoney, writing in the *Guardian* the following Monday, found some things to cheer about. 'The best material,' she wrote, 'was the interaction between Brand and his on-air team and Brand's verbal adventures in playful incongruity. The show needs more of that, and more music.' Unsurprisingly, the reaction from the amateur critics – the bloggers – was very mixed. Radio 2's own message board ran hot with comments about the first show and Russell's suitability for the slot. One poster wrote: 'I caught about 15 minutes on Saturday – no music (odd for a music station), just Mr Brand talking about his favourite subject: himself. In the context of his self-love ramblings, the terms juvenile, puerile and narcissistic spring readily to mind.'

Another said: 'I am "put out", as you put it, that this "major talent" (sic) is taking up one of the few slots I could actually sit down and listen to properly during the weekend... Unfortunately, if the "moaners and whingers" were to stay completely silent, it sort of gives a green flag to encourage more of the same to be introduced to R2, doesn't it?'

Other posters referenced Russell's past problems with drugs and his personal life, but some didn't believe this had any relevance in considering his talent. One blogger wrote: 'Lots of us have endured personal tragedy.' Another suggested rather hysterically that: 'Knowing the details of his personal life does not alter my perception of his "talent" one little bit, unfortunately. Would someone be better disposed towards Hitler or Stalin's excesses knowing that they had suffered drug problems, abuse as a child or the death of a relative at an early age?'

Even die-hard fans were not convinced by the move to a new station and whether a later and unfamiliar time slot worked for Russell's brand of banter-heavy, music-lite programming. 'Is it me, or was Russ really, really different last night compared to Radio 6?' wrote 'Mrs Russell B'. 'Maybe its just settling into a new slot, new station etc, but he seemed really reserved and to be honest I was a little bored at times. I love Russ to bits and I am a really big fan so will continue to see how it goes, but it seemed almost like he was much more structured and scripted than on Radio 6.' Many listeners also suggested that station boss Douglas would eventually move Russell to a weekday slot.

Morgan didn't appear phased by the reaction when he wrote the first programme blog. (Russell was not disposed to write it, Morgan told listeners, because he is a man out of time and much in demand. If Russell wrote a blog, it would be akin to seeing 'Samuel Pepys in a disco'.)

Morgan didn't enter into any defence of the programme or offer detailed interrogation of the differences of opinion. In fact, the view from the presenters was nothing more than: 'It's nice to be on R2.' It was going to be business as usual.

However, the new Radio 2 programme host did find an unlikely champion among the professional critics. The *Daily Telegraph*'s Reynolds pronounced herself a fan. More particularly, she was a fan of the voice that 'leaps from Romford to RADA'. Despite admitting she found Brand a 'pain' on TV, Reynolds thought he was an 'original' on the radio. She wrote: 'He is funny. He may even be nice. When he talks to his studio "zoo" of Matt and Trevor, he listens to what they say without bullying them in the manner of many other radio zoo keepers.' Reynolds wrapped up her supportive review by adding: 'I originally thought this show was intended for girls getting ready to go out. I realise now it's more for people staying in, looking for a bit of a think and a cuddle. It's addictive.'

CHAPTER 14

Leicester Square

BY APRIL 2006 IT DIDN'T LOOK AS THOUGH THINGS COULD GET ANY BETTER FOR RUSSELL. AFTER CONTRIVING TO GET HIMSELF SACKED FROM MTV FIVE YEARS BEFORE, WHEN HE ARRIVED FOR WORK THE MUSIC CHANNEL.

This seemed an impossibility back in 2001. Then the idea of Russell having any sort of a career appeared far-fetched. But Russell's decision to get clean and his rising popularity over the previous six months meant he was a totally different animal to the manic, drug-crazed host of *Select*. It was this that convinced MTV's bosses to give Russell, another chance.

1 Leicester Square, which premiered 2 April 2006 at 8 p.m. on a Sunday (before moving to the later 10 p.m. slot on Monday nights), was - alongside *Big Brother's Big Mouth* another high profile comeback vehicle for Russell. It was a high-risk strategy for MTV, but one that immediately paid off.

MTV's new weekly entertainment fix was billed as

fearless interviews, special live performances and A-list celebrities debating everything from lactating men to pimping. The series itself was fairly formulaic. Each show would begin with an announcer introducing Russell, who would swan on the set and recline in a flamboyant, zebra-patterned chair. Russell would then usually introduce the musical guest for that week's show and they would perform a track. Then the announcer would pipe up again, this time to introduce the first guest, usually the biggest star booked for that show. An outrageous and obviously fabricated fact or anecdote would always herald this guest's arrival on a sofa parked next to Russell.

The group or band would also be interviewed in another area of the studio before Russell greeted his other celebrity guests at a mock bar, the 1LSQ bar. However, these chats were usually punctuated with a sketch and the regular Daniel and Len's Video Review. This featured Russell playing an old man character, Daniel, while Russell's friend and co-presenter on 6 Music and Radio 2, Morgan, portrayed Daniel's fictional grandson, Len.

Naturally, the video reviews usually took a back seat to Russell and Morgan's imaginations. They would construct elaborate off-stage lives for Daniel and Len with an ongoing storyline following Russell's character's struggle to seduce a social worker called Elaine.

The last segment of the show was usually filled by the For Pity's Sake Help Us feature, followed by another music track from that week's rock or pop group. For Pity's Sake... involved the show's audience posing some of their own personal problems for the celebrity guests to attempt to solve or, at least, dispense some advice.

Other short features that made appearances on *1 Leicester Square* included The Rats sketch, where two humanised rats commented on a topic or subject usually thrown up earlier in the show. Russell also lampooned sister MTV show *Pimp My Ride*, presented by the hip hop DJ Tim Westwood. In Russell's version – called *Pimp My Application* – the *1 Leicester Square* host parodied Westwood's over-the-top presenting style and exaggerated street patois while helping to pimp up someone's CV to ensure they became a more attractive job applicant. Presumably, the station's bosses weren't impressed by Russell utilising one of its own shows for comedic fodder. The spoof appeared just once.

Other characters occasionally thrown into the mix included a Prince Charles-alike model called Gatwick, and Dan the researcher. Dan, according to Russell, was the brains behind the obscure and totally unsubstantiated facts that the presenter would regularly reel off.

Incredibly, in a world populated by myriad chat shows competing for a small pool of A-list talent, Russell's series was successful in attracting a rich and varied cast and cutting-edge musicians. The debut kicked off with the Stereophonics, the Mitchell Brothers, Joel Beckett from *EastEnders* and Pink joining Russell for a natter. He also managed to bag a pre-recorded interview with hip hop guru Sean Paul (later shows also featured outside interviews with guests, including Kate Bosworth, Kelly Brook and Kevin Spacey).

With many other chat shows fronted by bland, interchangeable hosts, Russell's engaging and witty interviewing style was a big attraction for celebrity guests. It meant that many left the *1 Leicester Square* studio having revealed more about themselves than they – and probably Russell – had hoped.

Russell's increasingly hip credentials and his own friendships with rising bands also meant he was able to entice the cream of the music industry into the *1 Leicester Square* studios, including his favourites Dirty Pretty Things, The Streets, Embrace, Guillemots, Orson, The Zutons and Wolfmother.

One highlight of the series was Russell interviewing Hollywood star Tom Cruise. The megastar, in town for the London premiere of *Mission Impossible: 3*, talked to Russell about life, movies and his newborn baby, Suri. 'Suri is spectacular,' said Cruise, 'totally spectacular. I think she's going to have a spectacular life.' When Russell inquired about fatherly duties, Cruise replied: 'We have this whole thing: B and B. [Katie] breast feeds and I burp! It's fun, yeah.' Jamie Foxx also popped into the studio with baby toys and some love, Hollywood-style, for his co-star in the Michael Mann directed *Collateral*. 'I just want you to enjoy it,' Foxx told Cruise. 'And I just want to say that I love you.'

Foxx told Russell: 'I'll tell you what's amazing about Tom Cruise. I name Tom Cruise intangible, because of things he does. For one, he's good looking, he's charismatic, he has all the money in the world and he has a great career. And he's still nice. You don't see it normally. I've seen a lot of people do a whole lot less than Tom and they've got the 95 bodyguards and whatever. Not this guy.'

Other high profile guests throughout the course of the

series included the model Caprice, who gave Russell and *1 Leicester Square* viewers an update on the Gumball 3000 road race from London to Los Angeles.

Jackass bad boy Johnny Knoxville also let rip on subjects as varied as George Michael and sleeping around. David Hasselhoff told Russell that fans regularly feign fainting fits to get backstage at his shows. He also claimed that Princess Diana, who he met at a showbiz party, had been one of his biggest fans. Hasselhoff elaborated: 'She walked in and had a twinkle in her eye. She said, "You look good with your clothes on," and I said, "So do you." My wife said, "You're flirting with the princess," and I said, "Why not?" Luckily, my wife adored her too.'

Pulp Fiction and *Kill Bill* star Uma Thurman revealed that she had no plans to get naked on screen. 'Keep your bum in and get your sword out,' Uma told Russell Brand, who flirted with the actress. 'Well, that's the American way; bum in, sword out.'

Boy George also got a load off his chest on issues including Matt Lucas, East Europeans, penises and pop stars. One thing that got the former Culture Club singer fired up was Elton John's gay wedding to long-time partner David Furnish. 'I've spent many years being abused for being gay,' said George, 'and I love being gay; I love being queer. But Elton John getting married, what is that? I was raised to be an alien, now don't tell me I can be normal. It's too late.'

Russell's regular radio sparring partner, Noel Gallagher, also got himself an invite on to *1 Leicester Square* and, characteristically, laid into one of his music rivals – James Blunt. Russell and Gallagher's relationship developed after the Oasis star went to watch one of Russell's stand-up shows and their friendship meant that Russell was able to coax one of the most frank and hilarious interviews from the musician. Russell revealed that Gallagher believed the comedian used him to 'prop up' his career. Russell disagreed. He thought Gallagher diminished his appeal.

Among Gallagher's pet beefs was the Rich List. Gallagher told Russell, 'I should fucking be in the Rich List. I'm looking down it saying "If I haven't got more fucking money than James Blunt..." He's been going for a year. A year. James Blunt has supposedly got nine million quid, right. Nine million. He's only been going for a year. I've been going for twelve solid. I've spent a lot on sweets, but I should have nine million in the bank. That much I do fucking know.'

While verbally tussling with Busta Rhymes, Russell also got the rap star to reveal that he would love to 'give it' to Missy Elliott. In the X-rated interview, Russell suggested Missy was a female version of Busta and asked whether he'd like to 'get mucky' with a female version of himself. The rapper replied, 'I would love to give it to Missy. Missy's sexy as hell, with those big juicy lips she got. I think we'd probably have a bunch of creative super genius children.'

Talladega Nights actor Will Ferrell also gave Russell something to think about when he groped him during the filming of the show. This intimate encounter occurred after the mic in Russell's back pocket became dislodged and Ferrell stepped in to help. As the actor got to grips with Russell's arse, the normally unshockable host looked as if his eyes were about to pop out of his head. 'Not many people start an interview by just bumming me,' he gasped. After wrapping the exchange, Russell judged it his favourite interview.

However, MTV dropped a bombshell on 13 November 2006 when it suddenly announced that it was axing *1 Leicester Square* to focus on entertainment series in the mould of *Virgin Diaries* and *Pimp My Ride*. An MTV spokesman said: 'It is always a difficult decision to end any show but Russell and the team have done a fantastic job.' The spokesman added that a New Year's Eve special would be Russell's last *1 Leicester Square* broadcast.

With Russell's increasing media profile during 2006, it wasn't going to be long before proper telly came calling. This finally happened in May, when Russell moved – albeit briefly – from the ghetto of digital TV and its modest audience numbers to full fat, multi-million, prime time, proper, national telly – *Friday Night with Jonathan Ross*, no less.

It was Russell's first major exposure to mass-market Britain, his first big TV interview. This was the point at which Russell was going to move from being simply the property of Fringe festival comedy hounds and *Big Brother* obsessives to become known to middle-aged soccer mums, silver citizens, playground poodles and production line humps. Russell was poised to charm and chat to Britain, and Britain was going to embrace him.

The 12 May broadcast had a great line-up. Alongside Russell on the green room couch was Uma Thurman, who Russell had interviewed on *1 Leicester Square*, one of Britain's finest actors, Sir Ian McKellen, and former Blur guitarist Graham Coxon, who was providing the musical accompaniment that night.

The show went like a dream for Russell. It was a high point of his career to date. In the *Observer Magazine*'s review of the year on 24 December, it was listed as a major 'tipping point' of 2006. Miranda Sawyer wrote that Russell stole the show and that 'a saucy, tight-trousered, back-combed ego is unleashed on a grateful nation'.

As guest and host stood and shook hands Russell could rest assured that he had cemented his reputation as a funny man. More than that, he'd enhanced his reputation. And more importantly than all of that, he'd roped in thousands, if not millions, more fans to enjoy the Russell Brand experience.

CHAPTER 15

Cuddles

SOME REPORTS LINKED KATE MOSS WITH RUSSELL BRAND, BUT THESE HAVE NEVER BEEN CONFIRMED. THE MODEL HAD BEEN DISCOVERED AS A TEENAGER AT NEW YORK WAITING FOR A FLIGHT WITH HER FAMILY. AFTER HOOKING UP WITH THE PHOTOGRAPHER CORINNE DAY SHE BECAME A FACE IN *THE FACE*. IN FACT, SHE QUICKLY BECAME *THE* FACE OF THE 1990S – AND NOW SHE'S THE FACE OF WHATEVER THIS DECADE IS CALLED. THE NOUGHTIES? THE NAUGHTIES MORE LIKE, AS FAR AS KATE'S CONCERNED.

By 2005, Moss was in a relationship with Pete Doherty, the hell-raising rocker from The Libertines. Turns out that Pete was too much of a libertine for The Libertines and he was ejected from the group when he refused to address the problem of his heroin habit.

Liberated from The Libertines, the group he co-founded and co-led with his mate Carl Barat, Doherty formed Babyshambles, a band over which he had sole control. A few hits followed, but not as many as hoped. Free to indulge his every whim and without strong characters like Barat to try to rein him in, Doherty persisted in living the high life – and getting high.

In September 2005 Doherty went into recording studios, where he was working with producer Mick Jones, legendary guitarist and songwriter in The Clash. When Kate Moss dropped in for a visit, she, Doherty and Jones were secretly photographed indulging in what appeared to be some recreational drug use – namely, snorting cocaine. Nothing was ever actually proven, but the screaming tabloid headlines denouncing 'COCAINE KATE' were enough. The snaps of fat lines, thin models and scrawny rockers made the front pages of all the red tops. The press went mad.

This was just another day at the office for Doherty. He's been busted for drugs numerous times in 2005 and 2006, and had even served time in Pentonville Prison. But for Moss, being splashed across the front pages of the newspapers was bad news. Suddenly, all the lucrative modelling contracts contracted. As the sponsors and advertisers distanced themselves from Moss she decided to lay low for a bit and fled the country.

With her career seemingly in tatters – temporarily, as it turned out – it seemed as though Moss's relationship with Doherty was over.

Enter Russell.

The 'ever so heterosexual' Russell had always been a babe magnet. Well, as soon as he'd shed his teenage puppy fat and reinvented himself as a camp, Essex-boy dandy. According to his father: 'He's always been popular with the girls – he was known as Golden Boy at college.

He's a young man and I don't see the problem with him seeing lots of women. He's not promising to marry them.'

In fact, marriage is the furthest thing from his mind. For Russell, it's usually all about sex. 'Yeah, sex is sort of a hobby,' he says. 'I like it. Would you believe that there are people who are trying to spoil that for me now? It beggars belief. I know, it's shocking isn't it? Shocking way to carry on. I really likes it. It's distracting ain't it? To have sex. Right across the sexual gamut really from onanism – the sexual act you commit by yourself – to the most exciting, spicy conjugal arrangements, numerous partners.'

Russell's definitely got something women like. Maybe it's his six feet two inches, or the TV fame, crotch-sculpting black jeans, dark, smouldering Byronic looks, bird's nest hair and quick wit. Whatever it is, Russell's not afraid to take advantage of it.

Russell reckons that he has bedded lots of women. Tons of them, literally. How many? Well, he hasn't got an exact score, but he claims it's well up on ex-Rolling Stone Bill Wyman's 1,000 fuck mark. 'I reckon I could take Wyman down,' joked Russell. He also estimated that his count was probably nearer 2000. But that was a joke. *GQ* magazine wanted a number and he pulled that one out of the air for them.

Russell started his sexual activity at 15 – a late starter, he confesses. But he has made up for it in the ensuing years. In fact, he has been pretty relentless. At his sexual peak he reckoned he was bedding around five women each day. One for breakfast, two for lunch and the remainder for tea. It was pretty mad.

In a good week around 20 young girls would have

benefited from his pulsating purple. His delicious dinkle has been offered in a bewildering menu of configurations, from a simple two-ball bunk-up, a threesome and a cross-pollinating foursome. 'I've also had nights when I've looked down my bed and seen a plague of women devouring me,' he reported.

He did have some standards, though. The maximum plague of women allowed under Russell's rules is three. Logistically speaking, he explained, three partners is the very maximum. After that 'nobody is quite sure what they are supposed to be doing'.

There have also been prostitutes and orgies, but no bald midgets. Not yet. Whores were fair game: Soho's finest ladies of the night – and not so finest – plus Thailand's hottest hookers. That's where Russell got the taste. He didn't mind paying for it if he had to.

There have been the indeterminate sex sessions. Brand has a vague recollection that a couple of game ladies proposed a bunk up in their hotel room. Time passed, and he was probed awake some hours later. However, no comely cupcakes awaited him. Sharing his bed was an old woman, several kids and a man in a sarong. The man wasn't happy. In fact, he was quite angry. Russell's explanation was illuminating, if only for the information that this escapade must have taken place in the sort of hotel that doesn't have en suite as standard. He recalled: 'Evidently I'd gotten up in the night in this girl's hotel room, gone to the toilet and ended up in another room. What I love most about it is that there must have been a point when I got into bed with them naked.'

Russell has also had a go at gay sex. He has even

154

confessed that a homosexual lifestyle would probably sit easier with all his preening and poncing around. He wanked a man off in a pub toilet for his TV series *Re:Brand*, and he also apparently tried the back door rhumba on a male accomplice during an orgy. It wasn't a success, though. Apparently, the subject of his erection wasn't 'even a good-looking man'. However, Russell has also contradicted himself on the matter of chocolate speedway merchants. He has stated clearly and categorically that there has never, ever been any man-on-man action where he's concerned. He said that he felt 'nothing towards men physically'.

He accepts that while there may be question marks over his sexuality, he claims that he is resolutely heterosexual in every way. His admiration and infatuation for 'all things female' knows no bounds. When it comes to describing his sexuality, Russell explains it thusly: 'I have this kind of roaring heterosexuality. Traditional, uncomplicated hetero-sexuality, an almost clichéd Robin Askwith thing. People have always asked, "Are you gay?" But it's just not me.'

The onset of fame meant that Russell got to fuck even more birds. Celebrity has been very helpful to the cause in that respect. He didn't even have to put the time in seducing women. Indeed, the amount of seduction required decreased by almost 'preposterous proportions' as soon as fame hit.

Fortunately, the fact that women might simply want to sleep with Russell because he is on the telly does not unduly worry him. He has often advertised his availability at gigs and does nothing to discourage that mentality because he sees 'huge personal gain emerging from that mindset'.

With his charm and dedication to the cause, Russell estimated that in the pre-fame days his hit rate was pretty good. He reckoned he would be able to turn two or three chicks out of every ten approached – a 20 to 30 per cent success rate. Post-MTV, post-*Big Brother's Big Mouth*, post-radio and TV shows, Russell believed that if he hit on ten birds he would be unhappy if more than one or two walked away without feeling the might of his dinkle. That's better than 80 per cent.

However, Russell draws the line at simply walking into a bar, pointing at a good-looking woman and snapping his fingers. That isn't Russell's modus operandi. He's too respectful of women for that. Russell believes women are ladies, goddesses even, and should be treated as such. He resents being referred to as a sexual predator, which is what Dannii Minogue called him after appearing on Russell's MTV show *1 Leicester Square*. A 'vile predator', to be exact.

She claimed: 'He is completely crazy and a bit of a vile predator. I certainly don't think he has cured his sex addiction, that's for sure. He wouldn't take no as an answer. He always goes that step too far. Never quite far enough to slap his face, but usually too far.' Dannii also thought Russell used too much make-up.

The accusation upset Russell. He couldn't understand it. He answered by saying: 'I'm just a man. I'm a big chatty. I like girls, you know? "Vile predator?" If that's the language you're going to use about someone who really ought to be described as "having a bit of an eye for the ladies", then what sort of language are you left with for Peter Sutcliffe and Ian Huntley?' He went on to add: 'I resent the word predator. I like to think of myself as a conduit of natural forces. After all, the most natural thing in the world for people to do is fuck.' For good measure, he added: 'I've always tried to avoid misogyny and aggression when it comes to women.'

To be successful – or for him to be successful – women, Russell argued, should simply be treated well and made the centre of attention. His argument is that everyone naturally wants to fuck, but women sometimes suppress this urge, possibly through pride or because they fear for their reputation. Russell claimed to be able to unpick these responses.

Although Russell is an 'easy lay' that doesn't mean he is without emotion. It doesn't mean he can't fall in love. He can fall in love with the best of them and it happens all the time – every day, for about eight minutes, he has said. 'I'm really not a nasty little pervert,' he argues, 'I am just looking for something bigger all the time, less ephemeral.' Elaborating on this theme, Russell confessed that he would be happy for a woman to come along and rescue him from the sex-obsessed rhetoric that punctuates his conversation and the serial fucking that interrupts his everyday life. He claimed: 'I think I need to meet a woman who can help me stop all this, definitely. I would gleefully leave this lifestyle right now to settle down and have children.' He even believes that one day he can be faithful to one woman.

The evidence suggests otherwise.

Russell is all-hetero love machine, a serial womaniser. 'I'm single, if not a little promiscuous,' he said, 'but not a sex addict. That is compulsive and destructive behaviour. That is uncontrollable.' Russell can control his desires. He just likes sex. Loves it.

And Russell wanted to have sex with Kate Moss. Their mutual pal Sadie Frost put the two together, sending Moss to watch Russell perform at a pub gig. Russell eyed up the supermodel and purportedly told her: 'I know you want to shag me, but you're just going to have to wait a couple of hours until I've finished the show.' The gig over, they retired to society Mayfair club, Annabel's.

But Kate Moss was a private person. For someone with such a high profile remarkably little is known about her 'real' life. She keeps a tight circle of friends around her and the golden rule for all of them is: never talk.

When Russell talked about his interest in Kate he was cast out of the charmed circle. He got the message in the end but it was too late. In an interview with *GQ* he claimed: 'If it were left to me, I'd tell you everything. But it's not just me – other people don't like me talking about whatever it is.' From there on in, whenever Kate's name was mentioned Russell clammed up. It must have been agony for him because it is his nature to be indiscreet. But he was not allowed to talk about it. No comment. He'd comment on everything else, but not that. He would not confirm or deny that he'd had relations with that woman.

But maybe one day he will. It's a fair bet that Russell's did-he-or-didn't-he liaison with Kate will eventually find its way into his stand-up routine.

So that, whatever it was, was that. Russell was out and Kate went back to Pete.

Once more back on the market, Russell continued to

find willing partners. Since his run-in with Kate Moss, Russell has been coy about mentioning names. He claimed that some of his conquests would be 'ashamed' to be associated with him and that he had too much respect for them to drag them into the spotlight of his showbiz life.

That hasn't stopped the media from keeping count and naming names. Of course, it being the British press they don't always get it right, but that never seems to bother them – or stop them. In one example, according to which tabloid you read, Russell was supposed to have bedded three girls in one night during the Edinburgh Fringe in August 2006. While the papers agree on this, everything else is up for grabs. According to one source Russell was 'not on the small side', while another rated him 'pretty mediocre' in bed. One lovely claimed that there was 'nothing to him – anywhere', while another announced that he was 'well equipped downstairs'.

Using the main weapon that he had at his disposal, Russell used his stand-up to pour scorn on many of the ridiculous sex tales he found himself at the centre of. In his successful 2006 tour, Russell complained that in June 2006 The *People* newspaper had entirely swallowed an account of his relationship with glamour model Cassie Sumner. The report was headlined SLEAZY TV RUSSELL BEGGED ME FOR A THREESOME WITH A CHEAP KING'S CROSS HOOKER. The whole thing was made up, Russell claimed.

The article made a series of allegations. Russell had asked Cassie to punish him, it said, adding that he liked squeezing into her undies. It also asserted that he flew into tantrums when Cassie bought the wrong cat food and that Russell begged her for sex on their first date.

The piece, subtitled 'Lover Tells of BB Host's Depraved Lust', also had it that Russell made 'madcap' demands on his lover. It went on to allege that the pair's relationship hit the rocks when Russell revealed his 'obsession' with hookers.

Up on stage, Russell took the opportunity to rebuff and refute every single ludicrous claim, joking that it was hard enough squeezing into his own underpants.

Russell's work on *Big Brother's Big Mouth* has had one perk, in that it gets him close to the housemates. Particular former 'friends' include Becki Seddiki and Makosi Musambasi. Makosi reliably informed one tabloid that Russell was 'an insatiable lover' and knew what he was doing between the sheets. But, she added, she couldn't trust him to be faithful.

Among the many other women Russell has befriended, or otherwise, are ITV presenter Kat Shoob, Abba impersonator and former schoolmate from Italia Conti Elke Heywood, glamour puss Abi Titmuss, promotions girl Jen Smith; rock 'n' roller Courtney Love, fashion buyer Jessica Renton, and model Coralie Robinson.

If Russell so much as talked to a woman the gossip columns immediately announced that they were an item. If he walked down the street with a young lady, the scandal sheets went into a frenzy. When he was spotted with producer Suzy Aplin, the rumour-mongers predicted a romantic future for Russell and Suzy, an ex of DJ Chris Evans. The truth of their relationship was that Aplin was producing Russell's DVD, which was released later that year.

The papers teamed Russell with the most eligible females in the land, though there was no evidence for it. Sadie Frost was one and Peaches Geldof was also supposed to be an object of Russell's affection. This was based on the fact that Peaches had made plans to spend the summer in Ibiza, where Russell would also allegedly be staying. After their run-in at the *NME* Awards, Peaches's father, Sir Bob, decided to intervene. An ever-reliable unnamed source reported that 'Bob freaked out at that one' and told Peaches that she couldn't go to Ibiza.

To keep up with all the fun, The *Sun* installed a special 'Russell's conquests' phone line in September. Anyone who had benefited from Russell's charms was urged to get in touch and spill the beans.

The sex certainly got Russell in the papers. Not a week went by without some commentator poring over Russell's libidinous adventures, real or imagined. It didn't matter that they didn't know what they were talking about. They wrote and wrote and wrote. And so Russell's fame – his infamy – spread. People began to discuss him around the office water-cooler. Was the comedian the real McCoy, they asked, or some kind of 21st-century poncing pretender?

On the fake side, the argument ran that Russell had pinched, magpie-like, his character traits, verbal cadences, dress sense and even his voice from a variety of easily identifiable sources. Perhaps *EastEnders* soap character Dot Cotton was the inspiration for his voice. Or had Russell pillaged the *Carry On...* movies for his vocal intonation? And what part did 1960s camp playwright Joe Orton play in Russell's development?

Russell's rapid elevation was used against him. The *Independent*'s cultural commentator and columnist John Walsh took up the cudgels on behalf of the fakers. In his 'Tales of the City' column on 15 August, Walsh confessed he couldn't fathom Russell out. 'To watch him lurch around the studio,' he wrote, 'gurning and ranting away in that hectic flood, alternately ignoring the audience and sitting on its lap, is to rediscover the concept of the Man You Love to Hate.' Although Walsh admitted that Russell's satirical thrusts were actually 'rather clever', he concluded that the presenter was 'egregiously fake'. He added: 'I don't think I've ever clapped eyes on a television performer who is so flagrantly a construct: a mascara-ed Frankenstein's monster made up of a dozen different rock-star affectations bolted together and subjected to a few thousand volts of lightning.'

To prop up his argument, Walsh bizarrely suggested the people he believed had inspired Russell's development. Paul Rodgers, gravel-voiced singer with early 1970s rockers Free, had apparently convinced Russell of the merits of skin-tight trousers; the comedian's insults and mannered language was a nod to Richard E Grant's character in *Withnail and I*; his beard was deemed similar to Bee Gee Barry Gibb's face furniture; Gary Glitter was apparently the inspiration for Russell's make-up; he had borrowed his walk after watching a new-born foal; his microphone was inspired by Queen's Freddie Mercury; and the scarf accessory was borrowed from John Wayne in *Stagecoach*. Walsh ran with his theme of pastiche and construct. 'It's too postmodern to be true,' he told his readers, 'like a song being sung in seven different styles simultaneously.'

The attack was lame and unnecessary. The references that the columnist – jokingly? – put forward as role models seemed ludicrous. The comedian wasn't even born when Paul Rodgers was still able to wiggle into a pair of figure-hugging strides and belt out 'All Right Now'. It was a slim argument. There was no mention of other stars who based their images on borrowed ideas – like Gary Glitter himself, for instance, or Freddie Mercury, or just about anybody else in the public eye. To fail to do so was missing their point of celebrity and completely undermined Walsh's whole argument. As a comedian, it only mattered that Russell was funny – or not. The question that Walsh should have asked was: did Russell entertain?

In what was obviously a slow news week, two days later the *Independent*'s sister publication, the *Independent on Sunday*, rose to the challenge of questioning Russell's credentials. This time, they asked, was he a real rebel?

Russell had never claimed to be a rebel but that didn't trouble the journalist, Liz Hoggard, who consulted Phillip Hodson, fellow of the British Association for Counselling and Psychotherapy. He stated that much of the bad-boy behaviour of the celebrity rebel pack was 'about adolescents who haven't really grown up, who haven't got a life'. A rebel is someone who refuses to accept authority, is opposed to cherished beliefs and disdains established dogma. Hoggard applied this criteria to Russell and others, including pop star George Michael, Scottish politician Tommy Sheridan, novelist Irvine Welsh, gay rights activist Peter Tatchell and the models Naomi Campbell and Kate Moss.

Although, the piece accepted that a rebel could be a 'dandy, a poser... a curious mixture of shyness and arrogance, gaucheness and charm', which seemed to fit Russell's personality profile well, the broadsheet newspaper had low hopes for his ability or desire to topple society's narrow codes of behaviour. Russell's name, for one, seemed to count against him. The paper suggested that Russell is 'the ultimate media creation'. Russell's decision to go straight and clean up – 'doing yoga, drinking green tea and practising Buddhism' – didn't score too high on the rebel meter either. He was, the piece concluded, a 'synthetic rebel'.

The *Daily Telegraph* also waded into the debate. According to the paper, Russell inspired 'violently opposing emotions in women'. Two of its toff writers were wheeled out to lead the debate. 'Is the Loud Mouth a Love God?' asked Tara Winter Wilson for the pro-Russell camp, while posh totty It-girl Celia Walden took the anti-Russell position. Tara came out swinging. She pulled out some early crisp right jabs, telling her paper's readers that 'like Marmite, you either love or hate him'. Tara then pummelled the metaphor into submission, claiming that: 'like Marmite he's dark and divine with a sharp salty acquired taste'. She followed this with a final flourish. Russell, she pronounced, was the country's 'most eloquent and cerebral' standup.

Not to be outdone, Celia Walden emerged from her corner full of fight. All she could see when it came to Russell was fakery and PR trickery. 'The public is force-fed the blandest of characters who've been chiselled into life by PR men,' she wrote. 'Russell Brand, to my mind, is one such creation.' She argued that until Brand hosted *Big Brother's Big Mouth* he was a 'nobody' and then, squeezing himself into tight jeans and adopting 'quasi-Dickensian speech', achieved some sort of vacuous celebrity, backed up with a few grubby celebrity conquests. Was Kate Moss one of these, she asked? If she was, so what? Take her out of the equation, plus all the other celebs that Russell was 'linked' to without any proof, and all that was left were his dabblings with the young female contestants who stumbled out of the *Big Brother* house to be pounced upon by a waiting Russell.

This was hardly enough to make him a love god, she claimed. 'If he is really as good as he says he is, why do none of his conquests seem to hang around for long?' she queried. Ouch! Celia even dismissed his 'trademark logorrhoea of archaisms' as being carefully aimed at a crowd of boneheads who might mistake it for 'real intellectual standing'.

But she saved the best – or worst – until last. 'My real objection to Brand's brand,' she wrote, 'is that it is nothing new. Pseudo-Wildes have been done to death in Britain. They get less witty every time.'

For Russell, all the tabloid interest both impressed and depressed him. 'Being in the tabloids gets a bit boring,' he said. 'It's not what I'm about. It's a tiny fraction of who I am. I'm not just some bloke going around being lecherous. I like being charming but I've not got a sexual motivation.' Although some of the scandalous tabloid tales made rich material for his shows, sometimes the bitchy barbs hit home. 'I really do care what people think about me,' he confessed. 'It really, really hurts my feelings when I read some things. I think, "Why would someone say that? And why would people believe that?" It makes me very sad that they're so judgemental.'

But then again, Russell loved all the attention. 'I've always wanted to be famous,' he admitted. Russell said that he thought fame would bring him validation – it would suppress the need for him to justify himself. He liked recognition and the sense of power and notoriety that came with it. In fact, when Russell wasn't being written about, he wrote about himself – how he met Keith Richards, what he said to Sadie Frost. Russell lapped it up and the papers lapped him up.

Russell's encounter with the Rolling Stones guitarist was intriguing. The *Observer Music Magazine* wanted someone to interview Keef. It decided it would be fun to send along his doppelganger. Compare *Exile on Main Street* period Keith with Russell. There is little difference.

When Russell received the offer to hook up with the Stones legend he jumped at the chance. Who wouldn't? 'Of course I want to meet Keith Richards,' he told the magazine. The resulting article, however, told the reader more about Russell than about Richards. The meeting was actually very brief – no more than introductions.

Russell then watched the Stones perform. He told readers, eager for more information about their hero Keef, that 'the stadium was perhaps 90 per cent full.'

Still, Russell liked what he saw. 'If they're not as good as they were in the Sixties, neither is anyone else. They have not been replaced.'

OK, so it was not exactly Pulitzer Prize-winning stuff. And

anyone lured into reading the mag based on the picture of Richards on the cover would probably have been disappointed. But the point was Russell had been asked to do the job. He was a celebrity now, someone with opinions, and the *Observer* wanted him to share them.

Other editors wanted Russell's opinions, too. What did he think about the war in Iraq? 'It's a stain on this nation and its government.' How about the rise of YouTube? 'It's a delightful phenomenon that will soon supersede television.' Once he got going, there was no shutting Russell up. You want opinions? Russell's got them.

Here he is on global warming (unable to resist slipping in a gag, naturally): 'We're all facing impending doom! We're so blasé, like we think that it'll be all lovely summers and mild winters. Let's see how much people like it when their grandchildren have to live under the sea. A lot of tabloid newspapers don't like it if people have slightly darker skin. Imagine how they'll cope when their grandchildren develop gills.'

Soon after his interview-that-wasn't-an-interview with Keith Richards, Russell was hired by the women's monthly magazine *Red* in January 2007 to interview his old pal, Sadie Frost. Russell proved unable to conduct the interview without revealing more about himself than Sadie – literally. He lounged around in a skimpy and loosely-tied bathrobe that hardly covered his modesty, let alone his beloved and much vaunted ballbags.

On 17 November, London's *Evening Standard* newspaper jumped all over Russell's ubiquity. It crow-barred his hip image into a throwaway feature about London. Russell was selected as a 'team leader' in the

'Urban Fix' spread in the glossy weekly *ES* magazine. As the sort of 'Experience' Russell would go for, *ES* avoided any mention of orgies and plumped for something eminently sensible: a talk by journalist Godfrey Hodgson, who was a witness to President Kennedy's assassination in Dallas. The piece wasn't particularly racy and – bar the cufflinks – none of the suggestions seemed particularly Russell-flavoured.

CHAPTER 16

Shame

SUMMER 2006. THE SUMMER OF SHAME. RUSSELL WAS PREPARING FOR A NEW COMEDY STAGE SHOW. IT WAS TO BE CALLED *SHAME*.

According to the tabloids, Russell's preparation did not run smoothly. On 31 July the *Sun* reported that the comedian had 'stormed off stage' at the Red Rose Comedy Club in north London as he road-tested his new material. The report suggested that the audience at the small comedy club on Seven Sisters Road in Finsbury Park had been underwhelmed by Russell's material. They had been talking amongst themselves, it claimed, as Russell laboured on-stage. Russell was reported to have ranted at one woman and stormed off stage. He apparently relented and returned to apologise, blaming the outburst on 'depression'.

Russell's preparations may also have also been disrupted on 16 August, when the comedian got into a massive bust-up with security staff at King's Cross station. Decked out in fancy dress, Russell was on his way to a friend's party in Camden. The party's theme was religious icons and Russell was dressed as St Peter. As he attempted to board a train at the London tube station, security staff spotted a toy sword under Russell's arm. Presumably, they thought it was a real weapon so they chased Russell down the platform. A row ensued and the sword was confiscated.

Russell travelled up to Edinburgh in the middle of August with the idea for new show in his head. He was going to try his luck again at the Fringe. But this time things were different. Sometime between booking a week's run at the 120-seat Assembly Rooms and his arriving in the Scottish capital, Brand had become a star.

In August 2006 Russell was now a somebody, a tabloid fixture and red top Romeo. It was Russell's first taste of returning to the city, where he had cut his teeth as a comic, as a celebrity.

The run of gigs would be a test of whether his dalliance with C-list celebrity had blunted or sharpened his comedic edge. The subject of Russell's new show augered well. It was called *Shame. Time Out*'s comedian of the year was going to squat over a mirror and examine his dirtiest, darkest disgraces.

In the old days, Russell had been able to distract himself from feeling clumsy, embarrassed and ashamed. The drink and drugs helped him to do that.
But this was a healthier, cleaner Russell. He could not hide behind the drugs anymore.

Naturally, the most exciting comedian of his generation was the hottest ticket in town. The tiny Assembly Rooms was bursting at the seams on his first night, 22 August.

The show was a roaring success. 'My life,' he told the audience packed into the Wildman Room of the venue, 'is a series of embarrassing incidents strung together by telling people about those embarrassing incidents.' It was a line he'd used on the *Friday Night with Jonathan Ross* show.

It was an intimate setting with a small stage area. A wooden stool and a table on which a bottle of Highland mineral water had been placed were the only items on stage. The Libertines announced Russell's arrival and he appeared before his audience in trademark skin-tight, grey jeans, polished black leather boots and a white shirt topped off with a grey, pinstriped waistcoat.

Russell probed the feelings of guilt and shame that surround harmless acts. With self-deprecating charm welded to a loose, flowing physical presence, Russell recounted an incident that took place when he went on a skiing trip to Val d'Isere in France. A 'conscription skiing holiday', he called it.

He went with a group of around ten men and one woman, Hannah. The men were all northerners 'Men that emanate from their cocks,' according to Russell, adding: 'Cock men, I call 'em... Everything they do is from the cock, every movement. Watch, I will demonstrate them drinking. Watch [mimes drinking]. The cock moved! The cock is involved in every action.'

At Lyons airport Russell – the beta male in the group of alpha cock men – was charged with looking after the bags of his friends as they came off the baggage carousel. That wasn't something Russell minded. In fact, he quite liked it. 'I like the carousel bit of the 'oliday. If your bags come quickly – 'citing. Ooh, ooh, it's my bag.'

But also waiting at the carousel for their bags was a group of Cockney hard men, testosterone-filled geezers. Trapped between a bunch of hardened cock men and a group of Cockney hard men, Russell realised that he was going to have problems when the bags arrived – Hannah, it transpired, had brought the girliest of girly pink bags with her, and it was Russell's job to retrieve it from under the noses of the mob.

In his show, Russell explained his sense of dread. 'I'm thinking, "I've got to collect that bag in a minute." Right, so I've got two options in this potentially humiliating situation: one, I could just let the bag go by, right? Let it go round the carousel, pretend it's not mine. Also, I start thinking, all right – my masculinity is not as typical as theirs. It's not an archetype form of aggressive masculinity. I'm still a man. I don't have to be ashamed of what I am. I don't have to spend my life apologising for being a bit unusual. I don't have to be afraid no more. I can just be me, right? I can take that bag.'

Better than that, Russell revealed he would not only snatch Hannah's pink bag from the carousel, but he would also confront the group of men. Well, not exactly confront them, but let them know he wasn't the girly bag's rightful owner. Tell them he used more manly bags for his skiing holidays. Probably all black ones, with black handles and tough penis-shaped logos. Unfortunately, when Russell engaged them he did so by cooing in a girly voice: 'Oooh-oh.'

It was a slight anecdote. A story of camping it up around a carousel. But Russell expertly – using mincing mimes, tough guy postures and a variety of voices –

turned it into an engaging and witty story, a story of shame and embarrassment – something that would make Russell curl up and wince every time he replayed it in his mind. It fit the show perfectly and was a good opener, but he didn't allow the clever yarn to end there. Russell's comedy is about wringing out the wit and there was more shame to shape into the salacious skit.

He described how an automatic door barred his exit. With his feeble exchange with the ringleader of the Cockney cowboys still ringing in his ears, Russell walked up to the door – which unhelpfully failed to open. He stood before it, perplexed. Was is broken? Or on a delay? What was he doing wrong? And, more importantly, were the Cockneys watching? Of course they were. When the door eventually opened Russell heard his tormentor mockingly call out: 'That was complicated, wasn't it?' Outfoxed again, Russell could only reply in a mincing voice: 'I can see you boys are going to be trouble.' Not a good punchline, he admitted. But it was too late, he'd said it now and it was out there. The fabled quick wit of Russell Brand. Not. However, it made a good story for *Shame*. 'You know when you've said something like that,' he told his audience, 'that's it. It's out in the world now. It's part of your life, ain't it? With you, that's it, you've said that thing. Humiliating. I've gotta live with that knowledge.'

Russell's ease with sexuality emerged during one part of the *Shame* show. He openly revealed his drug and alcohol addictions and then turned to his latest compulsion: sex. 'I used to deal with my sense of shame by drinking and taking huge amounts of drugs. Now I like to have it off,' he explained. Sex, he told the audience, provided him with 'absolute context. Nothing else exists in that moment. You don't have to feel shame'.

He also talked about talking dirty. He claimed: 'Talking dirty is good because it stops intimacy from forming. Otherwise, you might begin to talk properly and she'll say, "Oh, my brother's diabetic," and you begin to worry and say: "Is he OK? Perhaps we should get him a biscuit."'

Without embarrassment, Russell also gave future female suitors a little tip if they wanted to please him in the sack. He told them he liked a finger stuck up his arse, which he called 'an internal Narnia'. He also revealed his thoughts on the subject of saliva: 'It is my view that there ain't a single sexual act, from the humble wank right up to the sexual apotheosis that is bumming, that ain't enhanced by spitting.'

In *Shame*, Russell focused on pretty much every aspect of self-service sex. He even demonstrated how he shoos his pet cat away when he is in mid-masturbation mode: 'Morrissey, go on, go out. Daddy's busy... It's difficult because cats don't wank. He looks so innocent and confused and stuff, you know? It's not part of feline behaviour to masturbate. He thinks it's a game.'

However, he also referenced Michael Hutchence, who he said had 'wanked himself to death'. Russell advised that any masturbation that led to death should be halted. He joked: 'If, during a wank, you start to die, maybe put the telly on or something. Don't think, "No, I've committed to this wank now." If, during a wank, a tunnel of light appears with Christ at the end of it, don't let that spur the wank on. Don't think, "Oh that Jesus, I'll fuck 'im in the stigmata". Stop the wank. Stop the madness, I tells you.'

However, amid this onslaught of sex, sex chat and sexual positions, Russell also revealed a romantic side to his nature. On describing some carnal interchange he said: 'At the same time as being apes we are truly angels an' all.'

Inevitably in the *Shame* show, Russell dredged up his appearance at the *NME* Awards earlier in the year, when Bob Geldof had called him a cunt. Shameful. His mortification at this embarrassing event was played out all over again. Russell repeated his big punchline from the night: 'No wonder he's such an expert on famine, he's been feeding off "I Don't Like Mondays" for 30 years.' The comedian also invoked some accurate impressions of the testy pop-star-turned-charity-worker. He also did a convincing impersonation of Shaun Ryder. He described the former Happy Monday's singer, who had fought his own battle against drugs, as being 'like a didgeridoo' and 'a shambling, rambling narcotic casualty... the Queen Mum of junkies'.

He also picked apart the tabloid newspapers, while confessing to having a love-hate relationship with them. He said he'd read the *Sun* most of his life, but recognised the corrosive effect it had on him. He joked: 'I always thought of the *Sun* as sort of a friend, really. But, do any of you have a friend really that you fucking hate? That has infiltrated your life and is trying to surreptitiously make you a bit racist with the promise of £1 day trips to France and bingo.'

Like a superfine sub-editor, Russell pored over a copy of the red top and trashed a story about a paedophile who was found to be living in a tower block overlooking a school. Russell stomped over every lazy assumption in the article.

He scoffed at every inappropriate verb in the piece. He pounced on every misplaced adjective. He dumped on every ridiculous pun. The headline to the article had been PERV'S EYE VIEW.

Russell asked if it was appropriate for the paper to attempt its 'cheeky little pun' when it was also affecting moral outrage. Also, he guessed it would be easier for the paedophile to get his kicks from the internet than to squint from his high-rise apartment down to a school yard. 'The word perv is a little bit flippant don't you think? To describe a paedophile as a perv is a bit too light-hearted a sort of a word,' he commented.

There was a whiff of narcissism to the second half of the set. It was mostly concerned with the idea of celebrity in general, and Russell's growing celebrity in particular. Russell's routine concentrated on his own problems with the tabloids – especially their misrepre-sentation of him and the puffed-up prose used by reporters. He hilariously deconstructed an article in the *Star* about a supposed spat with the society It Girl Tamara Beckwith. He had been accused of trying to borrow some eyeliner from her.

Russell protested that that was not true. He had never met Beckwith. He said he'd never even been in the same room as her. Russell called it complete fabrication, from inception to denouement. There was not a single word of truth in the report, he said. Well, maybe just one. After all, the paper had called him Randy Russell Brand and he wasn't going to argue with that.

Nevertheless, the *Star* had managed to puff out a 300-word story about Russell and Tamara, specifically how he had narrowly avoided receiving a smack in the mouth from her. In the same way he attacked the *Sun*'s use of grammar, Russell analysed every letter, syllable, word, comma and full-stop used by the *Star* in its fabricated story before unloading industrial quantities of ridicule on red-top culture.

Russell was described in the story as the big-haired pixie. But his best gag was his deconstruction of the *Star*'s description of Beckwith as a plum-voiced fox. Russell joked that the *Star*'s attempt to fuse 'plum-voiced' (meaning posh) with 'foxy' (meaning sexy) to describe Beckwith had misfired. He argued that the image you actually create with 'plum-voiced fox' is of a 'perverted Beatrix Potter character. You get a fox in a waistcoat with a pocket watch'.

He then poured scorn on the reporter who had accused him, Russell, of lacking imagination. If the paper was prepared to print a lie about Russell meeting Beckwith, why he wondered, didn't it at least make the lie interesting? How about: 'the Neptunian underworld king unleashed a barrage of eels from his abdomen and each of the eels was carrying a Zippo lighter, and as they flew by they spelt across the sky in fire: "Tara, could I borrow your eyeliner please?" If you're going to make stuff up, go mental.'

Russell delivered the final punchline with a tongue-in-cheek request to the ladies in the audience. He told them that he was available for more than weddings and barmitzvahs. He declared that he was very much a sexually obtainable celeb. He smiled lasciviously at the audience and told them: 'You might be thinking, if you're a single woman, "He's nice but he's so unobtainable." Let me tell you: I'm not unobtainable.'

He then bid farewell with: 'Hare Krishna, good night.'

It was majestic gig and a critical triumph. There were no dissenting voices.

Writing in the *Independent* on 23 August, columnist Johann Hari said: 'If you tossed a Victorian dandy, a homeless smack addict and a thesaurus into a blender, you'd get Russell Brand. From the moment he almost dances on the stage ... you can see why the host of *Big Brother's Big Mouth* is the celebrity of the summer of 2006.' Hari conceded that Russell might have forced his way into the national consciousness by dint of his 'charged, bizarre presenting' and 'supermodel-bagging libido', but he cautioned that this should not deflect from the fact that Russell 'is an original talent, a rare break from the steady stream of solid comics with solid jokes and solid laughs and no aftertaste at all'. The critic added the new show had a texture and a depth that he did not expect. 'He has chosen shame as his theme, and he is marinated in it... After this strangely sharp, bitingly honest show, the Brand brand will continue to prance higher and higher.'

Other comedy critics were also effusive. The London *Evening Standard*'s Bruce Dessau commented that Russell, 'looked every inch the star' as soon as he swaggered on stage. Dessau told his readers: '*Shame* is not perfect, but it is an effective showcase.'

In *The Times*, Dominic Maxwell was also converted to the Brand cause. He stated that Russell was able to skilfully 'throw in bursts of comic trickery'. The *Daily Telegraph*'s comedy watcher, Dominic Cavendish, proclaimed Russell as the 'man of the moment'. He wrote:

'For the time being he's absolutely earned his right to be this year's cock of the walk.'

It was Russell's crowning moment. He had been gifted the greatest accolade a stand-up comedian could receive: universal praise.

But, typically, drama was not far behind. The following night's Edinburgh gig and the rest of the run at the Assembly Rooms was cancelled, with only hours to spare, when Russell was struck down by a bout of laryngitis. Four nights at the 1,200 seat Edinburgh International Conference Centre were added to appease fans, but Russell's illness and the rescheduling also nixed his planned appearance in front of a rock 'n' roll crowd at the Carling Weekend Reading Festival on 27 August.

His act wasn't the only thing to be spoiled by his illness. Russell also had to pull the plug on a romantic evening with a young lady. Dr Sarah Kennedy had won a date with Russell through a competition in Edinburgh's *The List* magazine, but his sore throat meant he or the doctor would never get the opportunity to indulge in some tonsil hockey, should the mood have taken either of them.

Russell hardly had time to absorb the glowing reviews for *Shame* before he and his radio comedy team were embroiled in more drama. But unlike Russell's previous scrapes with the law, this was serious. The cops were talking rape. Russell was suddenly faced by the biggest threat yet to his career – his liberty.

Russell won't forget 28 August 2006 in a hurry. The night before, Russell had come to the end of his sell-out Fringe run of *Shame*. He decided to celebrate by throwing a party in the apartment he'd been renting in Edinburgh's New Town district. He'd already had a couple of blow-outs during his run, in one instance inviting the audience back to the Tonic Bar on North Castle Street. He'd bedded a few beauties, too, but he wanted this party to be special as it marked the end of such a critically lauded set of performances.

Among the group of partygoers, including Russell, Matt Morgan and Trevor Lock, was a 20-year-old student. She was a fan of the comedian and had come to see him in *Shame*. The party went ahead as planned and was a success, seemingly. However, the next morning the young student was less than happy. According to reports, she claimed that she could not remember anything about the night before after being offered a drink at the party.

A police source told one newspaper that, 'she remembers having a drink, but nothing after that', and that she woke the next morning feeling uncomfortable, 'as if she had had sex'. Fearing she might have been raped, the girl's friends persuaded her to go to hospital, where tests confirmed that she'd had sex. Armed with the results, she made a complaint to the police. After interviewing the student and examining her for forensic evidence, the police suspected that the woman's drink might have been spiked with a strong sedative such as Rohypnol, the so-called 'date rape' drug. The Lothian and Borders police opened an investigation.

Russell appeared to have been blissfully ignorant of the unfolding scandal. He jetted off to Marrakesh in Morocco for a well-earned break. On 4 September the news that the Scottish cops were digging around leaked out. Inevitably, the newspapers smelled scandal. The press hounds pounced.

In their early filings, the tabloids had no reservations about linking Russell's name to the alleged rape. The tabloids thought they had another Fatty Arbuckle-style outrage on their hands. Disgracefully, in provocative and potentially career-destroying language, the papers suggested that Russell would face a DNA test as soon as he set foot in the country again.

'Russell Brand in Rape Quiz', was one sensational sub-editor's fiction. The *Daily Star* also didn't hold back. It fanned the scandal flames by pitching Brand's name right at the top of a piece titled, 'I Was Drugged and Raped in BB Star Brand's Flat'. The inference was clear: Russell was somehow implicated in a rape case. What a nightmare. It didn't look good.

Russell's management company distanced their client from the ensuing scandal. It issued a terse statement that left no room for interpretation or spin. It read: 'It becomes necessary for Russell Brand to state he has no knowledge of, let alone any involvement in, the alleged assault of an Edinburgh woman. Mr Brand understands that a woman who, with a number of other people, visited his rented flat during the Edinburgh Fringe has made a complaint to the police. As it was Mr Brand's flat the police have asked to speak to him on his return from holiday. Mr Brand is happy to assist the police with their inquiries.'

Russell's unequivocal statement prevented news-papers from continuing to print ambiguous articles hinting at his involvement. But when he arrived back from Morocco he walked straight into a media maelstrom and was quizzed by the cops.

Then came a bombshell, a twist in the tale that no one wanted. On 7 September, officers made a trip down to London and arrested Trevor Lock in connection with the alleged sex attack. The Lothian and Borders police issued a statement the following day that confirmed that 'A 33-year-old man has been arrested and charged following an incident in a flat in North Castle Street, Edinburgh, on 28 August. A report will be submitted to procurator fiscal.'

Lock denied all charges relating to the rape, but the strain of being accused obviously had a devastating effect on the comedian and he failed to show for the 10 September broadcast of the 6 Music show. Typically, Russell remained loyal to his good friend. The comedian sent out messages of support throughout the programme that Sunday morning. Russell suggested the theme of that day's programme: innocence. He also dedicated the Morrissey song, 'In the Future When All's Well', to Lock.

The case couldn't have come at a worse time for Lock or Russell. Russell's nationwide *Shame* tour started in Derby on 22 September. It was a major tour, taking in everywhere from Telford to Tunbridge Wells – and Lock was supporting him. 'Ever since that twerp Goddy make Adam wear a fig leaf on his dinkle, man has been living in shame,' said Russell. 'On this tour, I'm gonna expose my shame and let my dinkle roam free!'

Although the strain of the investigation must have taken its toll, the tour went ahead and Lock went with it.

He also returned quickly to the radio. In the meantime the allegation was reviewed by the procurator fiscal, the Scottish public prosecutor, to determine whether there was a case to answer.

CHAPTER 17

Bubbles

Russell's football team, West Ham, is not about glamour. It doesn't do glitz or have many showbiz supporters. There's Alf Garnett, of course, and a couple of boxers – Lennox Lewis, Frank Bruno – oh, and David Essex. Add to that half the cast of *EastEnders* and you're almost there.

Until recently, Ray 'I'm the daddy' Winstone was probably the club's best known supporter. Until Russell came along. With the fame he achieved in 2006, Russell became a terrace celebrity down at Upton Park. He was someone to cheer in the stands, or a person who could lift the gloom at 4.55 p.m. when the ref was about to blow his whistle on a 0–0 bore draw on a cold, wet, wintry afternoon.

Russell's credentials are impeccable – 'I am a lifelong Hammers fan begat by a Hammer's fan – my dad.' His new-found celebrity did afford him some privileges. Post-match, he has been an enthusiastic visitor to the players' lounge, mixing it with Nigel Reo-Coker and Anton Ferdinand. It has probably also helped him avoid a good kicking from some Green Street regulars.

He is asked to pose for pics and sign autographs before games, but Russell's profile is unlikely to stray anywhere near the full wattage, Hollywood-style glamour that forgives all sins – his barnet, for one. Russell's camp persona sits uneasily with the East End, which means Russell may never be fêted in the same way as Big Ray Winstone, never mind achieve the adulation that Jack Nicholson generates from the bleachers while watching the LA Lakers. 'Watching me cheering Matty Etherington in my shrill falsetto must come a poor second to watching Tobey Maguire slapping Magic Johnson on the back,' Russell admitted.

The club's uneasy relationship with its ex-drug addict supporter and new celebrity season ticket-holder (at most games Russell takes his place in the Doc Marten stand and sits next to a 14-year-old girl) was demonstrated in late 2006. The comedian was interviewed for the club's programme, but Russell's thoughts on West Ham's difficult season never made it into print. The piece was canned when the club discovered Russell was a former heroin abuser. It was a decision that begs the question: where had the person who commissioned the piece been living until then? Only residents of Planet Zog could fail to have known about Russell's struggle with dope.

Russell's own relationship with fellow supporters was also tested. He narrowly missed a good kicking on 10 September, a Sunday, at the first game he'd been to that season. The match was West Ham v Aston Villa. The

Hammers had already won a London derby against Charlton and had played a couple of away fixtures at this early stage in the season. They were not flying, but they weren't doing badly either.

As he sat in the stands and waited for the game to begin, Russell mused on a couple of new arrivals at the club, two South Americans, the Argentine stars Carlos Tevez and Javier Mascherano. The jury was still out on them. How would they fit in? Could they fit in? Would their arrival upset the team's delicate balance?

That was a theme Russell pondered. He realised that this pair of 'gigolos, these Johnny-come-lately saviours of the club' could unsettle the fire-power of Bobby Zamora or upset the creative artistry of Dean Ashton and Hayden Mullins. He said the glamorous recent arrivals had 'upset the domestic balance of the side like J-Lo and Angelina Jolie tottering into an Essex discotheque.' As if to bear out Russell's thesis, Tevez's introduction into the Villa game appeared to affect striker Marlon Harewood. Russell thought Harewood played the first half like a 'tentative mutt on its final journey to an indifferent vet'.

However, the more Russell watched Tevez in that game, the more he liked what he saw. Tevez, he said, 'played with the commitment and dedication of a man who will be there decades'. Bravely, and perhaps unwisely, he predicted that Tevez would become an Argentinian Billy Bonds. High praise. Ex-player and manager Bonds was Hammers through and through. Cut him in half; he's claret.

At half time Russell felt the call of nature and headed to the toilet. As he made his way through the throng,

Russell was accosted by comedy fans who wanted his autograph on their match-day programmes. Always one to oblige, Russell signed away. But then Russell became the focus of attention from another group of lads. This group didn't want his autograph – they wanted his blood.

The first Russell knew of it was when the chant went up: 'Who the fucking hell are you?' This was followed by a new one on Russell: 'Brandy is a wanker.' Then, with the topical skill of a Fleet Street newshound, Russell's recent rape rap in Edinburgh was invoked with the imaginative chant: 'Sex case, sex case, 'ang 'im, 'ang 'im, 'ang 'im.'

Russell wasn't scared. The tone of the taunting was ribald rather than out-and-out hate. But it did unnerve him – and bum him out. The rabble were suggesting that Russell was not a real Hammer. To reinforce their point they sang: 'Where were you when we were shit?'

They believed that Russell was no lifelong fan. Just as they probably perceived in Tevez a chancer and a mercenary, so they saw the comedian and TV presenter as an opportunist, a fair-weather chump hitching his allegiance to the Hammers for a whiff of street cred. The unlikeliest lickspittles have tried to align themselves with the beautiful game to prop up their image. Was Brand – Brandy – any different?

Russell's mind raced to find a (peaceful) way to reverse his predicament; he had no recourse for reply. He'd turned hostile audiences before with his quick wit, a gag maybe, but this was not the time or the place. But then the terrace choir handed Russell just want he wanted – the stage, his chance to shine. The chanting turned from taunting to a plea: 'Give us a song Brandy.'

It was a test. If Russell wasn't word perfect with the famous West Ham terrace song 'Bubbles' ('I'm for ever blowing bubbles/Pretty bubbles in the air') he would reveal himself to be exactly what his tormentors thought he was – a twat off the telly.

Russell knew that, and he relished the opportunity to turn the situation to his advantage. But what to sing? 'Bubbles', that wistful and mystical ode to transience and loss ('They fly so high, nearly reach the sky/Then like my dreams they fade and die') was the obvious choice, but maybe it was too obvious. Although it might demonstrate that Russell knew a little about West Ham, he could just as easily have learned the words to that ditty during the first-half action. He might still have been fingered as an interloper, a fraud, a fair-weather fan if he plumped for that.

Russell wracked his brain, flicking through the jukebox of Hammers' hits in his head. He knew all the greats –'Chim Chimeney', 'Stick the Blue Flag up Yer Arse', 'Come on You Irons' and 'Let's All Have a Disco' – but the one he eventually went for was the insider's classic, 'We All Follow the West Ham'.

Russell steeled himself. He flung his arms skyward and retreated into his youth to drag out his best flat Cockney vowels. Slipping at least three octaves lower than his usual affected speaking voice, Russell dug deep and delivered: 'We all follow the West Ham/Over land and sea/We all follow the West Ham/On to victory.'

By the end of the first line, he'd got the lads' attention. Their eyes softened and their heads lolled. Russell judged that he'd converted his tormentors by the second or third verse. They knew he was a Hammer. A real fan. By the time Russell got to the line 'All together now', he found himself leading the choir. The lads joined in. Full throttle, Russell led them through to the end of the chant: 'We all follow the West Ham/On to victory!'

Russell was as proud as punch. Prouder. His one-time aggressors were now fans – not just of West Ham but of him, too. He'd turned them. Some ran over to congratulate him after the sing-song. One displayed a unique bonding ritual by throwing his beer over Russell's head. Russell felt like he belonged. 'I've never felt more loved,' he said.

It got better. On a roll, Russell flipped his mental jukebox again and delivered big time. He rose up and, slipping into the melody from Dean Martin's 'Volare', belted out: 'Zamora, oh-oh, Zamora oh-oh-oh-oh/He came from Shite Hart Lane/He's better than Jermain...' The beer kept on coming. It was a perfect moment for Russell. He had passed the test and had been accepted. A true Hammer, he skipped into the toilet to point Percy at the porcelain. The only downer was that some guy wanted to take a photograph of Russell with his Johnson in his hand.

Back in his seat, Russell watched the second half play out to a 1–1 draw. But that was not the point. What fun he'd had. Russell had found a sense of belonging. The occasion, he said, 'Will live in my memory as the day that West Ham became a club... where one of digital television's campest men could lead a joyful battle hymn.'

It could only have been bettered by the club renaming the North Bank the Randy Brandy Standy. Result, as they say in those parts.

With his success as a terrace crooner and his allegiance

to West Ham proven, it wasn't a great surprise that as autumn turned to winter in 2006, Russell struck upon an idea. He would attempt to start up a new terrace chant on the North Bank.

Russell had always been interested in football songs, though not always a willing participant. He said: 'I'm happy to stand up during some songs and, of course, when there's a goal. But often I like to peruse the game all sedentary and snug.'

Although he had eschewed 'Bubbles' for his test-by-the-terraces, he believes the song is the perfect sing-along number. He noted: 'The anthem "Bubbles" has no equal. Most football chants are belligerent, tuneless cries of violent loyalty or jaunty playful, digs.' Russell insisted that 'Bubbles' is not a clarion call to arms, but is about futility. In that respect it's perfect for West Ham. Futility sits well with the Hammers. The team often blows chances.

The chant is so powerful that it has moved Russell to tears. He describes it as: 'A song that compares the inevitability of a bubble bursting to lost opportunity and wasted hopes sung by the ICF [West Ham's notorious hooligan fraternity] is a surreal anomaly.'

For Russell, the only song with similar portent is Liverpool's 'You'll Never Walk Alone'. But, he suggested, that terrace song is pedestrian by comparison. Russell suggested that not only is the Scouse song merely about walking, 'but also its themes are solidarity in adversity, not being afraid of bad weather and other ideas one would expect to encounter being yawped in unison. It's also triumphant in tone.'

Russell was stung into action to start his new chant

when Arsenal fans barracked his claret and blue army during a match by singing: 'You've only got one song.' That was a bit rich coming from the Gooners – the famously silent Highbury Library mob. However, their taunts did make Russell think. 'I've long been troubled by the lack of original terrace material,' he admitted.

His solution was to bastardise Billy Joel's non-classic 'Uptown Girl', the bug-eyed crooner's ode to his one-time wife, former model Chrissie Brinkley. Naturally, Russell's version was to become 'Upton Park'. He elaborated, 'It seems "Uptown Girl" by Billy Joel might easily become beloved of West Ham fans if, instead of "Uptown Girl/She's living in her uptown world" came the cry "Upton Park/ We're the Hammers from Upton Park/We're just a bunch of East End boys/Now we're going to make some effing noise/Some effing noise".' Russell hoped that 'Upton Park' could become an anthem to rival 'Bubbles'. It was a big hope.

Even Russell saw similarities between his proposed camp chant and what the Village People might have conjured. He also admitted that he would not have the confidence to be the first to stand up and conduct the terrace choir to sing along to his new soccer soundtrack. Upton Park was similarly unsmitten. The ground's announcer played the Billy Joel tune during half time at the West Ham v Sheffield United game on 25 November. It was a cue, but the East End hard men missed it. The terraces failed to break into Russell's effete anthem.

Russell also got into trouble with the publishers of the song when he sang his version of it on his Channel 4 show. He was fined five grand.

And by the beginning of December, Russell began to question his own motives. Had Project Billy Joel, he wondered, been an attempt to curry favour with his football-loving old man? Or his stepdad even? Was it an effort to show them that Russell could handle himself in the company of real men. Sensing that rowdy football fans seemed impervious to Joel's tune, Russell asked: 'Is it right to continue to attempt to infiltrate the terraces with jaunty ditties, or am I like a deluded missionary barging into an aboriginal village and dishing out boob inspector caps and sherbet dips?'

However, on 17 December there was a breakthrough. Russell found encouragement at a match against Manchester United, which the Hammers amazingly won 1–0. After the game Russell was spotted by a couple of jubilant West Ham fans. They stopped Russell and broke into song. His song. It was Project Billy Joel come to life. For Russell it was a 'proud moment.' He added: 'To hear my chant, if not sung en masse upon the terrace, I have achieved some level of penetration.'

Where West Ham's publicity machine (the club's weekly programme) had been afraid to tread, the *Guardian* was not. Learning of Russell's love for the beautiful game, the left-leaning broadsheet approached the comedian in the summer of 2006 to cover the World Cup. It wanted a column from him, a sort of irrelevant, sideways look at football. Russell was commissioned to write a column for publication every Saturday on the back page of the paper's sports supplement.

The *Guardian* went big with Russell. It trumpeted his

arrival by announcing a 'brilliant new column'. The accompanying picture byline was classic Brand: tight black shirt, open at the neck and augmented by a white scarf, wrapped twice and loosely knotted. No other sports correspondent looked like that.

After ranting at the media's outrages at his comedy, Russell found himself as tabloid-fodder-turned-press-commentator. He seemed to like the new role. After many months spent at the sharp end of the *Mirror*'s 3 a.m. girls' viperous pens, Russell now had his own vehicle for articulating his view of the world – albeit on the subject of football. Or, more accurately, West Ham's football. His columns never strayed too far from Upton Park.

This was Russell's first opportunity to directly connect with hundreds of thousands of readers – many of whom were higher up the demographic ladder than those devouring his antics in the *Sun*. He must have had this in mind because the tone of his dispatches were essentially straight. There would be a joke here and there, perhaps a witty bit of word play occasionally thrown in for good measure, but not the Woody Allenesque gag-a-minute stuff he used in his routines.

Once he got going, Russell found that he had a surfeit of material. It was a busy year for West Ham. His team went through a managerial change, plus it acquired new owners. It also experienced humiliation (a 6–0 drubbing at the hands of Reading was the nadir). For most of the 2006-07 season West Ham languished at the foot of the table, a prime candidate for relegation. Sadly, two of its greatest managers, Ron Greenwood and John Lyall, died in 2006, aged 84 and 66 respectively. And while all of this went on, there was Russell writing about it in his own inimitable way.

After tackling West Ham's ups and (mostly) downs, plus England's woeful World Cup performance in Germany, Russell began to spread his wings. Next up on his to-do list was tackling the bung scandal that shook football in September 2006. The BBC's *Panorama* programme had put soccer in the dock, contending that football was wracked by a culture of kick-backs, payola and bribes. At the centre of its allegations were the myriad agents operating within the game and, with little more than hearsay, it implicated Bolton manager Sam Allardyce and Portsmouth manager Harry Redknapp. Both men strenuously denied the programme's allegations.

Russell was on the side of Allardyce in his 23 September report, entitled: 'Not waving but drowning in a sea of bile'. Russell wrote that he hoped Allardyce was innocent. He regarded the manager as an 'ebullient, avuncular greengrocer', and hoped that time would show Allardyce was not guilty of 'mishandling his sprouts'. However, disappointingly, Russell also revealed his journalistic naivety. He confessed that he hadn't bothered to watch the *Panaroma* report on which the Allardyce allegations were based.

As the title of the piece suggested, the bulk of this dispatch was about the reception meted out to the Newcastle manager and former Hammer's boss Glenn Roeder on his return to Upton Park three years after he was sacked. Roeder had had a torrid time in the final weeks of his West Ham reign. Many supporters believed Roeder had abandoned the hallowed principles of West

Ham United. They thought he had ditched pass and move for Route One. Russell had witnessed the vitriol hurled at the hapless Roeder during his final weeks in August 2003. One unsupportable terrace chant directed at the manager during a game they lost to Leeds United had it that 'You've killed West Ham'.

However, this terrace tirade, followed by a hastily-convened boardroom meeting and then the swift dispatch of the underperforming manager, was lent some pathos. Roeder had been seriously ill. He had suffered a brain tumour in 2002.

As Russell pointed out, it seemed obscene to be questioning a man's motives for selling a star striker – Paoli Di Canio, in the case of West Ham fans – when he was 'teetering on the precipice of death'. Russell also cleverly invoked former Liverpool manager Bill Shankly's famous maxim: 'Football is not a matter of life and death; it is far more important than that'. In this context, he argued, quoting this seemed trite in the face of Roeder's health.

Roeder, who had fortunately made a full recovery to health, left West Ham and was hired by Newcastle. On 17 September, Roeder made his first return to Upton Park with the Magpies. Russell witnessed the claret side of the stadium turn on their former charge. Roeder made a cardinal error, when he acknowledged Newcastle's travelling support by waving at them. This was a signal, as Russell recorded, for Hammers fans to ensure Roeder would drown, not wave, 'in a sea of acrimony, antipathy and abuse'. The West Ham crowd turned on Roeder with venom. The former manager clapped and then punched the air and in return the home crowd booed. Then, some Hammers' fans attempted to attack the Newcastle boss. The fact that West Ham was losing (they eventually lost 2–0) might have played some part in this (over) reaction.

Russell could empathise with the West Ham fans. As the ground fizzed with anger and resentment at Roeder, Russell replayed his own experiences of being on the receiving end of hate-filled hecklers. He dragged up memories of his own death on stage. 'To feel such audacious wrath must be blood-curdling,' he said. 'I know myself; when I have been booed on stage, I still hear the jeering crowd as my head settles on my pillow.' But, he understood the crowd dynamic. And, as the braying continued, Russell admitted that he tried to compose another witty ditty that would instantly be adopted by the terraces. Caught up in the mob hysteria, Russell confessed he considered – for the briefest moment – whether it would be morally acceptable to conjure a rhyme around the word tumour. Fortunately, the moment passed before, in his own words, he 'could commit an atrocity of that nature'.

The experience gave Brand an insight into how his own audiences sometimes feel. 'It's interesting how one behaves,' he observed, 'when part of a crowd, the diminished responsibility, the intoxicating fervour.' And Russell believed, in this context, he was quite capable of behaving beyond the normal bounds of decency. Whether that would translate to a one-to-one, face-to-face situation, however, Russell was uncertain. Whether he would be so insensitive and callow to scream 'I hope you get cancer' into the face of someone else was a moot point. He posed this question: 'As one of thousands, I'm quite content to convey insensitive, incendiary sentiments. Would I be happy to express these views on a one-to-one basis?'

After the game, Russell encountered Roeder in the gent's loos by the players' lounge. He felt ashamed. Guilty and embarrassed that, just half an hour earlier to raise a laugh, to have a titter, he had been struggling to rhyme tumour and haemorrhage. Humour has its place, but Russell found it wasn't anywhere near a tumour.

Russell confined most of his *Guardian* reporting to the trails and travails of West Ham United. The club had been the subject of a convoluted takeover battle and in November they got a new owner. Eggert Magnusson paid £85 million for the club and took over from long-standing chairman Terry Brown. The move immediately put a question mark over the futures of Brand-favourites Tevez and Mascherano, who had been parachuted into the team during an earlier takeover attempt by the Iranian-born businessman Kia Joorabchian.

Russell fed off the terrace talk. He was optimistic that Magnusson could turn West Ham around. He thought the arrival of the new owner would herald a 'new golden age' for the Hammers. But Russell had one concern. He worried that Magnusson was head of the Icelandic FA, 'if people that head the Icelandic FA are anything like the English FA'.

With his comedy cap on Russell was able to recognise something that Magnusson gave West Ham. 'Eggert Magnusson is a man whose name is a gift to Premiership football; not since Arsene Wenger has a name been more pertinent. Magnusson has the word "egg" in his name, is bald, his head looks a bit like an egg, easily affording him the nickname "The Egg",' joked Russell.

Russell had hoped The Egg and Pards – Alan Pardew, the thoroughly decent Hammers manager – would together forge a new era at his beloved club. But it didn't happen. Even The Egg-man couldn't reverse West Ham's poor performances on the pitch. And after three losses on the trot, at the start of December, Pardew left the club.

A couple of days later, on 13 December, former Hammers player Alan Curbishley was hired. Curbs had pedigree. He'd played at West Ham when he was a teenager in the mid-1970s, when Russell was still in nappies. Curbs had then steered Charlton for 15 largely successful seasons. In an interesting twist, Pardew then joined Charlton.

Russell was elated at Curbishley's appointment and waxed lyrical about it. 'It is a time of Jacobean twists at Upton Park,' he wrote. 'Curbs from a post-Charlton wilderness, Pards to Charlton, ousted but with dignity intact and a misty veil of noble grief settling round East London's wounded streets.'

Although, Russell described Curbs as a 'rather humdrum Messiah', he was excited about the new man's arrival. He wrote: 'I was labelled a turncoat earlier in the season when, after eight successive defeats, I, prophetically now I see, suggested that Alan Curbishley might be a good replacement for Alan Pardew.' Russell was also encouraged that Curbs is not the kind of manager to favour cheque-book management, some-thing, the comedian believed, that would sit badly at the Hammers. He predicted:

'[Curbishley] may join the pantheon of West Ham managerial greats, alongside John Lyall, Ron Greenwood and Harry Redknapp. A firmanent of Cockney legends.'

CHAPTER 18

Dandy

GQ, THE *GENTLEMAN'S QUARTERLY*, THE MAGAZINE FOR MEN. THE STYLE BIBLE. THE MAGAZINE HOSTED ITS AWARDS BASH AT THE ROYAL OPERA HOUSE IN LONDON'S COVENT GARDEN. AND WHO WON THAT YEAR'S AWARD FOR MOST STYLISH MAN? RUSSELL, THAT'S WHO. IT WAS EVERYTHING RUSSELL COULD HAVE HOPED FOR AFTER THE MONTHS OF MEDIA RIBBING ABOUT HIS LOOK – HIS SKINNY JEANS AND SILK SCARVES. FED UP WITH SPECULATION AS TO WHETHER HE WAS METROSEXUAL, HOMOSEXUAL, PANSEXUAL, HETEROSEXUAL OR SEXSEXUAL, RUSSELL COULD AT LAST POINT TO THE AWARD AS EVIDENCE THAT HE WAS ALL THIS AND MORE. SEX ON LEGS, IN FACT.

He managed to cause offence at the awards when he made light of the then ongoing police investigation into the alleged date rape at his rented apartment in Edinburgh. In a crass and ill-judged aside he reported that: 'At the time the alleged attack was occurring I was having consensual sex with witnesses. Lovely night it turned out to be.' Lovely wasn't the way the alleged victim described it.

But, Russell had gained himself a reputation. He was a well-dressed man. It was official. *GQ* approved. To coincide with the awards, stylish Russell bagged the front cover of October's *GQ* magazine. He had to share it with six of the magazine's other big winners, but it wasn't a bad gig all in all. After all, his fellow cover stars were all Men of the Year too. The pull-out cover had Russell squished in at the right. Justin Timberlake snagged the centre of the little group of six, with Chelsea and England captain John Terry taking the left berth. Between Russell and Terry were Borat, alter ego of Sacha Baron Cohen, Timberlake, Rod Stewart and Ricky Gervais. Interestingly, Gervais, rather than Russell, walked off with the top comedian honour.

What is instructive is that the *GQ* editorial team, headed by Dylan Jones, decided Russell had more juice, more pulling power, more resonance for readers, than the ten other Men of the Year who didn't make it on the front of the magazine. They had to satisfy themselves with a place tucked inside the pull-out cover. And none – including Jamie Oliver, actor Cillian Murphy, motorman Jeremy Clarkson, presenter Jonathan Ross, music man Simon Fuller, Tory leader David Cameron, designer John Galliano and novelist Will Self – were shrinking violets.

Russell was not quite scratching his arse in the cover pic, but almost was. What he was actually doing was posing, archly, as ever. Russell had arranged his left hand to splay confidently, lightly, on his left thigh. But his right hand was the one to watch for. While his fellow award winners self-consciously grabbed at lapels or shoved hands in pockets, Russell opted for the open and ready to grab approach, his hand hovering dangerously close to his dinkle. Girls (or boys), he seemed to tease, here it is. Just slip the zipper and open the fly.

Inside, over a five-page spread, Russell pulled three more power poses: one leg aggressively thrust out, kung fu style; coy and sweet like the girl next door; then one leg in the air in a 'Bring Me Sunshine' dance move. Appropriately for someone who had just been voted the UK's most stylish man, Russell didn't allow his sartorial savvy to dip. He sported a waistcoat by Filippa K and jeans by J Lindeberg, drawn around snake hips by a bundle of chain belts. His £99.95 boots were by Beatwear, but Russell had supplied his own shirt and silk scarf. He had managed to outflank self-styled style student Ross in an Ozwald Boateng whistle and gave the flamboyant Galliano a good run for his money.

Russell has always liked clothes. He follows fashion. 'I like to dress up nice. I'm a bit of a show off,' he said. But a celebrity always needs help. Russell turned to stylist Sharon Smith at the end of 2005 to get some pointers and she became the architect of Russell's sartorial transformation.

The 'nerdy' jeans, jumpers, unstructured jackets and crap trainers in evidence on his MTV shows had been ditched. There were no more fashion *faux pas*. Since the start of 2006, Russell had begun to resemble a cross between Quentin Crisp, Oscar Wilde and Beau Brummell. Russell's move from man at C&A to *a la mode* was obvious to everyone, including the comedian's father, Ron. He said: 'He used to dress very normally until he got a stylist. Now he wears all those strange clothes. He doesn't usually talk in that strange old-fashioned way either. It's all part of his act.'

Russell's *GQ* honour validated his look. 'It means I can be a bit more confident in what I wear,' he said. 'If my hair looks bad, then it means that having your hair looking bad is now stylish.' Russell began to consult on mixing and matching his vintage pieces of clothing, customising and accessorising from the cool couple of fashionistas behind the achingly hip Junky Styling label, Annika Saunders and Kerry Seager.

Junky Styling was started in 1997. It customised and reworked second-hand clothes into new, unique outfits. Then it evolved into a wardrobe surgery service. And it was this service, which invited customers to hand over favourite, but damaged or outmoded garments to be reworked into a new made-to-measure designer creation, that Russell benefited from. He was in good company. Others using Junky Styling's services include the natty dressers pop star Gwen Stefani and actor Steven Berkoff.

With the *GQ* seal of approval, Russell would have been forgiven for believing he had arrived at style central to become someone envied and worshipped from Milan to Paris. But his elevation to sartorial sage wasn't universally accepted. Over the course of 2006 newspapers and magazines worked themselves ragged arguing the toss over Russell's credentials as a beacon of fashion and style.

While other comedians are judged purely on the material spilling from their mouths, it appeared the choice of material wrapped around Russell's neck was deemed fairer game for comment. Not even Billy Connolly's ludicrous fashion statements were given this much attention. The *Sunday Mirror* reacted to Russell's *GQ* nomination with undisguised disgust. 'God help us,' it pleaded. 'He wears women's clothes, he always looks like he needs a good wash, he's got a stringy body... he's got more of the girl about him than Julian Clary.'

The *Guardian* was no fan either. The broadsheet's fashion writer suggested that Russell's penchant for silk scarves had a whiff of the utterly un-hip hair metal band Whitesnake about it. His 'explosion of 80s' rock star hair' was perceived as a bar to true stylishness, and *NME* associate editor Alex Needham was wheeled in to provide a quote. Needham said Russell's hairy chest looked 'a bit wrong'. He also thought Russell looked too big for his clothes, 'like he is bursting out of them, which always looks bad for blokes'.

However, the same paper had reversed its opinion just a few months later. In its end-of-year style round-up, the *Guardian* anointed Russell as the male who had the biggest fashion impact throughout 2006. The paper's style awards suggested that 'with his furiously backcombed hair and skinny silk scarf, there is no denying that Russell Brand's born-again-decadent-dandy-look has had a huge impact'. According to the broadsheet's fashion experts, Russell's influence on fashionable youth had meant that sales of skinny evening scarves had gone through the roof at high street chain Top Man.

Although the newspaper conceded that the critics hadn't always been kind – 'the seams of Brand's skinny trousers often struggled to contain his oversexed flesh' – and confessed that his look was hardly original, it stated that Russell had now taken ownership of 'the look'. It was his. It belonged to him. It stated, 'possibly because no one has hammered home the sartorial point as hard as this presenter before'.

Russell's beard was even alleged to have had an influence on fashionable Britons. The paper hailed Russell and other beard-wearing men as being at 'the forefront of a new trend'. However, Tara Newley, daughter of actress Joan Collins, wasn't convinced. She used her 'If I Were Your Girlfriend...' column in the *Daily Mail* to offer Russell some unsolicited advice about his clothing choices. Newley wasn't having any of Russell's 'dandy chic'. Her advice was to stop hamming it up and start dressing up – in Dior, Jil Sander and Helmut Lang. Newley saved her most damning criticisms for the comedian's John Cooper Clarke-style hair. She described it as a cross between 'tumbleweed and the straw man'. According to the columnist, his 'barnet ticks all the wrong boxes' and she advised a shorter, more tousled look. Newley didn't elaborate on how a new barnet would improve Russell's comedy, his stagecraft or his presenter skills.

But not only was Russell slagged for his fashion sense. The blame for no end of ridiculous crazes and vogueish fads was laid at his door. Some commentators even suggested that Russell was partly to blame for a new breed of diet-obsessed, skinny, anorexic men -- or 'manorexics' as one red top coined the completely bogus condition.

However, some style counsellors did share *GQ*'s enthusiasm for Russell's unique dress sense. Support came from the unlikely source of the Bluewater shopping centre. Both Russell and Kate Moss were named by shoppers at Kent's giant retail complex as their favourite style icons. Pete Doherty, whose name seemed inexorably linked to both Russell and Moss throughout 2006, was voted the person shoppers would least want to share their retail therapy time with.

Russell was a brave choice for the conservative denizens of the home counties. Their selection conjured up an image of a mass gothic makeover at Bluewater with hoodie-clad chavs shunning their Nike sports gear to pile dandyish designer duds into their shopping trolleys.

ISSUES

CHAPTER 19

Issues

TOWARDS THE END OF THE SUMMER WORD GOT OUT THAT RUSSELL
HAD LANDED A NEW TELEVISION SHOW. HIS SUCCESS AT HOSTING
THE MAYHEM OF *BIG BROTHER'S BIG MOUTH* SAW E4 OFFER HIM
HIS OWN VEHICLE, *RUSSELL BRAND'S GOT ISSUES*.

According to Channel 4, it was a no-brainer selecting
Russell for the task. The station announced: 'The world's
in a shocking state, what with the tube always breaking,
World War III brewing and the ruddy weather. Now's the
time for an informed mass debate, and Russell's just the
man to get it out in the open and give it a darned good
thrashing.'

The show, again written with collaborator Matt Morgan
and produced by Russell's own production company,
Vanity Projects, was 30-minutes of live debate driven by
the comedian. A different and far-reaching topic – the
issue in the programme's title – was put up for discussion
each week. The first show aired on 5 September. The Dirty

Pretty Things' tune 'Deadwood' introduced the show to the great British public and the theme for the first programme in the series was: 'Is Our Lust for Beauty Making Us Ugly Human Beings?'

Lily Allen, who had presented Russell his *GQ* award, was the star guest on the debut programme. A specially invited audience (all asked to come armed with lots of 'opinions') was arranged in a conventional arc in the studio. In front of them, Russell paced the studio manically.

The debut programme posed a series of questions: Is beauty in the eye of the beholder? Do beautiful people get better jobs? Will our fascination with image be the death of individualism? However, this wasn't *Newsnight*, *Panaroma* or some other heavyweight, issue-based programme. As the series progressed, there was often much lateral digression from the subject at hand as Russell ran off at comedic tangents before reining the debate back. At the end of each *Russell Brand's Got Issues* show Russell promised an end 'event' to visually illustrate the show's debate. Because the first show was based on beauty, Russell used a crowd of naked people to demonstrate that 'people should be free of the shackles of beauty'.

Viewing figures for the show, which had benefited from a major promotional push, including TV trailers and a poster campaign, must have made disappointing reading for Russell. Just 148,000 people tuned in to the first show, roughly half the average for the 10.30 p.m. slot on E4. Worse, the show was beaten by almost all its main multi-channel rivals, with BBC Three's comedy sketch show *Little Miss Jocelyn* gaining 259,000 viewers. Despite the poor showing, Channel 4 stood by its new talent find, with a spokeswoman insisting: 'Russell Brand is one of the most exciting talents on British TV at the moment and his E4 series has made a positive start in a competitive digital world.'

But, the underwhelming start must have led to some head scratching. Playing in front of such a small TV audience must also have come as a shock to Russell, who had managed to pull in over 1.5m viewers for the first night of *Big Brother's Big Mouth* in *Big Brother* series 7.

Perhaps inevitably, the format was tweaked. A character, General Zod's nephew, and clips of people interviewed on the street were dropped in favour of Russell acting in skits. These took their inspiration from the week's hot issue. The second show in the series took the theme 'Yobs: Is It Time to Fight Back?' Lottery winner and super-yob Michael Carroll and interior designer Laurence Llewelyn-Bowen were guest panellists.

Other programmes in the series were: 'Is Sex Fucking You Up?'; 'The Paranormal'; 'The Nature of Celebrity'; and – one subject right up Russell's alley – 'Does True Love Exist?' Among the guests were Vanessa Feltz and Tim Westwood, the hip hop DJ and fellow MTV presenter with *Pimp My Ride*. In a reverse of the host/guest dynamic from May, Jonathan Ross also joined Russell on his couch for a frank discussion on sex. Ross also paid Russell the ultimate compliment by dressing exactly like the comedian host.

However, the ...*Got Issues* series never seemed to catch fire. There were plans to transfer – and promote – the show from E4 to sister station Channel 4 on 17 November but in the event this never came off. Instead, with the ratings failing to recover, the show was quietly shelved on 17 October. Russell was told to go away and develop another TV vehicle for his talents. Around the time of recording ...*Got Issues*, Russell appeared to suggest that he had lost some control. He was no longer master of his success; success drove him. He commented: 'I'd like to feel a bit more settled and at ease and not feel constantly driven towards achievement – devoured, consumed and discarded as a husk the moment it touches my lips.'

On 14 October, Russell took time out to appear at the first *Secret Policeman's Ball* benefit show for 17 years. He shared the bill at the Royal Albert Hall with Chevy Chase, Eddie Izzard, The Mighty Boosh and Jon Culshaw. The Magic Numbers and The Zutons provided the sounds. It was an ideal stage for Russell. The event was originally made famous by Russell's comedy heroes, such as Peter Cook and the Monty Python team.

The 2006 show featured some politicised sketches critical of the US detention centre at Guantanamo Bay. Russell used a tried and tested technique from his comedy armoury: he read from a newspaper report and then picked apart every idiotic word. This time he chose to have a rant at the *Sun*, which he described as a friend that he hated. In his brief – just under seven minutes – performance, Russell held the tabloid in his hand and let rip at the paper's coverage of Soham murderer Ian Huntley. It had reported that Huntley practised witchcraft in his cell. The paper was hysterical. Russell sarcastically punctured the story. He commented: 'I made my mind up about Ian Huntley when he killed those children. What? Ian Huntley is practising witchcraft – you're joking, I liked him.'

Interestingly, a previous mention of Huntley in a comedy routine had gone down in Russell's memory as one of his worst gigs. But his appearance at the *Secret Policeman's Ball* gig was a triumph. And with his sarcastic and surreal patter about murderers Peter Sutcliffe and Rose West bringing about peace in the Middle East, he won over many new fans.

On 22 November a new DVD called *Russell Brand Live* hit stores in the UK. It captured a performance at London's Shepherd's Bush Empire of the comedian on his *Shame* tour. A nice little stocking-filler for Christmas.

It was a big day for Russell. In addition to the DVD launch, Russell was back on stage that night. Comedians Matt Lucas and David Walliams had invited Russell to guest in their one-off *Little Britain* Comic Relief show at the Carling Apollo in West London. The pair, who had guested on Russell's Radio 2 show only weeks before, were the brains behind *Little Britain*, the hit character-based BBC radio and television sketch show.

The show made its debut on BBC Radio 4 in 2001. After transferring to television in 2003 it became a huge success with critics and audiences. Many of the show's catchphrases – delivered by grotesque characters, such as the wheelchair-bound Andy, the only gay in the village Dafydd and teenage tearway Vicky Pollard – gained currency in playgrounds and boardrooms across the country.

In November's spectacular sell-out show, in aid of Comic Relief, Russell was employed – and cast against type – by Walliams's transvestite character Emily Howard to play a plumber. However, Russell showed his true colours when he ripped off his boiler suit to reveal himself clad in black lace ladies' lingerie. The skit also provided one of the enduring images of the night: two of the UK's top self-styled ladies' men, Brand and Walliams, tussling with each other – with Walliams dressed as a middle-aged woman.

But Russell wasn't allowed to hog the limelight. Other stars with cameos in the show included the comedians Peter Kay and Dawn French, Jonathan Ross, DJ Chris Moyles and the actors Patsy Kensit, Dennis Waterman and Jeremy Edwards. The star-packed audience, which included Arsenal footballer Thierry Henry, actor Rufus Sewell and movie writer Richard Curtis, were also treated to a surprise when Kate Moss made her debut comedy appearance – hilariously, as Vicky Pollard's twin slag of a sister.

The supermodel, rigged out in a trashy nylon tracksuit and with her hair scrunched, took to the stage pushing a wagon train of prams. She delivered her lines with just the right amount of gobby insouciance. She told Vicky Pollard's former school teacher, Mr Collier, that: 'I'm the easy one. Total slag. I'm anybody's for a packet of Quavers.' When she left the stage to go 'off on the rob', Lucas's character yelled after her: 'Katie lose some weight, you fat bitch.'

It was a successful night for the show and also a good showcase for Russell to demonstrate that he can work well as part of a team.

A couple of nights later Russell was back on TV with his new vehicle, the imaginatively titled *The Russell Brand Show*. It aired on 24 November. According to the station's factual entertainment editor Angela Jain: '[Brand is] undoubtedly the man of the moment.'

The Russell Brand Show was put on late at night, in time for the post-pub crowd, and went head-to-head with Jonathan Ross on BBC1. Channel 4 billed the series, again produced by Vanity Projects, as topical shows with a mix of stand-up, sketches, music, chat and interviews. And that's just what they were. It provided Russell with another chance to showcase his talent on TV following the disappointing end of ...*Got Issues*.

However, it also meant that Russell was spread thin. At the end of 2006, his media and comedy commitments were staggering. He was all over the place. Russell was on the stage, he was doing standup on his national *Shame* tour, he was on the box, on Channel 4 presenting *The Russell Brand Show* and MTV presenting *1 Leicester Square*, he was on the radio, hosting BBC Radio 2's *Russell Brand Show*, and he was in the papers, writing his weekly sports piece for the *Guardian*. Ubiquitous didn't cover it.

Inevitably, with his fingers in so many media pies, Russell was criticised. Ridiculously, he was castigated for plugging his radio and TV work on other, sometimes competing, channels. His opponents cited his campaign to start a terrace anthem, about which Russell wrote in the *Guardian* and then discussed on his radio show as evidence of this cross-media marketing.

Channel 4's *The Russell Brand Show* was initially

commissioned for a run of five shows. The critics anticipated something special. London's *Evening Standard* believed that Russell would be a better bet at this time in the schedules and 'a wee bit more comfortable' telling jokes than Charlotte Church (the teenage classical-singer-turned-popstar who had previously occupied the same late Friday night slot).

The debut show, starting at 11.05 p.m., was a cracker. Two days after sharing the *Little Britain* Comic Relief stage, Matt Lucas and David Walliams joined Russell. Inevitably, the Dirty Pretty Things provided the title song and, after a short piece of stand-up from Russell, the host retired to a chaise longue in the decadently furnished studio. He was joined by a nattily dressed Walliams and Lucas. Russell gave both his guests presents: a chocolate bust for Lucas and a chocolate cock for Walliams. They reciprocated with a book and antique black top hat respectively, which Russell thought was a 'beautiful affectation'.

Russell interviewed the comedy stars and Walliams revealed that he hated Russell when they first met because his host was high on heroin. They met later in a yoga class and became close. Lucas commented that he thought Russell and Walliams were 'the two gayest straight boys'.

There was a sketch based around Tom Cruise's recent wedding to Katie Holmes and another with Russell emulating the cross-Channel swim that Walliams had made for charity. With just two guests to sustain the show over 50 minutes, the pace did flag from time to time, but things picked up when chanteuse Amy Winehouse was called upon to sing at the end.

Later shows in the series saw contributions from Courtney Love, the cast of the *League of Gentlemen*, Jade Goody, Sharon Osbourne and former boy band member Matt Willis. Russell also saw a childhood wish come true when Morrissey made a musical appearance.

Just prior to starting *The Russell Brand Show* the comedian used his new-found celebrity to put a little something back, hosting a charity gig for drug addiction centre Focus 12 on 2 November. Russell is a patron of the organisation. The cash raised by the charity gig went towards counselling and treatment for addicts.

The event, 'For Pity's Sake – Focus', was held on a bitterly cold winter night at Camden's plush pleasure lounge, Koko. On the bill: Noel Gallagher, Ozzy Osbourne's daughter, Kelly, The Holloways and Dirty Pretty things, whose September gig at West London's Coronet Russell had hosted. Unfortunately, Russell had had to bear the brunt of a chorus of boos that night before Carl Barat rushed from stage left to rugby tackle the comedian.

The original idea for the gig had been for Russell to do a comedy routine, with Oasis man Noel Gallagher providing the music. However, as more and more acts were added to the bill Russell's set got canned. 'I got to know Russell quite well and he kind of put me on the spot on his radio show,' said Gallagher, who joked that he rarely played solo sets because it upset his brother Liam. Russell added: 'I have become friends with Noel, which is why he along with Paul Weller agreed to appear at the benefit for Focus 12, the treatment centre for drug and alcohol addiction where I got clean.'

Despite the eye-watering £50 ticket price, the audience was a tricky one. Leery gangs roamed the opulent north London theatre pouring beer over anything that moved. Russell sensed that the rowdy crowd was not going to be responsive to his brand of humour. They had other concerns: as soon as the laddish throng spotted Noel's brother Liam in the balcony they began chanting the Oasis front man's name.

Russell joked that the room stank of cannabis and cocaine, adding that he was pleased to be 'raising money to get people off drugs instead of raising money to get drugs off people'. But he was fighting a losing battle, and as the chants of 'Liam! Liam!' rang out Russell couldn't get off the stage quickly enough, making way for the first band of the evening, The Holloways, whose set was also dogged throughout by shouts directed at the younger Gallagher brother.

When The Holloways finished, Russell returned to the stage to thank the younger Gallagher brother for attending. 'Thanks for coming Liam,' he said, before admonishing the rowdy crowd: 'I'm glad we're raising money for a rehabilitation centre because a lot of you need it.' Russell admitted later that he glanced up to the balcony and spotted Liam Gallagher, who he said was there 'to regard his elder brother's travails. Even from that distance he certainly has presence.'

With the audience more interested in the Gallaghers, it wasn't going to be a night for comedy. 'I'd never been at one of Oasis's gigs and had never encountered their fans en masse. Let me tell you, it was like no other musical event I've attended,' Russell said. 'I was under no illusions as to who the crowd had come to see on this occasion, but thought the 50 quid ticket price and acoustic nature of the evening might mean a relatively passive audience.'

Russell soon realised that his main job at Koko was to keep the crowd in check. He said, 'The Holloways were excellent, but each time one of their songs finished the crowd would seize the opportunity to begin one of their own – exclusively odes to Manchester City's most prominent players. I quickly realised that my job as compere was to contain the maelstrom as much as possible, which wasn't easy, and limit the chanting to the bits between other bands.'

When Kelly Osbourne came on to play a DJ set she was barracked throughout by the crowd. It was just as well that the aspiring DJ didn't do requests, seeing as the main one seemed to be: 'Get your tits out for the lads.' She didn't.

Next up was the Dirty Pretty Things. Russell claimed the band had only had 24 hours to prepare for the gig and weren't playing their equipment. They had stepped in at short notice for Kasabian, whose guitarist had been stricken with laryngitis. Despite the fact that the Dirty Pretty Things' set was in constant danger of being sabotaged by the chants for Liam Gallagher, Barat made a convincing case for proving that it was him and not Pete Doherty who had been the major creative force behind The Libertines.

He tore through an acoustic set and even dedicated the second song to Liam. In another first for the charity evening, Barat's band was joined by Charlatans singer Tim Burgess for a sterling rendition of 'North Country Boy'.

Russell watched from the side of the stage, liking what he saw. He remarked: 'The Dirty Pretty Things came on next and they too were remarkable and aided considerably, in the eyes of the pit, by the appearance of charming Tim Burgess, who belongs to the era from which Oasis emerged.'

Next up was Noel Gallagher himself. The Oasis guitarist arrived and sat centre-stage armed with an acoustic guitar and nothing else. He then sang his way through a number of what the singer described as Oasis 'b-sides and stuff'. In reality he performed songs such as 'Wonderwall', which the rabble sang along to like a terrace choir, and a beautiful version of 'Don't Look Back in Anger'. Gallagher also covered The Beatles' song 'Strawberry Fields Forever' and was joined on stage by Paul Weller for the pair to race through The Jam classic 'Thick As Thieves'. Gallagher later claimed that Weller had purposely and mischievously chosen the track because the Modfather knew that, with 14 chords, it would be a tough song for the Oasis man to master.

Russell confessed that as Gallagher performed, he watched Noel's interaction with his audience and fans. Was there something he could learn? 'I watched him and the crowd and pondered why he inspires such adulation,' said Russell, adding that he believed Gallagher has an 'almost paranormal ability to convert emotion into music'. The comedian added: 'It isn't an audio aesthetic with which [the audience] identify but something more profound.'

Despite the chants and his inability to command the audience, it had been a good night for Russell. He got to meet Liam Gallagher for the first time and was impressed by the Oasis singer's persona. The pair bumped into each other backstage and Gallagher steered the comedian, in a 'vaguely menacing' way, into a nearby room. Russell recalled: 'Liam came over and went, "All right mate, all right", sort of posturing and grandstanding like Muhammad Ali or Mussolini or something, but it totally suits him.' When Gallagher leaned in close, the comedian admits that he almost came. He said: 'There was one bit where he leaned his face into mine, so his nose was touching my nose, and it was so exhilarating that I thought he is either going to kiss me or head-butt me. But it was so exciting I didn't care which.'

Russell elaborated that the musician had nothing of any real import to tell him and just swore 'about nothing in particular'. But, between 'fuck this' and 'fuck that', he was struck by Liam's magnetism and charisma. Russell commented, 'Liam is just like the person in the video, the person on the posters, the person you see splashed across headlines. He is just like the distillation of fame, of celebrity, this charismatic sexy person.' The Oasis singer also volunteered to appear as a guest on one of Russell's TV or radio shows, but nothing definite was fixed.

Given Gallagher's bad boy image, Russell cautiously introduced him to his mum, Babs, whom he'd invited along for the evening. Russell was impressed that the singer didn't attempt to dial down his intense charisma even for her. Liam doesn't have a 'mum mode', Russell commented later.

However, Russell did have to swallow one bitter pill that night. Someone stole his coat.

CHAPTER 20

End of 2006

AS 2006 CAME TO AN END, RUSSELL FOUND THAT HIS TALENTS WERE STILL IN DEMAND. IT WAS A DEMAND THAT HE WAS AMPLY REWARDED FOR, ESPECIALLY WHEN HE WAS A POPULAR WINNER AT THE BRITISH COMEDY AWARDS ON 13 DECEMBER.

The glitzy bash, hosted by Jonathan Ross, went out live on ITV1 at 9 p.m. All in all, 2006 was a poor year for new comedy. Bar Russell, very few comedians or shows had made an impact. This was reflected in the nominations, which were dominated by Ricky Gervais's post-*Office* vehicle, *Extras*. For example, Gervais and his partner Stephen Merchant went head-to-head for the best TV comedy actor accolade after being nominated for their respective roles as Andy Millman and his hapless agent in *Extras*. The sitcom creator and his creative partner also had a joint nomination for best TV comedy series. With *Extras* threatening to sweep the board, *Little Britain*'s Matt Lucas and David Walliams

223

had a fight on their hands to retain the Best TV Comedy crown for their series.

In a weak male group, Russell was nominated for Best Comedy Newcomer alongside Kevin Bishop, from the comedy series *Star Stories*, and the *Friday Night Project*'s two front men, Alan Carr and Justin Lee Collins. Charlotte Church, Katherine Parkinson and Miranda Hart were nominated for the same prize in the female category. In addition, Russell was also up for the Best Live Standup Tour award.

Russell didn't have to wait long before picking up an award for his work on *Russell Brand's Got Issues*. His win was totally expected and, considering the competition, justified. Courtney Love, presented Russell with the gong, clearly delighted that her friend had won. Russell leapt up on stage in his rock 'n' roll threads and, perhaps mindful of his previous sometimes controversial appearances at awards ceremonies, kept his acceptance speech short and sharp. He said that it was nice to be acknowledged for his comedy rather than his presenter credits. He also publicly thanked his creative partner and friend, Matt Morgan, in addition to the 'loads of people who contributed to this glorious façade'. After a little banter with Ross, who warned Russell about trying it on with Church – 'she is going out with a rugby player', the awards host warned – the comedian hugged Courtney and returned to his table.

Jimmy Carr beat Russell to the Best Live Tour Show award and Church won the best female comedy newcomer gong.

The Big Fat Quiz of the Year returned for the third time on

27 December on Channel 4 with Russell as one of the guests and with Jimmy Carr as quizmaster.

Russell was paired with The Mighty Boosh's Noel Fielding. Rob Brydon and David Walliams made another pairing, with Jonathan Ross and Cat Deeley forming a third team. The whole show involved a lot of light slapstick, with jokes and banter about sexual diseases and Ross's salary. A number of guest questioners, including Boy George, Myleene Klass and Matt Willis, appeared.

Russell and Fielding looked like strange twins plucked from a Bauhaus concert in 1979. Naturally, they were tagged as the Goth Detective Team, but they won the quiz game with 39 points. Ross and Cat came second with 38 points, with Walliams and Brydon bringing up the rear with 37 points.

A couple of other honours went Russell's way as December advanced. The *Guardian*'s Saturday morning *Guide* chose Russell for its light-hearted inaugural end of year awards. He was given the Most Everywhere of the Year accolade. Writer Ben Marshall was obviously a fan. He wrote: 'Compared to the current crop of Yoof TV presenters, Brand looks like a cross between Oscar Wilde and Wittgenstein... he is great in small, moderately paced, doses.' However, Marshall did offer a cautionary note, adding that, 'wall-to-wall Brand is a bit like painting your home black and furnishing it with whoopee cushions and Aleister Crowley's pornographic poetry'.

A couple of big dates were also slipped into Russell's 2007 diary. It was announced he would be one of the headline acts at the prestigious Leicester Comedy Festival from 9 February. The annual event – the longest-running funny fest in Britain – promised more than 60,000 people chuckling through Russell's routines, plus those of another 1,000 acts, including Paul Merton and Jimmy Carr, over ten fun-packed days.

Organiser Geoff Rowe predicted the best line-up ever. 'There's a real desire by comedians to come here,' he said. 'Russell Brand's standup show is amazing.' The 2007 festival was shaping up to be a classic. Also on the bill with Russell, Carr and Merton were Tim Minchin, Sean Hughes, Count Arthur Strong, Shappi Khorsandi and We Are Klang. The festival promised to explore the links between disability and comedy and Russell was expected to unite with some of the best acts on the final night for a Comedy Heaven charity show. Leicestershire Aids Support Services and Amnesty International were lined up to benefit.

More good news flashed Russell's way. Just like at the start of 2006 he'd been hired to host the *NME* Awards, so at the beginning of 2007 he was booked to compere The Brits.

The move to hire Russell was explained by Peter Jamieson, co-chairman of the Brits. 'We always promised that Brits 2007 would be an edgy, exciting show,' he revealed. 'First, we announced we'd broadcast live. Then we announced Oasis as our Outstanding Contribution Award winner. And now there's Russell Brand.'

It was a major coup for Russell. In the space of 12 months he had risen from the digital ghetto to be considered a safe pair of hands in charge of a major live awards show and one of the most in-demand hosts on TV.

Russell acknowledged it had been a fine year. His

Annus Happilis. Or, as he might put it, his *Anus Happilis.* 'It's been a glorious year right across the UK, but specifically for me,' he admitted.

The comic spent Christmas hanging out with his mum, 'watching telly and saying: "It's better now, innit? Better now we're not all poor."'

Then, for New Year, he flew off to sun-kissed Mauritius with a new girlfriend, 20-year-old Laura Gallagher, sister of TV presenter Kirsty and daughter of Ryder Cup golfer Bernard.

Russell and bird didn't slum it. They stayed at the same hotel as Chelsea FC owner, Russian oligarch and billionaire Roman Abramovich. In fact, they spent New Year's Eve picking over a posh buffet and sizing up the nearby tycoon.

Celebrity Big Brother returned to the nation's screens on 3 January and Russell flew back from his luxury Indian Ocean resort to helm the accompanying *Big Brother's Big Mouth* series. The series comprised the usual motley crew of 11 'celebrities'. Some didn't even register on the C-list. Among the better-known housemates this time around were ageing pop singer Leo Sayer, former *A-Team* actor Dirk Benedict, The Jackson 5's Jermaine Jackson, lead singer of Towers of London Donny Tourette and the veteran film director Ken Russell.

The series promised to deliver a bounty of riches for the comedian as he and his studio audience picked over the bones of the celebs' lives inside the house. The first week hadn't finished before Ken Russell walked. After that, things got even more interesting as the show became embroiled in a racism and bullying row centred around

Big Brother mainstay Jade Goody and Indian Bollywood actress Shilpa Shetty. Russell earned plaudits for his perhaps uncharacteristically sensitive handling of the travails that affected the show. In the meantime, ratings for the show – which some said beforehand was tired and past it – soared.

Russell might not have forecast that, but asked by *Now* magazine his predictions for 2007 and beyond he did have some interesting thoughts. Not entirely seriously, he suggested that he would in future alternate between being 'deeply pious and celibate', to rampaging through life 'like a one-man funk band'.

He also hoped that oral sex would replace the handshake 'as the principal form of greeting'. Even among family members.

Russell also predicted the demise of the cult of celebrity. The end of the gravy train for the famous. 'People who've scaled the heights of popular culture will have to get careers in dog-fighting and prostitution,' he forecast. 'I'll be signing on again.'

His final prophecy was his wildest flight of fancy yet.

CHAPTER 21

Bye-Bye Big Brother

RUSSELL BRAND LAUNCHED INTO 2007 AS THE MAN OF THE MOMENT, WITH THE UK AT HIS FEET AND ITS LEGS OPEN. A SUCCESSION OF TV SHOWS, A NEW NATIONAL RADIO PROGRAMME, STAND-UP PERFORMANCES AT EVER-LARGER VENUES, DVDS OF THE SHOWS, A NEWPAPER COLUMN, AWARDS... HE HAD ACHIEVED THEM ALL AND THERE WAS MORE TO COME. HE WAS HOT TO TROT.

Fresh from winning a *GQ* Man of the Year award and *Time Out*'s Stand-up of the Year in late 2006, he was about to step out at another awards show. Only this time it was the biggest gig of his career.

The Brit Awards enjoys a special place in the annual awards calendar. The biggest gong-fest of the year for the British music industry, it has long been a calvacade of controversy, gross misbehaviour and sometimes comically inept presenting.

The event began in 1977, but only really caught the public and the press's attention in 1989. This was the notorious show when the ceremony was hosted by the Page Three model-turned-singer Samantha Fox and Fleetwood Mac drummer Mick Fleetwood – and screened live on national TV. Fox and Fleetwood proved to be the most shambolic double act in the history of awards shows. Comically mismatched and not just in terms of size – Fleetwood is about 6ft 7in and Fox is about 5ft 1in – they missed cues and they fluffed lines.

Sam Fox introduced Boy George as the Four Tops, a Government minister was booed by the audience, and a pre-recorded message by Michael Jackson was never broadcast, despite the show ending early. The result was one of the most cringe-worthy (or hugely entertaining, depending on your point of view) spectacles ever broadcast live on TV.

Then in 1992 came the KLF's performance of their dance hit '3am Eternal' – as a hardcore metal track, while frontman Bill Drummond fired blanks into the audience with a vintage machine gun. Famous conductor Sir George Solti walked out in disgust. The band didn't hang around to collect their Best Band award. Later, someone dropped a dead sheep outside the venue of the after-show party.

In 1996, Noel Gallagher had announced, when picking up one of new boys Oasis' three awards from INXS singer Michael Hutchence, 'has-beens shouldn't be presenting awards to gonna-bes.' Unfortunately, not long afterwards Hutchence really would be a has-been, when he accidentally hung himself in Australia.

But the biggest sensation of that night (and probably in Brit Awards history) came when Pulp's Jarvis Cocker invaded the stage while Michael Jackson was performing

'Earth Song' live. He ran around the singer, lifted his shirt and poked out his bum at Jackson in an overt gesture of defiance against what he considered to be the worrying messiah-like tendencies of the so-called King of Pop. Cocker ended up being questioned by police after claims that he had assaulted Jackson's child dancers. He was later released without charge.

Two years later, in 1998, Danbert Nobacon, lead singer of anarchist pop outfit and one-hit wonders Chumbawumba, threw a bucket of water over Deputy Prime Minister John Prescott as he sat at one of the tables enjoying his dinner. Afterwards, while their record company issued apologies, Nobacon (real name: Nigel Hunter) was unrepentant. 'If John Prescott has the nerve to turn up at events like the Brit Awards in a vain attempt to make Labour seem cool and trendy, then he deserves all we can throw at him.'

In 2000, the DJ Brandon Block managed to get into a fight with Rolling Stones guitarist Ronnie Wood on stage. Block, who had had a few drinks, was persuaded by his mates that he had won an award, so he marched up to collect it. Wood, about to present the award to someone else, aimed an insult at him. The DJ retaliated and the guitarist threw a drink over him. The same year, Robbie Williams demanded to have a punch-up with Oasis' Liam Gallagher, who had badmouthed him.

By then the reputation of the Brits for bad behaviour was so ingrained that for many years the show was considered too high a risk to be broadcast live to a primetime television audience. But in truth, during the Noughties the Brits become a much tamer affair. Pop stars weren't wild boys any more – they were now usually the malleable products of talent shows like *Pop Idol* and *X Factor* – and rock stars were now wearing ties. Record sales were dropping like a stone as kids downloaded their music for free, so there was less for the British music industry to celebrate anyway. Worst of all, audience figures for the TV broadcast had been falling year after year.

So what better way to inject some fresh excitement into this 30-year old institution than to revive it as a live TV event for the first time since the Fox/Fleetwood fiasco – and have a genuinely controversial, edgy yet entertaining figure as a presenter?

Step forward Russell Brand. He had already demonstrated that he fitted the bill with his headline-grabbing handling of the NME awards the previous year, having been called a 'cunt' by Bob Geldof and flung back a riposte that cut Saint Bob down to size. Since then his profile had got bigger and bigger. If the Brits organisers wanted excitement and controversy, they had come to the right man.

Russell did not disappoint. He opened the show, on Valentine's Day 2007, by poking fun at Robbie Williams, who was in the papers at the time for his latest trip to a rehab clinic, apparently for an addiction to prescription drugs. Russell pointed at a padlocked cupboard that formed part of the set and described it as 'Robbie Williams's medicine cabinet'. It was quickly tempered by another comment: 'Get well, England's rose – one day at a time, old bean. Oh, those drugs, – they're everywhere.'

After that Russell's patter between the awards was

liberally peppered with sexual innuendo about what he'd like to do with various female members of the pop fraternity – and he even managed to make a lewd suggestion about the Queen. That was bound to raise hackles.

Most controversially of all, Russell got political. When announcing the International Breakthrough award, he referred to the recently publicised 'friendly fire' death of a British soldier named Matty Hull by American forces in Iraq. 'I think a good international breakthrough would be if the British and American soldiers tell each other where they are standing,' he said.

Russell also addressed the rumours that Conservative party leader David Cameron had smoked drugs as a schoolboy. 'What worries me most is that he dressed up as a schoolboy to do it, the pervert. Though, perhaps let's not condemn him regardless. Who among us didn't smoke just a little bit of weed at school, just to take the edge off those irksome crack come-downs?

'Actually, as it turns out, it's about as good an anti-drugs campaign as you're going to get. Don't take drugs or you might end up leader of the Tories with a face like a little painted egg.'

Russell also made a joke that has been voted the funniest ever at any Brit Awards. It concerned the alcohol and drug problems of a well-known singer, whose notorious antics had become a daily source of material for the British tabloids. 'Amy Winehouse,' he announced, introducing the troubled star to the stage. 'Her surname is beginning to sound like a description of her liver.'

In a taster of much bigger controversy to come, the Brand brand of comedy was greeted by a 'flood' of complaints from the show's TV audience – at five million the largest for the Brits in several years. By the following morning, ITV had received 300 complaints, while the broadcasting watchdog Ofcom logged another 135 – most of them about Russell's risqué humour rather than the bad language that was regularly bleeped out during the live show.

This was described as 'a flood' of complaints in the media, but as Russell was to find out pretty soon, it was more like a minor leak. Russell was stoutly defended by ITV, who broadcast the show, even though it had started before the 9pm 'watershed' for adult programming. Russell was 'known for his flamboyant persona' and argued that his David Cameron routine had not glamorised or condoned drug-taking.

In March Russell co-hosted an evening for the Teenage Cancer Trust with Noel Fielding from *The Mighty Boosh* – a partnership they would repeat on Channel 4's *End of the Year Quiz* over the next couple of years. Furthermore, a second nationwide tour, called *Russell Brand: Only Joking*, was announced to follow the huge success of the *Shame* tour the previous summer.

A few days later Russell's elevation to the top rank of British TV comedy was confirmed when he hosted a segment of one of the year's big television events, Comic Relief, with the likes of Chris Evans, Graham Norton, *Big Brother* colleague Davina McCall, Paul O'Grady and Jonathan Ross.

Sacha Baron Cohen appeared as Borat, Rowan Atkinson played Mr Bean, there were appearances by everyone from Elton John to Ricky Gervais and from Billy Connolly to

Ozzy and Sharon Osbourne. After his success with 'Amarillo' at the previous show, Peter Kay performed '500 Miles' with The Proclaimers – and with Matt Lucas playing Andy from *Little Britain*. There was an entertaining celebrity edition of *The Apprentice* and perhaps most memorably of all, Catherine Tate played a number of her characters in sketches. These included mouthy teenager Lauren on work experience at 10 Downing Street, working for Tony Blair, who uses her catchphrase 'Am I bovvered?' back at her in scarily believable fashion.

Russell presented his section of the charity marathon – which also included moving reports of Comic Relief's work in Africa and elsewhere, presented by Ant & Dec, Take That's Gary Barlow and others – in the early hours of the morning, and he was able to announce that these efforts had raised around £40 million on the night.

But he also made another notable contribution. In a special show of *Little Britain Live*, celebrities including Kate Moss, Jonathan Ross, Chris Moyles and Dennis Waterman made guest appearances. So did Russell, in a sketch opposite David Walliams, who was playing his 'Edwardian 'laydee' character.

Russell entered wearing a boiler suit, brandishing a spanner, declaring: 'I understand you've got a problem with your plumbing.' He is soon fending off Walliams on a chaise-longue, but then Russell reveals he is similarly inclined. 'I know the game,' he says. 'I like to wear women's clothes myself. In fact, I'm wearing some right now. What do you reckon?' Russell then pulls off his boiler suit to reveal a bra, panties, suspenders and stockings underneath, to screams of delight from the theatre audience.

This was a rare (albeit very brief) acting performance from Russell. These had been few and far between for the past few years. His last acting gig had been on *Cruise of the Gods* with Steve Coogan back in 2002, and that had been during his self-destructive drug and booze phase, and had ended in him being sent home due to his off-set antics.

Apart from an appearance in Ben Elton's sitcom *Blessed* in 2005 and a few cartoon voice-overs. That was about it. Russell was up for the role of Super-Hans in Channel 4's brilliant sitcom *Peep Show*, starring David Mitchell and Robert Webb, but didn't get the part.

In 2006, Russell got a small role in a Hollywood movie shooting in the UK called *Penelope* – a romantic comedy starring Christina Ricci as a wealthy aristocratic heiress trying to shake her family curse. It also featured Reese Witherspoon, James McAvoy and a fair number of British character actors and comedians, including Lenny Henry, Richard E Grant (Withnail from *Withnail and I*) and Nigel Havers. Russell was cast as Sam the Jazz Club Owner, and was on screen for a couple of minutes.

He also had a part in *The Abbey*, a comedy pilot about a celebrity rehab retreat, playing drug-addled DJ called Terry. The show was broadcast straight after the Brit Awards on Valentine's Night on ITV – and was considered so unfunny that it was never picked up for a series. But shortly afterwards Russell also appeared in a serious role, playing the part of an ex-con in an episode of ITV's cop drama series *Cold Blood*. Acting, movies – and, believe it or not, Hollywood – now beckoned for the scruffy lothario. That meant he had to make a decision.

Ever since he had become host of *Big Brother*'s spin-off show, then called *Big Brother's Efourum*, back in 2004, the newly clean and sober young comedian had been on the up. His success and fame had grown because of *Big Brother's Big Mouth*. It had been a perfect vehicle for his talents – he was, after all, a bouffant-haired big-mouth capable of abusing the audience as he entertained them. The popularity of the show had exploded – it was consistently one of E4's highest-rating shows. In many ways *BBBM* had made Russell Brand – it had put him where he was. But now he had to leave the show that had made him because, frankly, he was getting too big for it. There were other gigs and commitments that were, well... 'citing.

But also the tide was beginning to turn for *Big Brother*. His final stint on *BBBM* was during *Celebrity Big Brother 5*, in which Jade Goody led a notorious racist bullying campaign against her fellow housemate, the Bollywood star Shilpa Shetty. It exploded into a major controversy and international incident. *Big Brother* and Channel 4 were roundly condemned for their handling of the crisis, with calls for the show to be pulled off-air.

Russell had been praised for his sensitive handling of the controversy on *BBBM* but after three years and 65 episodes hosting the show in his inimitable fashion, Russell quit following his final show at the end of *CBB5* – a show that featured all the contestants with the notable exception of Jade Goody and Shilpa Shetty.

Before Russell hosted the Brits in February, word was

out that he would not be hanging around for *Big Brother 8* in the summer. It was in early April that Russell officially announced his decision to stand down in order to pursue other projects. In typical Brand style he thanked the programme makers for 'taking the risk of employing an ex-junkie twerp' to front the show.

'The three years I've spent on *Big Brother's Big Mouth* have been an unprecedented joy,' he said. '*Big Mouth* has afforded me opportunities that are too exciting to turn down, so alas I can do it no more. And while I recognise this isn't as significant as the resignation of Beckham or the Cuban missile crisis, I just wanted to say thanks to everyone.'

But Russell was not quite done with *Big Brother*. His own personal, surreal and very funny history of the show – *Big Brother: According to Russell Brand* – was screened on E4 in May.

Russell continued to show up on the telly in his own right. After making his first appearance on Jonathan Ross's chat show *Friday Night With Jonathan Ross* in 2006, he appeared twice more the following year, in June and November.

In the June show Russell seemed to get the better of the usually quick-witted Ross with ease. Ross was gushing about Russell's performance in a non-comic acting role in the ITV drama *Cold Blood*, playing a character who was nothing like himself. 'Well, that *is* acting in its essence, Jonathan,' replied Russell, straight-faced. 'You're making me out to be a proper fool,' muttered a ruffled Ross. But the pair were becoming good mates – and that would have far-reaching effects for both of them.

But for the first time in a long while, Russell was really focusing on acting. He was about to undertake in his most significant movie role yet: playing Flash in the revival of the 1950s British movie series *St Trinians*. It looked like an inspired piece of casting.

The original *St Trinians* movies had featured a character called Flash Harry, a spiv-like fixer who greased the wheels of the the headmistress's outlandish and illegal schemes to keep her notorious girls' school in business. Harry was played by George Cole, who would find greater fame decades later as Arthur Daley in the TV show *Minder* – essentially an older version of same shady but lovable character.

Flash Harry had a sharp wit and was sharply dressed. What's more, he spent most of the *St Trinians* movies surrounded by gorgeous girls in gymslips and stockings. What could be a more fitting role for Russell?

He was busy filming the new *St Trinians* film in the spring. The movie would be released at the end of 2007 to very mixed reviews, but took a very respectable £12 million at the UK box office (which was quite a lot more than the low-budget movie had cost to make). That would ensure that further *St Trinians* adventures would get made – albeit without Russell.

Even as he was shooting his scenes in *St Trinians*, his next movie role was already lined up. This time, Hollywood wanted him – and it would prove to be his biggest break yet.

CHAPTER 22

Breakthrough

KATY PERRY HAD BEEN LIVING IN LA FOR A FEW YEARS NOW. SHE'D HAD TWO RECORDING CONTRACTS WITH MAJOR RECORD LABELS, AND HAD RECORDED TWO ALBUMS THAT HAD NEVER BEEN RELEASED. SHE HAD APPEARED IN A FEW VIDEOS – SOME FOR OTHER BANDS, SOME OF HER OWN. BUT BY THE BEGINNING OF 2007, THE ONLY PROPER RECORD RELEASE SHE HAD TO SHOW FOR SIX OR SEVEN YEARS IN THE MUSIC INDUSTRY WAS AN ALBUM SHE'D RELEASED IN HER MID-TEENS FOR A MINOR CHRISTIAN ROCK LABEL THAT HAD SINCE DISAPPEARED WITHOUT TRACE.

By this point, Katy had left her Christian roots far behind. 'It's so easy to know everything when you're a kid,' she says. 'God, I miss that. Then you start to wonder: "Dudeface is going to hell because he grew up in a family just like mine, except in another country and Muslim?" There's a lot of question marks in my life. This is a universe I can't control – and I'm a control freak.'

She was by no means estranged from Mary and Keith,

her devout evangelical pastor parents – their bond was stronger than a difference in religious belief. 'I'm happy where I came from,' she would confirm later. 'I love my family, and I like my upbringing. I think it was pure.'

But the grown-up Katy did like to party. Not in the Amy Winehouse league of over-indulgence, but she was drinking a lot. Too much, in fact. 'It was really difficult,' she admits. 'Drinking became a problem. It got out of control, until I said, "OK – back to work." I know I'm speaking for someone, even if it's someone silly.'

As for men, Katy was attracted to the creative types, the difficult personalities. 'It takes one to know one,' she has said. 'I'm not difficult, though. I'm complicated. OK, so I'm difficult. The closest I ever came to normal was dating a golfer.' Some of these boyfriends – and other guys – would provide inspiration for the new bunch of songs she was writing during 2006 – songs like 'Mannequin' and 'UR So Gay'.

But the special person she wanted to get close to was definitely an artistic type – but also a bit of ladies man. It was the brooding, tattoo-heavy MC of up-and-coming alternative hip-hop outfit Gym Class Heroes – Travis McCoy.

Katy met Travis in a recording studio in New York in 2006, and thereafter she would attend numerous Gym Class Heroes gigs, and hang out with him and his band. They became a lot closer during a period when the rapper was suffering a period of depression, and Katy helped him recover. 'There was this really, really dark point about two years ago when I just hit rock bottom,' explained Travis in 2008, when he also admitted to having been addicted to prescription drugs since he was 15 years old. 'I called Katy who was in LA at the time and said to her, "Do you mind coming out and keeping me company?"'

According to Travis he was in awe of Katy, and his initial approach was to play it cool – basically ignore her. 'I was smitten as soon as she walked in the room – she's a girl who demands attention. I have no game whatsoever, so I decided, "I'm just gonna ignore the shit out of her." In essence, that worked.'

But only up to a point. The situation was also pretty unsatisfactory for Katy, who was clearly having a problem getting Travis to commit. 'We weren't really together,' she said later. 'It was casual. But soulless hooking up didn't seem so hot to me. I always wanted to have a romance.' Katy likened her position with Travis to that of Penny Lane – the favoured groupie of the movie *Almost Famous* (played by Kate Hudson). But Katy was better than that.

Despite being dropped by two major record labels, she had already shown tremendous resilience and determination to keep control over her own music and image. Now things would start to pay off. At the end of 2006, Katy got a new record deal and this time things started to happen.

At the time she was working at an A&R company Taxi Music, to pay the bills. 'I was sitting in a cube, listening to all this horrible music people had sent in and critiquing it, because I was supposed to be helping them get ahead in the music industry,' she recalls. 'Then Jason Flom called me. That day I went out for coffee and never went back.'

Jason Flom was the president of Capitol Records. He had heard the masters of Katy's recordings for her last record label, Columbia – which her management company had been able to extract from them. Flom wanted to give Katy a chance – and he was prepared to give her the creative freedom she craved. 'Capitol Records picked me up and decided they wanted to make a *Pretty Woman* story out of me – without the prostitution!' Katy has quipped.

Katy started working with Lukasz Gottwald – better known as Dr Luke – a producer and songwriter who has created huge hits for Britney Spears, Kelly Clarkson, Avril Lavigne, Miley Cyrus and Flo Rida. Crucially, as well as recording the songs she had already written, Katy and Dr Luke co-wrote two new songs for the album – 'Hot N Cold' and 'I Kissed a Girl'.

As someone who plays guitar and writes songs, Katy would start writing at home. Then her producer would go to work on them in the studio, contributing music and sometimes bringing in other writers – another co-writer of 'I Kissed a Girl' is the British pop songwriter and former D-Mob singer Cathy Dennis, whose credits include Kylie Minogue's 'Can't Get You Out of My Head' and Britney Spears's 'Toxic'.

Most of Katy's songs were being built into catchy, punchy power-pop, bursting with her personality and attitude: her opinionated views, her put-downs of old boyfriends, her use of the language she used in her own life, her own experiences. Her songs were inspired by specific moments and dealt with specific events, real life and love – and heartbreak.

'For me, it's really easy for me to write about heartache, really easy,' she said in an interview just as she was finishing recording what would become *One of the Boys*. 'I don't know why. I think that's how I get through it, is writing about the heartache that I'm having about a relationship, or a boy or you know, someone I was in love with or hurt by or whatever.

'It's also easy for me to write from a humorous perspective. My dad's hilarious, and I got a lot of that from him. I guess that's in my bones – that comes out in my songs. I'm a somewhat strong-minded female, and so I think that also is a theme in the songs as well.'

Katy described her approach as somewhere between Lucille Ball – the great American TV comedienne of the 1950s and '60s – and Freddie Mercury, who she described as 'pretty much my biggest influence and idol'.

She also explained that various songs on the album were inspired by real men. 'There's the "UR So Gay" guy. "Thinking of You" and "I'm Still Breathing" are about the same person. And the "Mannequin" guy – some people think it's a dis when I sing, "You're not a man, you're a mannequin," but it's not. Writing that song actually fixed some things in the relationship. It was my way of saying, "I love you so much. Wake. The. Fuck. Up. I want you to be in my life. Oh, and please stop wearing my jeans."'

By the time the album was nearing completion in late 2007, there was already a good buzz about it. The first release would set the tone for the months ahead. A digital EP and video came out on YouTube for 'UR So Gay' – Katy's anthemic demolition job on an ex-boyfriend. It was a campy, over-the-top effort showing a self-obsessed emo male doll surfing on MySpace, while a blonde female doll engages in trickery to seduce him – and like Katy, turns brunette. It was Katy herself who came up with the concept of using the dolls, to make sure it was seen as a tongue-in-cheek track.

With its opening line of 'I hope you hang yourself with your H&M scarf' and its perky chorus of 'You're so gay and you don't even like boys', the video started picking up a decent number of views on YouTube. Magazines and blogs started picking up on it – and then Madonna said she liked it.

Even as 'UR So Gay' was attracting attention and then controversy, Katy was still putting the finishing touches to the album. '"I Kissed a Girl" almost didn't make it on,' she revealed later. 'There was some concern at the top, but I just let them sit with the song and they came around.'

Capitol Records decided to put Katy's personality and individual fashion style at the forefront of the campaign for the new album. They had found the angle that worked for her – she was kooky, she was full of personality, but she was also very feminine with a very individual style. And they now liked 'I Kissed a Girl' so much, it would be the first single from *One of the Boys*.

Chapter 23

Live Earth to My Booky Wook

After hosting the Brit Awards in February and Comic Relief the following month, it was no surprise that Russell was asked to be one of the hosts of the Live Earth benefit concert at Wembley Stadium – one of a string of concerts held all over the globe on 7 July 2007 to raise awareness for the growing climate change crisis. One hundred and fifty acts were to play in 11 locations around the world – in the US, Japan, the UK, South Africa, Italy, Brazil, China and Australia – to a global audience on TV, radio and online.

As well as introducing acts including the Foo Fighters, the Beastie Boys and Madonna on stage, Russell hosted a special version of his Radio 2 show that Saturday night, featuring live coverage and highlights of the concerts.

But unlike Live Aid (the mother of all multinational benefit concerts in 1985) and Live 8 (held just a couple of years earlier) – both organised by Russell's arch-critic Bob Geldof – Live Earth was a ratings disaster on the BBC. It was also widely criticised, not least for the carbon emissions it created in flying numerous music stars around the world to perform at the events. Further, Russell's lighthearted banter with Ricky Gervais during an interview with Sky News hardly suggested that he took the subject of climate change that seriously. His comments about 'everybody doing a little bit to help' were somewhat undermined by his jovial attempts to grab the interviewer's testicles.

Still, Russell could pretty much do no wrong. The same month he was taking his new stand-up show *Only Joking* on a sell-out national tour across the UK. Not surprisingly, climate change did not feature on his list of favourite topics for discussion. Sex, however, did. One of his best stories in the new live show was his description of filming a sex scene for his new movie – his first venture into Hollywood.

Forgetting Sarah Marshall was the latest film by Judd Apatow – Hollywood's hottest comedy producer/director and the man behind smashes such as *Knocked Up* and *The 40 Year Old Virgin*. It was the story of a guy called Peter Bretter, played by Jason Segel – one of several regular performers in Apatow movies and TV shows, and also the writer of the script. Peter goes to Hawaii on holiday to try to forget his ex-girlfriend, a movie starlet called Sarah Marshall (played by Kristen Bell) who has recently dumped him. But when he arrives at the resort, he finds Sarah is there too with her new boyfriend – a dissolute, snake-hipped, sex-mad English rock 'n' roller named Aldous Snow. No prizes for guessing who Apatow and director Nicholas Stoller cast to play Aldous.

Russell was in Hawaii in May and June for the movie shoot, which included a couple of memorable sex scenes with Kristen Bell. It was both funny and enlightening as Russell explained the process of shooting these scenes to audiences on his *Only Joking* tour a few months later. He described how in one particularly acrobatic scene, although he seemed to be naked, this was not the case. Instead his manhood had actually been trussed up in a little bag – a bit like the sack that they put over Saddam Hussein's head when he was hanged.

But this was nothing compared to the indignities suffered by his co-star, also apparently naked. During the scene Kristen had to wear plastic knickers that resembled flat liquorice, and a silicone jelly bra. According to Russell, she looked like 'a Bertie Bassett prostitute'.

Russell had certainly made an impression on the shoot of *Forgetting Sarah Marshall* – even among Americans who didn't know him from Adam (and most of them didn't). The correspondent from the influential movie website Ain't It Cool News who visited the set suggested to his readers that Russell was 'infamous for his outrageous behavior in the UK as much as he's famous for any actual comedy he's done'. He also noted that both he and co-star Kristen were winners of Sexiest Vegetarian Awards – Russell was PETA's Sexiest Vegetarian in Europe in 2006 and 2007, while Kristen was World's Sexiest Vegetarian in 2006.

The writer also noted that, like Kristen, Russell was clearly an experienced yoga practitioner. 'Take after take, they are flawless in their technique – and they're being asked to do some fairly elaborate handstands and downward-facing dogs and four-limbed staffs [a challenging push-up] and standing forward bends.' Which gives you some idea of how one of their sex scenes turned out.

But it was Russell's charisma, disarming charm and extraordinary lack of inhibition that really caught the visiting American media unawares. He was outspoken, he was flamboyant and he was lusty – the very opposite of the American stereotype of the repressed, buttoned-up Englishman. He raised eyebrows with his behaviour in interviews, where, libido in full cry, he made no bones about the fact that he was very interested in having sex with his female interviewer. In one classic example, being interviewed by the large-bosomed TV presenter Carrie Keagan for adult entertainment movie show *No Good TV*, he seduced her on camera with a breathless (and breathtaking) stream of patter that demonstrated why Russell's bedroom is probably fitted with a revolving door.

'Young lady, you're the reason I went through puberty,' he began. 'The comedy is very much a front for my sexual antics. I only do that to facilitate opportunities like this. Opportunities I'm not going to let slip through my fingers – although you will slip through my fingers, over the course of the next few hours, when I make bells ring in your stomach, make your eyes dance like fire, make you forget your name – which I'll never forget: Carrie, Carrie, Carrie – a word that rhymes with "marry". But why should we have conjugal rights when we could have marital nights, coital fireworks dancing between our thighs? Let me be shipwrecked with you...' And on he went.

Carrie Keagan was astonished and delighted. But

Russell's first proper impact in America would come when *Forgetting Sarah Marshall* was released there early in 2008. But before that, he had to do his stand-up tour of the UK, followed by a new show for Channel 4, *Russell Brand in Ponderland.*

Ponderland consisted of Russell delivering a series of monologues, stand-up style, in front of a studio audience. Each of the six shows tackled a different subject – childhood, science, crime, sport, love and holidays – with his brilliantly off-the-wall observations and irreverent humour interspersed with vintage television clips. As a no-holds-barred version of TV shows like *Tarrant On TV*, it was an excellent and often hilarious vehicle for Russell's mocking eye and surreal imagination.

In the first show, Russell drew on personal experience to discuss the complexities of childhood – like the fact that two of his biggest preoccupations (or fears) were rabies and quicksand. He also revealed that he was obsessed with the colour of his dad's willy – why was his own pink like a prawn while his dad's was a much darker brown, like an animal that had emerged from a wood? He actually phoned his dad Ron during the show to ask him about it.

Russell also revealed that the jingle from the Coco Pops advert – the one that goes: 'I'd rather have a bowl of Coco Pops' – had rung around his head all during his childhood. And it was still there. In fact it was the thing that always came into his head when he wasn't thinking about anything else. 'That is the screensaver for my mind,' said Russell.

In the second show, about science, Russell pointed out

that just eight years earlier we had all been living without mobile phones. If the person you arranged to meet outside WH Smith didn't turn up, you couldn't ring them – you just had to go home. 'My whole life was like the end credits of *The Hulk*.' He also reminisced about the early days of home computing in the 1980s, using the ZX Spectrum and the bizarre techniques used to play early video games such as *Daley Thompson's Decathlon*.

In the third show, on the subject of crime, he offered his insights into the thought-patterns of famous East End hardmen, wondering how mad Mad Frankie Fraser must have been, seeing as he was hanging out with people like the Kray brothers who were dishing out lots of GBH and murder themselves. And he marvelled at the sense of entitlement shown by Fraser (as demonstrated in the TV clips) who thought that because Woolworths kept their lights on and you could see the company safe from a street, that meant he had the right to take the money out of it. 'Like he thought his name was actually Mad Frankie Woolworths.'

Ponderland was screened on Channel 4 over successive nights in October. Russell's long-time comedy compadre Matt Morgan was creative director of the show, which meant he contributed to the writing of the material. Russell and Matt had also been working together on another big television project, this time for the BBC.

Russell Brand on the Road was a homage to Jack Kerouac's classic novel *On the Road* – one of Russell's favourite books – and involved Russell and Matt travelling across the US, visiting the locations in the book 50 years after it was written. As a teenager, Russell had been greatly inspired by *On the Road* – from Kerouac's spontaneous writing style to the Beat Generation lifestyle – and it's not hard to see parallels in his own stream-of-consciousness style and freewheeling attitude.

Russell and Matt began their journey in late summer at the writer's home town and final resting place in Lowell, Massachusetts, before travelling to New York and then setting off by car on their journey across the country towards San Francisco. On the way, they visited many of Kerouac's old haunts, met up with the real characters from the book and discovered friends from Kerouac's past.

The two-part documentary (broadcast in December) showed the other side of Russell. It was certainly not a mainstream show – it originally went out on the arts channel BBC4. Rather it was an outlet for his intelligence instead of his flamboyance and womanising.

It also helped to give the impression that Russell could be in two places at once, because throughout the whole of 2007, Russell was still doing his Radio 2 show (with Matt) every Saturday night and lots of other things. While shooting *Russell Brand on The Road* he broadcast the radio show from the US – and kept up with the football back home so he could write his Saturday column in *The Guardian*. But on top of all that, he had another project that was demanding his attention.

Russell's first book, *Irons in the Fire* – a collection of his articles in *The Guardian*, in which he chronicled the concerns of a moderately famous West Ham United supporter – had been published in early 2007. Before the end of the year, he would complete and publish another book – one that would have much greater impact.

Russell's autobiography *My Booky Wook* was published in hardback on 15 November 2007. It was a candid, warts-and-all memoir of everything so far: from his childhood in Grays to his first taste of fame at the Italia Conti stage school, to his turbulent years in the grip of drug addiction and alcoholism, to his redemption and subsequent rise to fame.

It was told in the classic Russell Brand style of florid, highly descriptive language – there was no question that anybody but Russell had actually written it – and it was a vivid, entertaining and hilarious read. The critics lapped it up. One reviewer wrote: 'The Russell Brand of *My Booky Wook* is surprisingly approachable. The comedian's playful love of language is evident from his occasional lapse into obscure or archaic words, and sits well with his penchant for childishness ... Inevitably, the main point of interest is Brand's addictions, drugs and sex, about which he writes with unexpected affability.' As Christmas approached, so did the public, buying copies by the truckload.

By the end of 2007, Russell could add 'successful author' to an expanding CV that already included being a successful comedian and TV personality and having a successful film (*St Trinians*) on general release. And now Hollywood beckoned.

CHAPTER 24

She Kissed a Girl

'LILY ALLEN DOESN'T WANT TO BE AN AMERICAN POP STAR.
I DO. THERE WAS A VOID FOR A GIRL WHO HAD SOME SASS.
I KNEW THAT GIRL WAS ME.' – KATY PERRY

By early 2008, Katy Perry was on the US music radar –
and 'UR So Gay' had put her there. This download release,
with a much-talked about video, had been picked up
nationwide on radio. People were blogging about it and
Madonna had mentioned it.

The song was also coming under increasing flak from gay
rights groups, who were quick to condemn it for being
homophobic – anti-gay. One said: 'It's official, it's cool to
make fun of gay people again,' while veteran UK gay rights
campaigner Peter Tatchell said that Perry's lyrics 'can be read
as implicitly demeaning gay people. I am sure Katy would get
a critical reception if she expressed comparable sentiments in
a song called "UR so black, Jewish or disabled".'

Katy would counter, in lots of interviews over the next few months, that she wasn't homophobic and that the song was based on a personal experience. 'The fact is that we live in a very metrosexual world. A girl might walk into a bar, meet a boy and discover he's more manicured than she is. And they can't figure it out. Is he wearing foundation *and* a bit of bronzer? But he's buying me drinks at the same time!

'I'm not saying you're so gay, you're so lame. I'm saying you're so gay, but I don't understand it because you don't like boys! I totally understand how it could be misconstrued or whatever. It wasn't stereotyping anyone in particular: I was talking about ex-boyfriends.' Which is all slightly ironic, considering that she would eventually get engaged to a man not unfamiliar using eyeliner.

But Katy was pretty much ready for whatever would be thrown at her. *One of the Boys* had the energy of someone who had been waiting on the starting blocks for a while, but also had the experience and self-confidence to deliver. She was on the verge of a stunning success that would make her a household name – and far more controversy. But she was prepared: the years working with Glen Ballard – a record producer with the highest credentials – had served her well, even though their efforts had apparently come to nothing.

'[Glen] did develop me for a few years and through all kinds of events,' she said. 'Making this record has been like a three-year process, so I've had the opportunity to be a developed artist, rather than just being picked up, thrown with a manager and putting a record out. I'm very happy that that's been the case.'

Katy's record label decided to take a very traditional approach to the promotion of her album: at the start of 2008 they sent her out on a two-month tour of radio stations around the United States. They had figured, correctly, that her bubbly outgoing personality and strong-willed determination to succeed would help her connect with radio programmers across the country. They were right – so when 'I Kissed a Girl' was released it was quickly picked up by radio. What followed was a phenomenon.

Against a stomping glam-disco beat and highly catchy chorus, the lyrics say it all. Soon there was also an expensive-looking music video to accompany the song, which had Katy lounging in a boudoir, wearing vintage lingerie – soon to become one of her trademark looks – surrounded by attractive models in gorgeous underwear, who are all very interested in each other's soft skin and red lips.

The provocative 'I Kissed a Girl' caused a sensation. The song began to be heard on the radio, and the video premiered on MTV and other TV channels. Then it started climbing the charts, attracting more airplay. Soon it was picked up by the mainstream press, and by groups from both the right and left of the political spectrum in America. On the right, they were outraged that this young singer was promoting lesbianism. On the left they were peeved that Katy was using 'les-ploitation' to sell records. 'We had two groups that never agreed on anything both mad at us,' her manager Bradford Cobb has said.

It just meant more press and publicity for Katy. And every journalist she spoke to wanted to know: had she kissed a girl? Had she liked it? Was she gay?

'It's about not being gay,' she cheerfully responded on numerous occasions. 'It's just a song about curiosity.

'It's just an innocent kiss! You know, girls are at a slumber party and they are hanging out with other girls. We're all deathly afraid of that first kiss by that boy who we know is just gonna slobber all over our face.' But, she added, the song was also about the 'undeniable beauty' of women. 'Some women are just so beautiful, that female or male, you would probably kiss them.'

In some interviews she wouldn't go as far as confirming that she was straight, describing herself as 'metrosexual'. Certainly her provocative ways and eye-catching, vintage-influenced style were gaining her not only young female fans. There was also a growing gay fanbase – some extremely influential, like gossip-blog king Perez Hilton, who announced that he was a big Katy Perry fan.

But over and above the growing furore, there was no denying that 'I Kissed a Girl' was also a cracking pop song – one that would became the hit of the summer of 2008. In America it spent an incredible seven weeks on top of the Billboard Hot 100, selling 3.1 million downloads. It was just as big in the UK. At its peak at No 1, it was selling twice as many copies as the No 2 song on downloads alone. Eventually it became the fourth best-selling single of the year, with sales just short of half a million.

Katy had well and truly broken through. All that determination, self-belief and hard work had finally paid off. All of a sudden, she was a star. But what did her mum and dad think about this? The parents who had raised her in a strictly Christian household – with no pop music and no MTV?

The world quickly became aware of Katy's background, that her parents Keith and Mary Hudson were evangelical pastors who spent their lives travelling the United States spreading the word of God. Then the *Daily Mail* in Britain published that Katy's mother had described her music as 'shameful and disgusting'. It was suggested that they prayed for their daughter every time they heard 'I Kissed a Girl' on the radio, and they certainly didn't approve of the video either.

But Katy rejected the suggestion of her parents' disapproval out of hand, repeatedly denying that her parents were less than supportive of her. They certainly had strict Christian views, but they hadn't disowned her for holding different ones and doing her own thing. Quite the opposite: they were still close.

'My parents are definitely supportive and happy for my success,' she said. 'I think if they had it their way, then maybe I wouldn't be singing a song with this subject matter. But I'm an adult, I make my own decisions now.' Anyway, she said, her mum and dad weren't really *that* shocked: 'It was more like, Katy's always had something to say, now she's saying ... this.'

In fact her parents were to be spotted at Katy's live performances that summer on the Warped tour, where she was the only girl in a packed line-up of emo, punk and rock-rap bands criss-crossing the US – and the only one with a No 1 hit record. She had signed up for the tour early in the year, before 'I Kissed A Girl' had gone into orbit. She could probably have made her excuses and pulled out as her career went stellar, but Katy decided to fulfill this commitment and build her fanbase. In any case, she could rock with the best of them.

But her presence on the Warped tour could also be explained by the fact that Gym Class Heroes were on it too, and that she and lead singer Travis McCoy were now, at last, a proper item. She was letting it be known that her 'thug' had finally been tamed. 'He's thug-nificent,' she said. 'I can't believe I got a thug to commit!' Wearing a promise ring that McCoy had given her, she added, 'He's a big ladies' man, so I guess he wanted to put his stamp on me. It's like, "Fine – please just don't brand me with your iron, OK?"'

But it was also clear that her status had now changed: he could no longer treat her as a casual girlfriend. It was time for a proper romance. 'I said, "Excuse me, I've been coming to a number of your shows in the greater Los Angeles area for quite some time now. I've been your Penny Lane long enough, and now I want to be your Grace Kelly."'

For all the 'curiosity' of 'I Kissed a Girl', it was clear that Katy wanted a boyfriend who had something about him but would treat her right. Finally she had that with Travis – at least for now.

At the end of the busiest and most exciting summer of her life, Katy's next single 'Hot N Cold' was released – and would prove to be as successful (if not as controversial) as 'I Kissed a Girl'. She was also about to be welcomed into the heart of MTV: she was nominated for several awards, including Best Female Artist, at the MTV Video Music Awards in Los Angeles. There she would meet, quite briefly, an English comedian who, like her, was just starting to get a profile in the US and who, like her, was no stranger to controversy. He was also having a big night: he was hosting the whole show.

His name was Russell Brand – and she was impressed.

CHAPTER 25

Countdown to Romance

'SACHSGATE' WAS THE SECOND TIME IN A FEW WEEKS THAT RUSSELL HAD HAD TO ENDURE LOTS OF FLAK. IT FOLLOWED HIS HOSTING OF THE 2008 MTV VIDEO MUSIC AWARDS IN LOS ANGELES, WHEN HE HAD CALLED PRESIDENT BUSH A 'RETARD' AND MOCKED THE JONAS BROTHERS' PURITY RINGS. AFTER THAT SHOW THERE WEREN'T JUST COMPLAINTS. SOME CRITICISM CAME IN THE FORM OF DEATH THREATS.

But not everyone was offended. A few days after the VMAs, Katy Perry was in London and she made a point of mentioning him when she was being interviewed by Scott Mills on Radio 1. 'I met Russell Brand who I'm in love with,' she said. 'I love him, he's so great. He's got the worst sense of humour in the best sense of the way.' She also made the point that despite the controversy, Russell had actually been a great success hosting the awards – and most people thought like she did.

Russell would no doubt have been pleased – and no

doubt directed his charm, albeit briefly, on the lovely Ms Perry when they met. In fact, there are rumours that he suggested to her on the night of the VMAs that she play a cameo in his new movie *Get Him to the Greek*.

By this point, Katy was promoting 'Hot N Cold', her next single from *One of the Boys*. It would prove to be as big a hit as 'I Kissed a Girl'. In the video for it Katy plays a bride at the altar waiting for her man to say 'I do.' But when he starts showing signs of saying 'I don't,' the church congregation starts rocking and she gives him a piece of her mind, singing about his flip-flop failings as she chases him around town, and then takes on different characters to torment him.

'Hot N Cold' reached No 3 in the American charts and No 1 in the UK, and like 'I Kissed a Girl' it was certified triple-platinum in February 2009 after selling over three million downloads in the US. It has now sold more than four million downloads in the US alone.

By the end of 2008, *One of the Boys* had sold nearly a million copies in America, and two more singles would boost its sales further: the emotional 'Thinking of You' (with a tear-jerking World War II-set video of Katy trying to forget her tragic soldier sweetheart) and the far bouncier 'Waking Up in Vegas'. The album had not been universally well received by the critics when it was released, but it was certainly packed with hit songs.

After completing the lengthy Warped tour, Katy then toured Europe in the latter part of the year, confirming that she was becoming as big a name there as in the US. That was emphasised when she was offered an extraordinary opportunity for a newly popular artist: she was asked to co-host the MTV European Music Awards in November.

She made a very big impression too. Katy opened the show – held at the Echo Arena in Liverpool in November – by singing 'I Kissed a Girl' while dressed as an American footballer and astride a giant lipstick. She then went on to make 10 costume changes – beating Christina Aguilera's previous record of nine. Her outfits included a frock with a print of Barack Obama, a fairground carousel and one that was half gents black tie (complete with moustache) half ladies evening wear.

Katy's performance followed a fruity theme, which gave her ample scope for suggestiveness – as when she rode a giant banana. While wearing a short pink dress and standing on two cherries she told the crowd: 'I've got to be careful getting off these suckers – I might pop one.' In fact, her quips were so full of innuendo the *Sun* said she would 'give Russell Brand a run for his money.' She also happened to win her first big music award at the EMAs: for Best New Act.

In early 2009 Katy began the *Hello Katy* tour – her first headline tour – across America and then into Europe. By that time her easygoing wisecracking had earned the wrath of the thin-skinned Lily Allen. Asked in an interview to describer herself, Katy had said: 'I'm like a fatter version of Amy Winehouse and a skinnier version of Lily Allen.' Lily was not amused and let rip in a radio interview, saying Katy had been signed by her record label as an American version of her, because the label wanted 'to find something controversial and "kooky"' like her.

'You're not English and you don't write your own songs – shut up!' she added.

Katy said later she was sorry for the 'skinnier than Lily' comment. 'I was just kind of joking and trying to be funny. I didn't mean anything by it. Comedians are not necessarily to be taken super seriously.' Whether or not she considered herself to be a comedian, she was again straying into Russell Brand territory.

Rather more significant for Katy as she headed out on the road in January was that she was single again. She and Travis McCoy of Gym Class Heroes had split up in December. They had made a serious go of it during the course of the Warped tour but her 'thug', who had given her a promise ring in the summer, was no longer in the picture. But it wasn't quite over yet....

* * *

Meanwhile, as 2008 drew to a close, Russell was having to shrug off an avalanche of controversy and criticism from various quarters. But he was well equipped to do so. Having been through the twin addictions of heroin dependency and alcoholism, he had the mechanisms to deal with pressure – meditation, yoga, stroking and talking to his cat Morrissey – and of course, sex.

There were other consolations too. At the 2008 British Comedy Awards in December – a show that was due to be hosted by Jonathan Ross until he pulled out in the wake of Sachsgate – Russell won Best Live Stand-Up Performer. He had also won Best Biography of the Year at the British

Book Awards for his No 1, no-holds-barred memoir, *My Booky Wook*.

On top of all that, a second series of *Ponderland* was screened on Channel 4, where Russell, in his inimitable fashion, tackled more six more subjects with the help of TV clips. This time the topics for discussion were pets, family, education, food, class and Christmas.

In the first show Russell recounted his experience of having a gerbil called Barney, who turned out to be less of a bloke than he'd thought, immediately producing numerous offspring. They themselves started producing more gerbils and then eating each other's babies, but he found he couldn't stay angry with those 'murderous, incestuous, infanticidal, cannibalistic little slags'.

In the second and arguably funniest show, on education, Russell opened proceedings by confirming what many had already suspected: that he didn't agree with the 'coercive indoctrination of a brilliant young mind' that had occurred during his own school days. But he fondly remembered the times when the teacher was sick and due to an administrative quirk no supply teacher was found – and all the kids would go 'all *Lord of the Flies* and a bit Rambo.'

He also read out a letter from his old school in Grays which, after a spell of truancy, described him as 'an immature boy who craves attention... His desire to be different manifests itself in him wearing his hair in a ponytail, childish behaviour and being insolent towards staff.' Russell described it as the genesis of his career right there: stupid haircut, attention-seeking and childish behaviour.

Just after the second – and final – series of *Ponderland* had finished its run in December, *Bedtime Stories* – the Disney-produced movie starring Adam Sandler in which Russell was appearing – was released in the US and the UK. Russell played hotel waiter Mickey, loyal pal to Sandler's character Skeeter Bronson, at the Hilton-type hotel where they both worked.

Apart from showing an irrational fear of a large-eyed guinea pig, Russell's most notable contribution to the movie probably comes near the end where he is the only person able to interpret Sandler, who has to talk about his plan for a new hotel complex with a burnt tongue. It did not have the same impact as his performance in *Forgetting Sarah Marshall*, but this was a very different kind of movie, being aimed squarely at the family market. If nothing else, it gave Russell his most mainstream exposure in America so far.

He was also about to make an interesting diversion into a very different sort of movie. Russell was cast as Trinculo the jester in a new version of Shakespeare's *The Tempest* starring Helen Mirren, who was to play the leading role of Prospera the sorceress (usually a male character, Prospero). Also signed up were Ben Whishaw, Alfred Molina and Felicity Jones.

Russell filmed his scenes at the beginning of 2009 – the movie was scheduled to be released during 2010 – and more movie projects were in development: a live action/animation family movie *I Hop*, with Russell voicing the Easter Bunny; and another animated film, *Despicable Me*, in which he voices Dr Nefario. A movie version of *My Booky Wook* was also being discussed until

Russell decided to put that one on the back burner. He was happier with the idea of remaking the 1981 Oscar-winning comedy *Arthur*, with himself in Dudley Moore's lead role. And there was *Get Him to the Greek*, which would resume shooting in the summer.

All this clearly rankled with some people – particularly ex-newpaper editor, *Britain's Got Talent* judge and vocal Russell-hater Piers Morgan. Speaking to *OK!* magazine later in the year, Morgan described Russell as 'disgusting'. 'That whole Russell Brand thing, I don't get it,' he declared. 'The idea that he is some huge international acting star is ridiculous! He's just a long-haired ex-junkie and shagging addict. I just don't get it. Why does everyone find someone that disgusting so attractive? It's just extraordinary.' Suffice to say, Piers just didn't get it.

But the fact was that Russell was now becoming well known across the pond. His autobiography *My Booky Wook* was published in the US – and hit the bestseller lists there too. As it begins with him in a sex addiction clinic, he was inevitably asked while promoting the book: are you a sex addict?

'I don't think I have a sex addiction. I just think I *like* it,' he replied. 'It's just a hobby. I'm an enthusiast. And, yes, I've got a sexy reputation. Sometimes I'll see my reputation walk down a promenade, and I'll think, "Oooh, you dirty bugger."'

Which wasn't to say that Russell didn't believe that sex addiction existed. 'Taking heroin wouldn't matter if you could just get on with your life. Chocolate only matters if you gorge on it so radically and in such a loopy fashion that you crash your car. At the same time, sex isn't a problem unless it starts to get in the way of your work – if you have to sneak off away from your desk and have a bit of monkey business.'

Clearly Russell didn't think he was at that point – even though his working routine meant he could sneak off and have sex any time he liked. And he often did.

But these were exciting times for other important reasons – in fact, the most important reason of all – his stand-up comedy. There would be a new stand-up show in the UK called *Scandalous* and Russell would do more shows in the US, the nation of his ultimate stand-up heroes like Lenny Bruce and Richard Pryor.

One of his first American shows, at the Hammerstein Ballroom in New York City in March, was regarded as a rousing triumph. Russell himself was certainly pleased – if nothing else because a well-known Englishman (although not to Americans) was in attendance: Stephen Fry.

Russell wrote afterwards that the presence of Fry 'pushed my vocabulary into overdrive. Barely a sentence passed without a needless polysyllabic word crowbarred in solely to impress everyone's favourite avuncular genius.' And Fry 'said he loved the show and praised me heartily. For me this is like a kick-about with [famous West Ham striker and ladies man] Frank McAvennie or fellatio from [large-breasted porn actress] Gianna Michaels – the apotheosis of approval.'

While in New York, Russell would also be photographed for *Vanity Fair* magazine as Charlie Chaplin, another English comedian who had made it big in America. Russell followed the New York show with a successful Australian tour, and then the first dates of his new British tour, *Scandalous*.

This new show would see Russell covering all his most recent crimes and misdemeanours – hosting the MTV awards, his progress in Hollywood and Sachsgate. It would also see him playing his largest venues yet – including the 18,000 capacity O2 in London. Among other things, he described the experience of his Bush 'retard' remark at the VMAs being greeted by 'blank billionaire faces – some of whom had guns' and realising his script was in fact a litany of insults against Americans and 'too dangerous'. But he told a few of them in Britain – including one naughty one about Michael Jackson.

Russell was also at the G20 protests in April, exercising his radical side – the one that had seen him make a complete tit of himself back at the May Day march in 2000. By now, however, Russell's behaviour was impeccable – statesmanlike even. 'I'm here to observe and participate peacefully in the protest,' he said. 'I always come to these kind of things. I'm very interested in learning and interested in why these people have come to this. I wonder what alternatives there are and I think it makes people cogniscent of them. I think it's also very beautiful.'

What's more, Russell was back on radio again – albeit briefly – with Oasis's Noel Gallagher. After Russell's resignation from the BBC, commercial radio's sports station Talksport cannily offered Russell and Noel a joint slot to discuss one of their favourite subjects: football. Russell had also retired from writing his column for the

Guardian's sports pages, so this filled a gap in his football output. It turned out to be a shortlived stint: soon other commitments would take Russell back to the US – in particular, to continue shooting scenes for the movie *Get Him to the Greek*.

By now Russell was taking a small army of support staff – led by his manager, Nik Linnen – with him as he criss-crossed the continents. But Russell was no longer working with Matt Morgan, his co-writer and comrade-in-arms since his early days at MTV. Matt had actually stopped working on Russell's Radio 2 show the previous September – mysteriously described as 'M.I.A.' [Missing In Action] on the show's blog – and therefore managed to avoid any involvement in the Sachsgate saga. Matt was not replaced as Russell's on-mike or on-camera foil – it wasn't necessary. Russell's creative team now comprised of his producers – and effectively his British mates in America – Jack Bayles and Gareth Roy.

In June, back in LA, filming *Get Him to the Greek* really got going. This time he wasn't just a supporting member of the cast, he was one of the main attractions – along with Jonah Hill, with whom he had shared some excellent scenes in *Forgetting Sarah Marshall*. In that film Hill had played an adoring maitre d' at the Hawaiian hotel where Aldous Snow, Russell's character, was staying. This time Hill was playing Aaron Green, an idealistic intern at a record company, who gets tasked with bringing Snow from London to LA for a very important show at the city's legendary Greek Theatre.

Also in the movie, playing the record company boss, was P Diddy, aka Puff Daddy, aka Sean Combs. He and

Russell would become friends during the shoot, and the part would afford Russell more contact with other A-list pop, rock and hip-hop stars, including Christina Aguilera, Lars Ulrich of Metallica and Pharrell. And as the script required that Aldous indulges in serious mouth-to-mouth action with two top girls in the pop world, Russell got to snog Pink. Then came the moment when he had to kiss Katy Perry.

Katy has since described her reaction to this encounter with Russell – a man she had only met briefly at the MTV Video Music Awards the previous September, but whose work she clearly admired. 'My scene called for me to make out with him. And on the way down the stairs after the scene, I was hopping like a bunny. I hop like a bunny when I'm happy – I get a bit childlike.'

Quite possibly her screen smooch with Russell was particularly exciting because it looked like Katy's on-off romance with Travis McCoy was now beyond the point of recovery. Having broken up at the end of 2008, the pair had patched things up in April after the *Hello Katy* tour had ended, but they had drifted apart once more. Katy, it seemed, was on the lookout for a new lover.

* * *

At the same time Russell was dabbling with monogamy again – and failing miserably. The previous summer, while shooting *Bedtime Stories*, he had begun dating the Australian actress Teresa Palmer. He was soon talking enthusiastically about changing his womanising ways and settling down with her – until it ended after a couple of months and he returned to womanising.

Then, while shooting *Get Him to the Greek*, Russell met Christy Peterson, a 22-year-old model who was an extra in the film. Christy would later claim that Russell was a one-girl man with her for a whole three months during the summer of 2009 – before he spectacularly fell off the wagon in a three-way romp with a groupie and a pole-dancer, while Christy was shopping with Russell's mum Barbara.

According to the model (who was being paid by a leading British tabloid for the information), Russell's commitment to honesty – an important element of his recovery from his various addictions – meant that he had to let her know what he was intending to do before he did it, and gave her a blow-by-blow account of his activities when she returned.

'He wanted me with him 24 hours a day and when I said I had to work he'd become distraught. I really believe Russell thought I was the woman who was going to save him from his demons. But although he didn't want to hurt me, he can't control it. He's replaced his heroin addiction with an addiction for strippers and prostitutes.

'It was three months into the relationship when he explained it. I was in bed when he opened his laptop, put on a porn film and started pleasuring himself like I wasn't even in the room. Then he said, "I thought being with you had cured it, but I'm having urges to have sex with other women again."'

Apparently Russell confessed he had never gone longer than three months of fidelity – and admitted he had started sleeping with 'a handful' of other girls.

'As ever, it was all about him,' continued Christy. 'This is a man who Googled himself every night before going to sleep. Russell's such a great person in so many ways, but until he beats his sex addiction he's going to break the heart of every woman he falls in love with.'

CHAPTER 26

A Night in New York

As Russell has said, after his first year hosting the MTV Video Music Awards he had become notorious in America. People had threatened to kill him, but the death threats had finally petered out. So, in September 2009, Russell Brand returned to host the VMAs – the biggest MTV jamboree of the year and one of the most star-studded music events anywhere in the world – for the second year running.

That was quite an achievement – although he was now a much more high-profile figure in America than he had been 12 months earlier. The 2008 VMAs, the movie roles, his numerous appearances on TV chat shows and the American publication of his autobiography *My Booky Wook* – which had made it into the bestseller lists in the US – had made sure of that.

Russell also now had very high profile, high-rolling friends. A month before the VMAs, Russell would join hip-hop star and tycoon P Diddy on his Lear jet to fly to

Vegas for the weekend. The pair had bonded while filming *Get Him to the Greek*, in which Diddy plays the record company boss desperate to get Russell's character, the debauched rocker Aldous Snow, to play an anniversary concert that will save the music business. Diddy posted a video of the pair on the plane, discussing plans for what appears to be a celebrity version of the movie *The Hangover* – with Diddy repeating the famous line: 'What happens in Vegas, stays in Vegas.' But as Russell has to point out to his new friend 'Puffy' (as he calls him in the clip) he doesn't actually do hangovers any more – he's a recovering alcoholic.

But there was no question about it. Russell had managed to do what very few British comedians have done – and only Ricky Gervais of the current generation of British comics has come as close to achieving – he'd made it big in America.

'This year will be a controversy-free festival of love and discrete orgasms,' Russell declared in the lead-up to the 2009 Video Music Awards. MTV clearly thought otherwise – well, the controversy bit anyway. The publicity generated by Russell's performance in 2008 had been pure gold for the network, and in the lead-up to the new show MTV ran polls that asked viewers 'who should Russell take on?' at this year's awards. 'We are thrilled that despite numerous death threats from Jonas Brothers fans, Russell Brand has accepted our offer to put his life on the line and host the VMAs again this year,' quipped MTV general manager Stephen Friedman.

For his part Russell was reported to be directing his scorn towards the new vampire-teen phenomenon of numerous TV shows and movies – notably the *Twilight* series starring fellow Englishman and heartthrob Robert Pattinson. And in the lead-up to the show, he was up to his old tricks again, like propositioning middle-aged African-American talk show host Sherri Shepherd – well known for being celibate – on TV. (When Sherri's co-host Whoopi Goldberg asked Russell whether he's had many 'sisters', he replied, 'Yeah, loads.')

The first big trailer for the 2009 VMAs harked back to the previous year's promos featuring Russell and Britney Spears, in which Britney cheerfully fended off this lustful mystery English fop. In the new trailer they were in different places, thinking about how they were going to deal with each other at this year's awards after last year's encounters. Russell was worried that he had been too forward and had offended Britney; Britney (wearing a bikini by an LA swimming pool) was thinking she'd offended Russell by not being nice enough to him... until the picture switches to Russell while Britney is thinking and he realises he can hear her thoughts. So he sends out a telepathic message telling her to sleep with him.

Elsewhere, in a self-produced video on YouTube, Russell announced that he favoured Britney's 'Womaniser' for the Video of the Year at this year's awards – and he hoped she had written the song about him.

The new Russell/Britney promo stressing their sexual chemistry was funny, but with the 2009 VMAs being held in New York, the main theme of the build-up to the show was a tribute to the classic 1950s musical *West Side Story*, which is set in the city. In another expensive-looking trailer-cum-video a number of current stars – including

Ne-Yo, Cobra Starship and Taylor Swift – recreated the song 'Tonight' from the musical with VMA-related lyrics.

And following each other – but not together on screen – were Katy Perry and Russell Brand. Katy was on a New York apartment block rooftop at night, tending to her roof garden and looking very sexy in her perfectly 1950s outfit. Then on came Russell, Artful Dodger-like in top hat, singing a saucy introduction which made reference to Katy Perry.

Katy arrived at her second Video Music Awards after another amazing year. She was now established as one of America's biggest pop stars. She was also footloose, romance-wise. Things had not worked out with Travis McCoy and there was no significant other in her life – although a newspaper reported that she had been seen 'locking lips' with the American singer John Mayer – another renowned ladies' man who has squired both Jennifer Aniston and Jessica Simpson – a few days before the awards.

Katy was also a big Russell Brand fan. Having said so publicly after the previous year's awards – at a time when he was getting considerable flak elsewhere – she had had her first encounter with him a month or so before this year's awards on the set of *Get Him to the Greek*. In his Aldous Snow character Russell had had the arduous task of kissing Katy Perry – and Russell and Katy's on-camera snogging had evidently made a big impression on both of them.

Katy came away from the experience skipping like a happy child. And according to sources close to Russell, from that point on he just was waiting for a chance to turn on the full force of his charm on Katy. The 2009 MTV Video Music Awards was going to be his chance.

He had clearly not failed to notice Katy's superbly curvy figure. Katy herself said she had come to appreciate the power this gave her over men. 'I didn't know how to use my curves growing up – I was a little boxier. But now I understand that I'm so attractive because I have that curvy thing. I'm not like Jennifer Lopez and Kim Kardashian, but it's there. That hourglass is in there somewhere.'

It certainly was – including a bra size of 32DD. In fact, not long before the VMAs, she revealed that as a God-fearing child in Santa Barbara, she had prayed for big breasts. 'I remember really vividly kneeling by my bed as a nine-year-old, saying my prayers and asking God to give me boobs that were so big that if I laid on my back I wouldn't be able to see my feet. Eventually that request was granted.

'A bit of divine intervention displays the power of prayer,' she added, mischievously. 'Every time before I go on stage, or go out where I know there will be a lot of press, I take a skipping rope and spend about ten minutes, fully clothed, skipping. I look like Rocky. This way I can ensure that everything is firmly in place and I won't have a wardrobe malfunction. Don't want those boulders doing a show of their own!'

Katy had possibly been on the skipping rope for about an hour in the sensational number she wore to the VMAs on 13 September. She arrived at the venue – the Radio City Music Hall – in a stunning silver mini-dress that clung to her well exercised figure and sported a distinctively cartoony special feature – two silver spikes sticking out from each side. She was nominated for more awards again this year, and she was also going to perform a song near the top of the show.

As for Russell, he was about to give a commanding performance as the host of the night's proceedings. As Jack Bayles, one of his English producers has revealed, the countdown to the show itself involved nerve-racking decisions about which jokes would work for an audience that included a considerable number of pop stars and celebrities with very large egos.

But the show started on an emotional note: Madonna came on stage to deliver an eight-minute tribute to the late Michael Jackson, followed by a performance from Janet Jackson of her and Michael's song 'Scream'.

Then Katy took the stage – surprisingly dressed in pants – to kick off the main show by singing Queen's 'We Will Rock You' with Aerosmith's Joe Perry (no relation) accompanying her on guitar. Then Russell – wearing a tuxedo and top hat – emerged at the top of a set of steps, his name emblazoned in 10ft-high lights behind him. He immediately started by making a cheeky reference to Katy's bottom in those pants – and noting that he and she were staying at the same hotel that night.

Katy wasn't the only pop star he was to proposition, but she remained prominent in his thoughts. He went on to debunk the rumours flying around that Lady Gaga wasn't actually a girl. 'There's been a lot of mudslinging and rumour-mongering and rubbish, people saying that she's a hermaphrodite,' Russell said. 'I think it's a disgrace that a woman cannot be successful, sexy and have an aggressive sexuality without people saying, "Oh, she must be a bloke." That is sexist. And I would like to condemn the male-dominated media for their disgusting treatment of this incredible woman. And if you haven't worked it out by now, yeah, I'm trying to fuck her.' The bleep man in the TV control room was having a busy night.

Russell also turned to politics. The year before, he had been outspoken about then-President Bush and raised the hackles of millions of Americans. This time he defended Barack Obama, now President – as Russell had requested of the MTV audience the previous year – but struggling to get his proposals for free healthcare for millions more Americans through Congress, the American Parliament.

Perhaps slighted by attacks on the UK's national health service by opponents of Obama's proposals, the left-leaning Russell waded provocatively into the debate by talking about the differences between Britain and the US. 'Instead of "truck" we say "lorry", instead of "elevator" we say "lift" – and instead of letting people die in the street we have free healthcare.'

But anything that Russell might have said this year was overshadowed by the extraordinary and outrageous behaviour of Kanye West. The hip-hop star already had a reputation for his antics at MTV Awards shows – having stormed the stage to complain when he failed to win the Best Video award one year at the MTV Europe Music Awards. But this year he surpassed himself: after young singer Taylor Swift had come on to accept her Best Female Video award, Kanye stormed on stage to inform her (and a viewing audience of many millions) that she didn't deserve to win it, because Beyoncé's video was one of the best ever made.

At the end of the awards – after Beyoncé had won Best Video of the Year for 'Single Ladies (Put a Ring on It)' – Russell ended the show by saying he intended to console Katy Perry – who had left empty-handed – and be her 'shoulder to cry on'. It was a comment that no one considered remarkable at the time, considering Russell's reputation. But he was true to his word – with a surprising outcome.

At the end of the VMAs, Russell was whisked to the exclusive Manhattan nightspot Avenue, where Lady Gaga was throwing an extravagant after-show party to celebrate her Best New Artist award. And Katy Perry was there too.

CHAPTER 27

Love Blooms

AFTER THE MTV VIDEO MUSIC AWARDS LADY GAGA'S PARTY AT AVENUE WAS DEFINITELY THE PLACE TO BE. SHE HAD EARLIER GIVEN A RIVETING PERFORMANCE OF 'PAPARAZZI' THAT ENDED IN HER SLUMPED ON THE STAGE, APPARENTLY FATALLY WOUNDED. NOW, CELEBRATING HER VMA AWARD, SHE DANCED ON THE NIGHTCLUB'S SOFAS TO HER OWN SONGS. THE OTHER BIG STORY OF THE NIGHT WAS, OF COURSE, KANYE WEST'S ANTICS THAT HAD UPSTAGED POOR TAYLOR SWIFT DURING HER BIG MOMENT.

But while it wasn't headline news in another eventful VMA night, the activities of Russell Brand and Katy Perry on a banquette at Gaga's aftershow party didn't go unnoticed.

The following day, their encounter was reported in New York's top newspaper gossip column – Page Six of the *New York Post*. An 'onlooker' had reportedly seen them together. 'They were sitting together, flirting and whispering to each other with their faces very close,' said the source. 'Then Russell leaned in for a long kiss. It didn't look like this was the first time. He was looking extremely pleased with himself.'

Russell's reputation for womanising meant that this was to some extent only par for the course. So this was simply a bit of post-VMAs fun by a couple of footloose stars out for a good time and nothing more. Wasn't it?

Certainly if you were scanning the newspapers in the following few days to find stories about a blossoming romance between Russell Brand and Katy Perry, you would have been disappointed. There was surprisingly little – even in British newspapers, always hungry for Brand gossip.

But what happened between Russell and Katy that night in New York was really quite special. The true facts, and their reverberations, only became public knowledge a couple of weeks later. By that time, Russell and Katy had already enjoyed their first holiday together.

Their post-VMAs encounter in New York was followed by days of flirting over the phone, as they both went back to their respective homes. Then, a few days afterwards, Russell sent Katy a love poem – possibly of his own composition – expressing his considerable ardour for her. He also attached a note saying: 'Please send me a poem back.'

He got one. Katy messaged Russell a photo – a shot of her cleavage with one word written across it: 'POEM'. Katy clearly had the hots for Russell just as much as Russell had the hots for Katy.

By all accounts, Russell 'killed himself laughing' when Katy sent him that photo. He liked her style. This was a girl obviously up for some fun. So he picked up the phone and invited her to fly off to Thailand with him for a week. Katy accepted the invitation.

To be sure, this was a familiar Brand tactic with girls he liked. He had done it before with several others – and South East Asia was a favourite destination, because of Russell's interest in Eastern religions, mysticism and meditation, and its air of tranquility and peace. It was a great place to achieve the required state of bliss for himself and whoever was accompanying him. In other words, a week-long bout of sun, sand and serious shagging has been his *modus operandi* for years.

So Russell took Katy to Thailand and that's when they started to get to know each other. They really hit it off – and it wasn't just about the shagging. There was a meeting of minds too. There was real chemistry. There was poetry.

Russell and Katy became the Owl and the Pussycat: Russell the wise owl, a fount of wisdom, and Katy the sex kitten. Edward Lear's famous nonsense ditty was one of the poems that Russell recited to Katy on their holiday – telling how the two animals sail off in a beautiful pea-green boat, and Owl sings: '*Oh lovely Pussy! Oh Pussy my love, what a beautiful Pussy you are,*' and the pair are eventually married in '*the land where the Bong-tree grows.*' It became a private joke between them – they would use the pairing as nicknames for each other.

It was only on their return that the wider world became aware that they had even been together on holiday. It was a blissful Katy who went public – accidentally? deliberately? – via Twitter on 1 October. No names were mentioned but she wrote that she had just enjoyed a 'magical' week in Thailand, adding that she'd been 'schooled on Morrissey, Oscar Wilde and Peter Sellers... inspired.' As it was well known that this trio were heroes of a certain English comedian, people were soon putting two and two together.

A couple of days later, Katy posted an even more intriguing message via Twitter: 'Pssst... I've got a secret. HUGE news coming in a couple days! No, my ego is not prego.' What could she mean?

And what about Russell? He also mentioned on his Twitter feed that he had spent a week in Thailand, but there was nothing about Katy's presence. Instead, he focused on other subjects – Buddhism and elephants. Even after Katy's semi-revelatory tweets, this still seemed, in all likelihood, like one of his familiar flings. Then, a couple of days after Russell had returned to London, he was spotted taking two girls back to his place in Hampstead. Same old Russell then?

But then something strange happened. Katy had also travelled to London, and the first time she and Russell were spotted together by the British press was when they were seen coming out of his £2 million home in Hampstead, walking around his leafy neighbourhood and enjoying a cooked breakfast in a local café.

Then Katy left to attend the spring fashion shows in Paris – where she was seen arm-in-arm with another man and having lunch with him – ironically in the restaurant L'Avenue (the same name as the New York club where she'd first canoodled with Russell). Maybe she had dumped Russell already, having heard about him and the two girls?

But a day later, after being approached by reporters as he left his home, Russell made a surprise confession when quizzed about Katy. 'I think I'm in love,' he said. He wouldn't divulge any details nor make any jokes about the saucy stuff either. 'I don't think I should be drawn on that.'

And a day or so later – after Katy had skipped Lily Allen's performance at the Chanel show, apparently due to an upset between the two – Russell joined Katy in Paris. He just had to be with her. They were photographed together for the first time, going into the Fendi fashion house catwalk show – Katy in a powder blue 1960s-style mini-dress with suspenders visible above her white stockings. Their relationship was out in the open. And the man she was spotted having lunch with at L'Avenue turned out to be her gay friend Markus Molinari the fashion designer.

The following day Katy and Russell were spotted hand-in-hand at the famous Père Lachaise Cemetery, visiting the grave of The Doors' singer and 1960s rock god Jim Morrison – a man also renowned for his sexual appetite and debauched behaviour – before attending more fashion shows that evening.

Katy was again using Twitter to strongly suggest her feelings for Russell. Explaining her recent lack of activity to her followers, she tweeted that she was 'in a love K-hole'. She might have been making an imaginative comparison to the catatonic state caused by taking the horse-tranquiliser ketamine (an American party drug) but the implication was clear.

As the two enjoyed the final day or so of this momentous trip to one of the most romantic cities in the world, Katy posted, on Twitter, lyrics from a Rufus Wainwright song, 'The Tower of Learning'. It was all about falling in love in Paris.

Russell had his own for Katy. They came from his great hero Morrisey, and a lesser-known 1995 track, 'Whatever Happens, I Love You'. The lyrics were simple and spoke of the fact that when everything else was set aside, his love for Katy would remain. The papers were saying he was going to have the chorus tattooed on an intimate part of his body.

Russell and Katy had only been an item for a couple of weeks, but they were already head over heels in love.

CHAPTER 28

Happy Birthday Katy

AFTER THE HEADY ROMANCE OF PARIS, KATY FLEW BACK TO THE US WHILE RUSSELL RETURNED TO LONDON FOR A FEW DAYS. BUT HE WOULD SOON BE BACK IN LOS ANGELES, WHERE KATY WOULD BE WAITING FOR HIM – AND WHERE HE FACED THE FIRST BIG CHALLENGE OF THEIR RELATIONSHIP: MEETING MUM AND DAD.

Meeting your girlfriend's parents is always a big hurdle for a young chap, but this was definitely going to test Russell's famous charm and gift of the gab. This was a man whose sexual conquests had run into thousands of females – to say nothing of a handjob on a gay man for the sake of a TV show. He was also a recovering heroin, crack and alcohol addict – and, if truth be told, quite possibly a sex addict too. On top of everything else, he was fonder of Eastern religions like Hinduism and Buddhism than any Western faith system. So how would he gain the confidence and approval of Keith and Mary Hudson, two evangelical born-again Christians who spent their time travelling America spreading the word of Jesus Christ?

It was true that although Katy had started out singing gospel in their church, she no longer shared her parents' strict beliefs. She had strayed from their path a good time before she met Russell. But far from being estranged from her parents, she still had a strong, loving relationship with them. And so, quite naturally, she wanted them to meet Russell – and Russell to meet them.

Why was this so important? Because, unbelievably, marriage was already being aired as a possibility. In any case, on 25 October it would be Katy's 25th birthday. There was no way around it: Russell would be meeting her parents.

Katy picked Russell up from LA International airport on 16 October, squealing with delight when she saw him. 'She looked like the cat who got the cream,' said an onlooker. 'She pounced on him as soon as he got in the car.' From that point, whenever the pair were seen in public they would invariably be kissing and cuddling as if they were, in the words of one member of the pursuing press pack, 'besotted teenagers'.

A couple of days after his arrival, Russell and Katy were spotted partying at H Wood, one of LA's hippest nightspots. When the club's DJ, realising that Katy was in the house, started playing 'I Kissed a Girl', Katy put on a show for Russell with a female friend. They started giving him a lap dance then, near the end of the song, they pulled each other close for a kiss – before pulling away at the last moment and laughing. Then Katy fell on a saucer-eyed Russell for a proper kiss.

Katy was certainly acting like a besotted teenager – impetuous, impulsive and head-over-heels happy. That included hiring a plane to skywrite 'I Love You' over Russell's home near Sunset Boulevard.

With Katy's birthday approaching, it was Russell's turn to come up with something special. Perhaps unsurprisingly, he was spotted visiting the exclusive sex toy and lingerie shop Coco De Mer a few days before the big day. But it was widely reported that he also had an even more imaginative gift in mind.

After going to see the movie *Where the Wild Things Are* at The Grove leisure complex in Hollywood, Katy had been greatly taken with the petting zoo set up temporarily next to the venue, with real animals in one section and amazing animatronic creatures in the other. Katy had wanted to milk the fake cow and ride the fake pony, but didn't want to be photographed. As a result, the media claimed, Russell was organising for the petting zoo to visit her home for her birthday – at an estimated cost of around £20,000.

Whether or not Russell actually went through with the petting zoo surprise for Katy, they definitely celebrated her 25th birthday in style. Her party was held at Hollywood's Sunset Beach club, where Russell made a very rare appearance out of his customary uniform of black skinny jeans and T-shirt. Like Katy and everyone else, he was wearing all-white – although neither of them ended the evening that way. Katy had hired a team of face-painters for the all-white themed party, but apparently things got rather out of hand. By the time they left, their clothes were spattered in red, blue, purple, pink, orange and other colours – with Russell sporting Katy-sized handprints on his chest.

It seems Russell also met Katy's folks at the birthday bash. Her dad, Keith, had a gift for Russell too – a copy of the book he had written called *The Cry*, which Keith described as a guide designed to 'release the desperate longing for God's intervention in your life'. In return, Russell handed him *My Booky Wook*, with its detailed accounts of his adventures with drugs, alcohol and women.

It must be doubtful if this initial encounter quelled Keith and Mary Hudson's doubts about this foppish Englishman's commitment to their beautiful daughter, despite their obvious passion for one another. Whatever the Hudsons' feelings, there were plenty of others who had their doubts.

Over the following days Katy and Russell were spotted in her hometown of Santa Barbara. With their romance now generating serious coverage in the tabloids on both sides of the Atlantic, it was inevitable that someone would soon comment about the likelihood of 'sex junkie' Russell Brand's ability to curb his womanising instincts. Step forward Georgina Baillie – Andrew Sachs' granddaughter and the subject of Russell and Jonathan Ross's huge radio controversy 12 months earlier. Perhaps understandably, Georgina took a swipe.

'Everyone knows you don't date Russell Brand seriously,' she said. 'Russell likes the idea of having a serious relationship, but when you've got all these different flavours of ice cream offered to you on a plate, you're not going to stick with vanilla, are you? I don't think he's capable of monogamy.'

She was entitled to her opinion, but Russell was talking about the very thing that would make the jaws of hardened Brand-watchers drop in astonishment. He was no longer content with his philandering lifestyle. He was talking about settling down and having kids.

'I am feeling broody. I've grown weary of the carousel,' he announced. 'Regardless of what happens in my current situation, I am unlikely to be satisfied with the calamitous promiscuity of the preceding five or six years.'

Calamitous promiscuity? Could this be Russell Brand talking? The *Sun*'s Shagger Of The Year for three years in succession and favourite 'swordsman'? Maybe meeting Katy's parents had had an effect on him after all.

Before they headed back to London at the beginning of November, Russell was with Katy in the studio – the famous Sunset Sound studios in Hollywood, where rock giants like The Rolling Stones, the Beach Boys and Jim Morrison's Doors had all recorded. Russell, messing around, started to recite the poem *The Owl and the Pussycat* into a microphone. By all accounts, Katy blushed at the line 'O let us be married, too long have we tarried' – and then she joined in, singing a refrain to Russell's speech.

It seems everyone who heard it was completely transfixed. It was beautiful.

CHAPTER 29

A Big Surprise for Rusty

At the beginning of November, Russell and Katy headed back to London together. Russell was going to be performing the final shows of his *Scandalous* stand-up tour, and in a few days Katy would be hosting the MTV European Music Awards in Berlin – also for the second year running. It was where she would demonstrate her devotion to her man in spectacular, headline-grabbing fashion...

On Monday 2 November, Russell was at a Music Industry Trust dinner at London's Grosvenor House Hotel, hanging out with his mates Noel Gallagher and Jonathan Ross. A year after his and Russell's very public troubles over Sachsgate, 'Wossy' was to receive the Trust's award for his services to the music industry from George Michael.

Russell and Jonathan were clearly still big pals. 'I'm showing my support for Jonathan,' he commented at the dinner. 'I definitely want to do more work together – I love working with him. He'd do fantastically well in the US – he's the best chat show host in the world.' Food for thought for Ross, who would announce his departure from the BBC – no doubt partly due to the continuing fallout of bad publicity generated by the Sachsgate scandal – a few weeks later.

There were rumoured to be plenty of females at the bash who were keen to gain Russell's attention. But he wasn't interested. As Noel Gallagher told a journalist: 'He's a changed man is Russell.' The famous dinkle was now the property of one lady only.

Then it was Katy's turn to step up to the challenge of fronting an MTV awards show before a live TV audience of millions. The MTV European Music Awards (or the EMAs, as opposed to the American VMAs) was being held in Berlin on 5 November, with another platoon of stars showing up and performances from Beyoncé, Shakira, the Foo Fighters, Katy herself and more.

When she had hosted the previous year's bash in Liverpool, Katy had worn no fewer than 11 outfits – including an American football uniform and a fairground carousel frock – and appeared to ride a banana and stand on two cherries. This year she was promising a more daring and risqué show highlighting her natural assets.

'I'm going to highlight what God gave me – what my momma made – with lots of booby things,' she explained. 'There will be a lot of costumes but fewer clothes. I am using lace, feathers and garters. Some of the outfits will be almost just "nip slips" but not quite fully exposed. Last year it was fruity and kitsch and fun. But this year the fruit has gone sour.

'It's darker, sexier, it's sultry, it's romantic – maybe with an undertone of S&M – but not really!' she added quickly. Her inspiration was the Oscar-winning musical *Cabaret*, set in decadent 1930s Berlin. 'I've been glued to the TV watching Liza [Minnelli]'s song and dance numbers. So I've picked up my make-up tips from her and got that overall 1930s dark romantic vibe.'

Katy was also asked if she'd had any tips from Russell. 'We're stepping on each other's turfs. I've learned a couple of things from Russell over the last months that might not be appropriate for this! MTV asked me back because I have this "no fear" attitude. I don't care if I do fall over or if a boob does fall out!'

Katy didn't fall over and no boob fell out, but she didn't disappoint. She wore an array of stunning costumes – each more outrageous than the last. She walked down the red carpet at Berlin's O2 World Arena in a demure floor-length pink Marchesa gown, but then went on to reveal lots more flesh in a series of sexy skimpy outfits that set the burlesque *Cabaret* theme in Katy's very own Kitty Kat Club. At different times she wore lace, feathers and latex rubber, an orange ball gown with shapes cut out of the flared skirt, and hot pants with spikes. 'Last year I broke my MTV cherry,' she announced. 'This year I'm more experienced – if you know what I mean.'

She certainly did her *Cabaret* thing – dancing around a chair wearing a German military hat and ringmaster-style basque outfit. And rather like one of her style inspirations, burlesque star Dita Von Teese, she appeared in a giant stiletto. She told the crowd: 'They say if men have big shoes they have big... The confusing thing is I borrowed this from Lady Gaga!'

But the real headline-grabbing moment was when she took to the stage wearing a basque, knickers and a garter – in the claret-and-blue colours of Russell's beloved football team, West Ham United, with a club badge over each breast. What's more, there was one word emblazoned across the back of her knickers: RUSTY – a reference to the man whose Twitter monicker is Rustyrockets. Could Katy, widely praised for her performance at the EMAs, make her feelings for Russell any clearer?

Not surprisingly, Rustyrockets himself was quick to express his delight. 'Wow. Now MY GIRLFRIEND has worn a West Ham basque while hosting the EMAs. What a day!' he tweeted on Twitter. 'I might revive Gandhi and ask if he wants to be mates. I'm off to meditate now, though unless enlightenment includes Richard Pryor and Bobby Moore caressing me, how can this be improved?'

He added: 'I will be taking Katy to a game at Upton Park – West Ham vs Everton [the following Sunday]. And, before it begins, no I won't be taking her up the Arsenal.' Later he said, 'I don't think she realised the impact that would have on me! She looked amazing in it.'

Did he take Katy to Upton Park that Sunday? Probably not, as Russell had a big gig that evening: the final show of his *Scandalous* stand-up tour at the Royal Albert Hall. But two weeks later, West Ham cannily launched a limited-edition lingerie range inspired by Katy's undies – at £300 each. They had been in touch with Siobhan Dillon, the freelance celebrity stylist and costume designer who had designed the basque, after she had revealed how she made the whole thing from real West Ham shirts. 'I used the collars along the top of the brassiere and used the two badges on the front,' she had explained. 'I had a team of three girls working with me on the outfit. It was made entirely from three shirts, but we had to take the Aertex out and replace it with some lining.'

Meanwhile, during Russell's final *Scandalous* show, he had some news for the audience: he had promised to be faithful to Katy. 'I've taken a pledge,' he informed the full house of 5,000. 'I can't break it now. There will be no more threesomes.' Was there an audible sigh from the audience?

Asked that weekend if he was in love, Russell had answered: 'It seems that I am.' Questioned further, he was asked how he knew he was in love after his years of womanising. He replied: 'Because of this overwhelming urge to change and to be beautiful to everyone and to be kind.'

CHAPTER 30

A Lovely Christmas

THE FOLLOWING DAY WAS KATY'S LAST IN LONDON BEFORE SHE FLEW BACK TO LA. BECAUSE OF THIS, SHE CANCELLED AN APPEARANCE ON A BRITISH TV SHOW – *CHRIS MOYLES'S QUIZ NIGHT* – SO SHE AND RUSSELL COULD SPEND THEIR LAST NIGHT TOGETHER. RUSSELL PHONED THE PORTLY MOTORMOUTH DJ HIMSELF TO OFFER HIS EXCUSES AND APOLOGIES.

Moyles was fairly miffed, but that was nothing compared to the apparent fury at EMI, Katy's troubled record company, which regarded Moyles's TV show as a major PR opportunity. Instead, Russell and Katy went out to eat at Dans Le Noir – a trendy restaurant in East London where diners eat in total darkness – and went home early.

As Katy was returning to LA, her *MTV Unplugged* show was about to be premiered on MTV.com – and Russell himself was given the freedom of the *Sun*'s Bizarre column to inform their readers of its imminent arrival. It was an opportunity that Russell could not resist.

Under a photo of Katy in her West Ham kit, with the word 'RUSTY' visible on her knickers, Russell wrote: 'A less dignified man might say: "Not the first time I've decorated her bottom." Katy Perry's *MTV Unplugged* will be premiered online at MTV.com on Monday. From my unbiased perspective it seems it will be magnificent. I wouldn't want people to think I was "plugging her un-plugged". Naturally I would never be so vulgar as to make a crass "plugging" pun at this point as I am an English gent.' But not too much of a gent to indulge in some good old English vulgarity.

Russell was soon back in LA with Katy. There was work to be done that he had been neglecting during the past few weeks of blissful happiness. There was a new documentary – a sequel to his BBC show when he followed the path of the characters in Jack Kerouac's 'beat generation' novel *On the Road*. This time he was to work with legendary Hollywood bad-boy director Oliver Stone. Then there was the second volume of his autobiography. After the massive success of *My Booky Wook*, he had won a lucrative book deal for a sequel – but the planned publication date for late 2009 had already come and gone. There were also his various movie projects, including the remake of *Arthur*.

Meanwhile Katy had commitments of her own: she was back in the studio to record her all-important follow-up album to *One of the Boys*. Just before she left LA to host the EMAs in Berlin, she had announced that work had started on the album, and she was planning to collaborate with a platoon of top producers to craft her some more magic. These included The-Dream and, Christopher 'Tricky'

Stewart – who wrote 'Single Ladies (Put a Ring on It)' for Beyoncé and 'Umbrella' for Rihanna, Max Martin, Ryan Tedder, Calvin Harris – and Lukasz 'Dr Luke' Gottwald, who had helped to guide *One Of The Boys* to glory.

But another big moment was coming for the couple. At the end of November there would be a proper getting-to-know-you holiday break for Russell, Katy and the rest of her family. Russell had met Katy's parents at her birthday party but this would be a few days together – the sort of thing you only do if you're really serious about somebody.

Although they had raised Katy and her brother and sister in Santa Barbara, California, Keith and Mary Hudson now had a travelling ministry, roving the breadth of the United States from their base in Temecula, a small place 74 miles south of Los Angeles. But the get-together with was not to happen on American soil, or even in the UK. It was to be in the popular Austrian ski resort of Ischgl, where Katy was performing to open the winter season. An Alpine retreat would be the perfect opportunity for Katy's folks and Russell to get to know each other a little better, while Katy could release her tomboy side – she's an experienced snowboarder.

Katy's pastor-parents had already declared their views about their daughter romancing a former heroin addict and recovering alcoholic, to say nothing of his treatment for sex addiction. Mary had made it all very clear back home in Temecula.

'Russell must go towards the light and not towards the darkness – only God can take the very worst person and turn them around for good,' she told the congregation at The Way Family Church, shortly before they flew out to Austria for the big Alpine summit. 'You just have to see how the Lord's will is done. I mean, how many times have your kids disappointed you so profoundly that you wanted to get up from the chair and knock them out?'

You could hardly blame the Hudsons for being wary of this English guy of ill-repute going out with their daughter. But in fact Keith and Mary already seemed prepared to give Russell the benefit of the doubt and regard him in a fairly positive light. They had clearly read his book but they were willing to accept him.

'There are parts of Russell's book where he's really hungry for positive influences in his life,' Mary Hudson said. 'I think the two of them are hungry. They are basically looking for God and they are seeking the truth – and they are going to find it.'

Then Keith chipped in. 'We all have a past,' he said. 'I was in the Jimi Hendrix and Janis Joplin era, and I used to take LSD. [Russell]'s got a real spiritual hunger. He really likes us because he has a whole new different concept on Christianity now that he has met us.'

When the family – including Katy's sister Angela and brother David – all met up in Ischgl at the end of November, things got under way with Katy performing a storming show of her hits at the ski resort in a suitably seasonal costume. It was what she called her 'slutty sexy Santa outfit' and she dedicated it to 'all her ex-boyfriends'. Later on, when asked by a journalist if she would be joining the 'gondola club' – the skiing equivalent of the mile-high club – she replied: 'Sure, why not? I'm freaky.' Then she and Russell took a gondola ride to a mountaintop restaurant.

Katy clearly wasn't toning things down in Austria for the sake of her mum and dad, so it's no wonder that Russell was nervous – as he explained a few days later. For a start, he pointed out, Katy's dad Keith looked intimidating. 'Have you seen a picture of him? He's got a shaved head and he's tense-looking. But if you're a proper Christian, it means that you've got to be a gentle, loving, compassionate soul.'

But rather like Katy, Keith and Mary proved susceptible to Russell's charms, his well-read intelligence, his sharp wit – and his Englishness. 'They love the old-school Englishness,' he revealed. 'There's a thing where the mom said, "Nothing's impossible," and I went, "Well, of course, Nelson Mandela said that everything is impossible until it's done." And she went, "Oh," and she really enjoyed that.'

Russell was cautiously enthusiastic about Mary and Keith when he was talking to DJ Christian O'Connell on his show on Absolute Radio. 'Obviously when I heard that my girlfriend had preacher parents, I thought, "Well, this has got a huge scope for disaster," but it's actually been quite good so far. I've been bringing out quotes. I'm doing well, you know, because I'm committed to it and they're lovely, lovely people. It's been nice.'

Russell was back in London, doing a round of media interviews as the DVD of his *Scandalous* stand-up show hit the stores for Christmas. Inevitably he was deluged with questions about Katy, and it was evident he really couldn't be happier or more relaxed. This really did look like a new Russell Brand.

'She's amazing," he told O'Connell. 'I'm having a right laugh. She's a good person to spend time with and it's changed me. It's made me stop doing stuff that I probably shouldn't have been doing.

'I didn't drink or take drugs, so my main hobby was, like, meet girls, chat them up. Once you stop doing that, everything's a lot more relaxing if you're not, everywhere you go, thinking, "Right, shall I chat to her?" Now I'm just talking to people, do a bit of yoga, meditate, look out the window, think about the cat – you know, it's a more chilled out pace of life.'

Another interviewer noted that the press had been unusually positive about his and Katy's relationship – perhaps sensing that this really was something special. 'I don't know. I certainly am – it's been fantastic,' Russell responded. 'She's a lovely person to spend time with. You learn to divorce yourself with how it's dealt with by other people, and get on with how it is between the pair of us. Press attention can be a little annoying but there isn't much you can do about it. It's part of it, and in a way it's nice because you feel you're hiding away in an igloo.'

On GMTV, Lorraine Kelly asked the question many people really wanted to know: would he be popping the question?

'I don't know, get married, you say? That would be good, wouldn't it?' he replied. 'I want to have children – that would be good.' And now he'd realised that all those girls for all those years – it was simply all about him looking for Ms Right. 'It was a deep craving within me –

I mistook it for lust. I thought I was promiscuous, but it turns out I was just thorough – to get the right one. I'm ever so happy.'

But it wasn't all sweetness and light: Russell accused *Daily Mail* journalist Nathan Kay of writing lies about him. The reporter claimed that Russell had spoken to him about marrying Katy Perry, and didn't want Katy's parents to join them on holiday. Writing on Twitter about the article, Brand tweeted: 'The *Daily Mail* tell lies. "Nathan Kay" is a pustule of untruth. I suppose we ought be grateful they've stopped supporting Hitler.'

* * *

So what would Russell be getting Katy for Christmas? Would it be simply a Christmas gift? On 11 December Russell was spotted browsing the diamond rings at Cartier on Bond Street. The *Ponderland* star was clearly pondering handing over a serious wedge for the best diamond ring he could find in the best diamond jewellery store in London.

Was this sensible behaviour for a man renowned for his dependence on drugs, alcohol and sex? There were always going to be doubters, and an LA-based clinical psychologist and 'addiction expert' called Dr Seth Meyers popped up to make the case that Russell and Katy should take a far more cautious approach to their relationship. It was, after all, just three months old.

'Addicts sometimes make impulsive romantic decisions,' Dr Meyers told gossip website HollywoodLife.com. 'The inclination is often for the addicts to jump into the relationship as a means of self-medicating. Serious romantic relationships can trigger strong addictive feelings, which can lead to relapse.

'Addiction affects everyone,' the psychologist continued. 'It has a great impact on the romantic partner. [Katy] might end up worrying more about Russell than herself. This is dangerous because it can create co-dependence.'

So how long should they wait before tying the knot? 'Marriage is something maybe you think about after you've had at least two years of sobriety and have been with your significant other around two years.'

But Russell and Katy would not be taking Dr Meyers' advice. When they were thousands of miles apart, the lovebirds kept talking by what Russell has described as 'the kinky miracle of iChat', by which he meant they could talk to – and see – each other most of the time. But Christmas was approaching and they would have to get closer than that. Would there be a Christmas proposal? Russell actually denied it. 'I've done enough damage to Christianity without tarnishing that special day,' he quipped.

But there was a sense that momentous things were about to happen. Russell was reported as saying that he could not relocate to the US permanently because of Morrissey – his cat – but he was now spending as much time in LA as he was in London – and he wanted to spend all his time with Katy. When he returned to Los Angeles a couple of weeks before Christmas he would make a big decision about his future with Katy. He would buy a house.

Russell's drug- and alcohol-free existence meant that

he also fitted well into the health- and body-conscious LA lifestyle. With Katy making almost daily visits to the gym, Russell had also got into the celeb routine of regular exercise to maintain the body beautiful. In the warm climate of southern California, Russell would usually go jogging in his West Ham football shorts, a singlet – a favourite Brand item of clothing – and, quite weirdly, long socks that looked like he'd borrowed them from Katy. But his exercising regime, including visits to the gym, meant that he was now appearing more toned and even muscular.

Of course there were other good-looking, well-fit guys around in LA – not least Robert Pattinson, the English star of the vampire movie series *Twilight*. In mid-December it was reported that Katy had been spotted 'flirting outrageously' with Pattinson in a Hollywood karaoke bar. That night, Katy had given Robert a lift home in her chauffeur-driven car. The next day Russell would fly home to the UK for Christmas after being given a loving farewell at the airport by Katy – but now the press were implying that Katy was playing behind his back with 'R-Patz'.

This quickly drew a withering response from Katy. 'Read a bunch of yesterdays news – B**LOCKS,' she steamed on Twitter, showing a fine command of English terminology. 'Ppl should know by now that I don't do vampires, but I do DO @rustyrockets [Russell's Twitter username]. Don't get it TWISTED!'

Katy would soon follow Russell to London – where a new experience would await her. London was covered with heavy snow and Rustyrockets was planning to turn his hometown into a winter wonderland for her.

Russell wanted Katy to see London at its best at this joyful season of the year – it was actually threatening to be a white Christmas for once – so they walked from his home onto nearby Hampstead Heath, where Russell took his delighted girlfriend on a thrilling sledge-ride down the long and steep Parliament Hill. After that, they walked hand-in-hand on the Heath, he took her to a carol service at London's greatest church, St Paul's Cathedral and then to a musical – *The Lion King* – in the West End.

They were like any other normal, very happy young couple, so completely into each other that no one else came close. The paparazzi took their photos of them as they walked happily through the snow in Hampstead, but as Russell had said, they were living in their own little igloo of love.

A couple of days later Katy would use Twitter to joke that she was busy coming to terms with the differences between UK English and the version she was used to speaking: 'Chips/crisps. Trash/bin. Trunk/boot. Bathroom/loo. Zebra/Zahbra. Vitamins/Vitaminz. Lady bug/Lady bird. I need English lessons.'

Russell also gave Katy another new experience in English culture when he took her to watch a big pre-Christmas football match. Of course, it was to Upton Park to watch his beloved West Ham United.

West Ham were playing their London rivals Chelsea in a important Premier League match – Cheryl Cole, whose husband Ashley was playing for Chelsea, was also in the crowd. Form suggested that the Hammers, struggling at the foot of the league, would suffer a hammering against table-topping Chelsea, but whether or not Katy was wearing her claret-and-blue basque to the game (and she did buy a claret-and-blue Santa hat in the club shop), she proved to be a lucky charm for Russell's team as they managed a 1-1 draw. But quite possibly not even a West Ham defeat would have dented Russell's happiness at that point.

In a few days Katy would get a Christmas present that would indicate that his heart no longer resided mainly in East London. Russell had bought a $3.2 million house in Los Angeles – a four-storey, four bedroom, four bathroom love nest for Katy and himself in the hills above downtown LA. (Katy's Christmas gifts to Russell were some nice wheels so he could get around Los Angeles – once he'd passed his driving test, that is.)

Russell had spent a lot of time in America over the past couple of years. He had been in movies, appeared on chat shows, done some stand-up and hosted the MTV Video Music Awards two years running. But this was different. It was clear: Russell was moving to LA – permanently.

But before that, he and Katy would be heading somewhere else. Between Christmas and New Year they left London for much warmer climes. They were going to India, for a very special New Year's Eve.

CHAPTER 31

We're Engaged!

AS FAR AS THE WORLD KNEW, RUSSELL AND KATY WERE IN LONDON, OR MAYBE IN AMERICA. IN THE DAYS LEADING UP TO CHRISTMAS THEY HAD BEEN TOGETHER AT RUSSELL'S HOME IN HAMPSTEAD, MAKING THE MOST OF A SNOWY, VERY FESTIVE CITY. BUT THEY HAD ALSO JUST LOCKED THEIR DOOR AND SPENT A LOT OF TIME TOGETHER AT HOME, LIKE ANY OTHER YOUNG COUPLE WHO WERE COMPLETELY INTO EACH OTHER. BUT THINGS THEN TOOK AN EXTRAORDINARY TURN, PROVING THAT RUSSELL AND KATY AREN'T REALLY QUITE LIKE EVERYBODY ELSE.

Rumours that Russell and Katy were engaged started to emerge between Christmas and New Year. On 27 December the *Sunday Mirror* reported that Russell had actually popped the question in the lead-up to Christmas – and she had said yes.

But something wasn't quite right. Quite possibly, that was the engagement ring. Was there a problem with the diamond ring that Russell had apparently bought at

Cartier in early December? Maybe. Because, according to the story, Russell would present 'a suitable ring' on New Year's Eve – probably in New York.

In fact, it soon became clear that they weren't going to be anywhere near New York as 2010 began. Or England, or California for that matter. They would be in India.

Katy had flown back to America to spend Christmas Day with her parents. But it was over a curry in London, when Katy had expressed her love of Indian culture, that Russell had surprised her. He was going to take her to India. It would be Katy's Christmas present – or at least one of them.

Two days before New Year's Eve, Katy posted a photo on Twitter, of herself and Russell hugging in front of the Taj Mahal. Beneath it she wrote: 'He built this for me.' The following day she tweeted: 'In India, the motto... you gotta go with the flow...'

They were staying in the ancient city of Jaipur, in Rajasthan, northern India, at the luxury Taj Rambagh Palace hotel. And when New Year's Eve came... well, Russell had planned it all with meticulous precision. Earlier in the day he had taken Katy to an ancient fort and bought her a traditional Indian dress – costing £600 – to wear for the night ahead. He would also wear a traditional Indian outfit for what would be a very special candlelit dinner.

Russell had asked the hotel staff to set up a table in a garden near the hotel, with candles everywhere. And then they arrived, by horse-drawn carriage. The meal that followed was just the start. Just before midnight, a guru arrived to bless their relationship in a traditional Indian ceremony.

There, in a tent at the foot of a mountain in Jaipur, in a ceremony usually intended to lead couples towards marriage, Russell and Katy were granted luck and divine happiness. That ritual had a special status, as that evening coincided with a 'blue moon' – an extra 13th full moon in the calendar year – which only occurs every two or three years.

Then at midnight Russell topped even that experience. Showing an imaginative sense of the occasion, he had specifically requested that he and Katy should bring in the new year watching fireworks – on the back of an elephant.

As Russell admitted a few weeks later, this almost scuppered the crucial moment when he proposed to Katy. 'We were on an elephant just before it. It was at midnight, and it is not a good idea to be on the back of an elephant during a fireworks display. They can't tell the difference between an apocalypse and New Year's Eve!'

Then it happened. Russell and Katy were taken to the Mughal Garden in the grounds of the Taj Rambagh Palace, which had been decorated with flowers and candles. Russell had had the diamond engagement ring hidden among a bouquet of flowers. Katy found it and Russell asked her to marry him. Katy immediately accepted. More fireworks.

Katy confessed later that she'd had a good idea it was going to happen. 'Unfortunately, I still Google myself sometimes,' she said. 'I saw it on Google alerts. I'm going to be honest!' But she must have had a pretty good idea even without Google's help.

A few days later rumours were circulating that Russell

had proposed. Katy tweeted: 'Happy New Years everyone... under a blue moon.' Then, a few days later, as if reliving the magical moment: 'Peacocks on rooftops, parrots on telephone lines, camels in the streets, elephants on the horizon.'

The American gossip magazine *US* broke the story on 5 January. 'He kissed a girl, and she liked it' they trumpeted on usmagazine.com. 'Katy Perry and Russell Brand are engaged, sources confirm.' The rest of the media rushed to substantiate the story and Russell texted the *Sun* to confirm the news: 'It's true. Much love.'

Katy tweeted: 'So when do I start walking the streets naked singing that Alanis song?' She was referring to the song 'So Called Chaos', by her big musical inspiration, Alanis Morissette.

By the time their engagement was announced, Russell and Katy were back from India. Just as it was becoming public knowledge, Katy revealed something about Russell's appeal to her, in an interview with *Glamour* magazine.

'He could slay anybody with the things he says. He doesn't even need his fists.' She revealed that she had fallen for him the first time they had kissed, on the set of *Get Him to the Greek* – when afterwards she had 'hopped like a bunny'. But then she added something surprising – that Russell was a good influence on her.

'I'm excited to find a partner who can just be my teammate,' she said. 'And there's got to be respect. For me, that's hard because it's easy for me to steamroll guys. I need a man who tells me the party's over, that it's time to go home, because [we] have to work in the morning.'

It was an interesting and perhaps surprising dynamic of

Russell and Katy's relationship, but in strange way it made sense. They were both hard-working and ambitious. Russell had shown immense discipline to put his alcohol and Class A substance abuse problems behind him, and although Katy was by no means wayward, he could show her a thing or two on that score.

Katy seemed to have another subject on her mind. In a series of enigmatic tweets that poured out in the days after the engagement was announced, she seemed to suggest that she might be pregnant. 'Let me tell you 2010 is BUMPIN!' she wrote on New Year's Day. Then there was a possible hint at morning sickness – 'i love you @rustyrockets (awwwww...barf)' – and then she tweeted Russell: 'Hey @Rustyrockets I heard ur prego-ed. I love you @Rustyrockets.'

The first time Russell and Katy were seen as an engaged couple was in London in early January – when much attention was paid to the third finger of Katy's left hand. It was sporting some serious bling: a beautiful square-cut diamond engagement ring set in a platinum band.

But what was more, they were then spotted browsing baby bootees in a children's shoe shop on Hampstead High Street on a Sunday afternoon stroll. Then, lunching in the local Café Rouge, Katy made sure her scrambled eggs were well done – uncooked eggs are a big no-no for pregnant women.

But a few days later Katy then scotched the idea with the unsubtle announcement on Twitter that her period had arrived. But all this pregnancy talk merely had emphasised the sense that Russell and Katy would be getting married within a few months – possibly sooner.

The newspapers were already speculating on what kind of star-studded event the wedding was likely to be. Russell's close pals included Jonathan Ross, Noel Gallagher, David Walliams and Morrissey, while Katy also had several close pop star friends, including Rihanna and Taylor Swift. It was already looking like an extraordinary celeb-packed guest list – and possibly a little troubling if you wondered what the likes of Gallagher and Walliams would make of, say, Katy's pal Miley Cyrus). The *Sun* reported that Russell had already made his manager Nik Linnen his best man and asked him to start preparing his speech.

But when the couple returned to Los Angeles, the first priority was moving into their new home – and getting some work done. Katy went back into the studio with Dr Luke to work on the follow-up to *One Of The Boys*. She had talked about the new record when she'd started working on it back in October, saying it would show "whether I'm meant to do this, or I got lucky."

She also made it clear that she intended to do another bunch of highly catchy pop-rock songs, with more of her biting lyrical edge. She revealed that the songs would focus on dealing with fame, friendships and her relationships. That had been before her relationship with Russell had really got going, so she now had a great deal more material – and was busy jotting down ideas in a beautiful notebook Russell had bought her in India.

At the same time, Katy did have a new record out – her guest vocal on Timbaland's song 'If We Ever Meet Again' was released as a single.

Then came the news that she had just finalised a

lucrative deal to become the new face of Proactiv, the American acne cream, following in the footsteps of previous campaign models Jessica Simpson and Jennifer Love Hewitt. Katy would star in TV ads shown all over the world, in which she'd discuss her own acne issues. She was quoted saying: 'I got acne at the start of my career. It was to leave acne scars which I'm self-conscious about.' Talking about it now for Proactiv was reported to be worth around $4 million.

Katy was also making a big impression on TV – as a judge in the preliminary rounds of *American Idol*, recorded some months earlier but now being shown on US TV in January. In particular, her minor run-in with fellow judge, the pop songwriter and producer Kara DioGuardi when they disagreed about one auditioner made great TV. DioGuardi even started singing 'I Kissed a Girl', which got a frosty response from Katy.

Katy described the *American Idol* experience as 'awesome' and said, 'If I was offered that job as a permanent host, I would ditch my career and take on that career.' Presumably she wasn't being entirely serious.

Meanwhile, Russell appeared to be getting his head down too. The follow-up autobiography, new stand-up material and more movie projects were all demanding his attention. And if renouncing promiscuity wasn't enough, he was even considering another previously unthinkable act – cutting his hair. Before Christmas he had admitted, 'I can't keep always playing long-haired, scruffy men, otherwise my career would be limited. I was hoping one day to play Napoleon, but I can't play Napoleon as this shaggy-haired, bearded raconteur. But I did also want to play Rasputin, the monk, so that'll be good – I can look like this.'

Far more likely to get off the ground was his remake of *Arthur* – possibly with Meryl Streep in the role of Arthur's butler, played so beautifully in the original by John Gielgud – or perhaps (and in a way far easier to improve on the original) *Drop Dead Fred*, a comedy-drama about an unhappy young woman whose life is turned upside down by the reappearance of an imaginary friend from her childhood. There was also talk of him recording some podcasts with Noel Gallagher, and writing again with his old collaborator Matt Morgan.

Russell had also been working on a documentary project with Oliver Stone before things had got serious with Katy. Whether that was actually amounting to anything – Stone having also being focused on making *Wall Street 2* – it came up when quotes in the press from an 'insider' were released, scurrilously casting doubt on Russell and Katy's long-term prospects.

'Russell has the shortest attention span on the planet,' sniped the 'insider'. 'He literally can't divide his attention between two things at once. When he decided to really give a relationship with Katy a shot, he put the documentary on hold. He said, "I think I'm going to try giving monogamy a shot for once."

'It's probably not going to last. He gets too distracted. He's so focused on one thing at a time, and when something new comes along his attention gets totally diverted. He's focused on Katy – for now. But how long will that last?'

But among those who were now fully convinced that

Russell was made of the right stuff were Katy's mum and dad. At a dinner to celebrate their daughter's engagement at Los Angeles restaurant Il Cielo in mid-January, Keith and Mary Hudson both gave speeches praising Russell. It was a dinner thrown mainly for Russell's benefit – a chance for him to meet Katy's relatives and friends – and the message was: 'He's won us over. He's part of the family.'

Katy's brother David gave a speech first, joking that he was almost as much in love with Russell as his sister. Then he mentioned the possibility of a baby Brand-Perry this time next year. Russ gave him a thumbs-up and grinned, with Katy jokingly saying, 'No, no!'

Then came a more uncomfortable moment when Katy's father recalled one of Russell's crude jokes. 'The first time I ever came across Russell it was at the VMAs when he talked about my daughter's hole,' remarked Keith. 'I didn't quite understand. But after that, I got to meet him and realised he was pretty OK. He loves my daughter and I cannot wait to welcome him into the family – he already feels like he is one of us. He is a wonderful guy and I think he makes Katy very happy. Russell has our blessing.'

Then Russell got up and said: 'I am so in love with you, Katy, and cannot wait to spend the rest of my life with you.'

He clearly had been thinking about getting hitched. 'We are going to do the wedding naked! All the families will be naked!' he announced to *People* magazine, before admitting that perhaps nerves ahead of the big day were starting to manifest themselves as he slept. 'All my dream weddings don't make sense,' he revealed. 'The vicar will start melting. The people in the front row will turn into people from my school. And then everyone will only say the word "potato".'

But he also added that he couldn't wait to walk down the aisle. 'I'm getting married to a beautiful woman. I'm enjoying my work. What could be better? Nothing!'

At the end of January the happy couple stepped out in Hollywood together for a big night out – at a music awards show that neither of them were hosting: the 2010 Grammy Awards. It was Russell's first Grammys, and he had clearly learned that is one of longest awards ceremonies on Earth – which led to something of a public tiff on the red carpet.

They had been invited to a prestigious event – prior to the awards themselves – to celebrate the career of the American music industry bigwig Clive Davis. Russell, speaking to TV reporters as he and Katy entered, said he thought this was a Clive Dunn event, and started singing the theme tune to *Dad's Army* – 'Who Do You Think You Are Kidding Mr Hitler?' – to the bewildered interviewer and shocked organisers of the event.

Then he added: 'Grammys – I know why it's called that. That's how much coke you need to cope with it.'

Katy, who caught the end of the exchange, didn't appear best pleased. 'Stop it and behave!' she scolded him. 'I don't want to upset the Grammys – I want one!' Later, several po-faced Hollywood fashion-celeb websites would affect horror at Russell's cocaine references, snatching at them as evidence that Russell really wasn't suitable material for Katy. Making jokes about drugs was clearly a sign that you were using them, they hinted, but Katy would know better.

At the Clive Davis dinner Katy was radiant. Her outfit for the Grammys included a reference to her magical Indian trip: her clinging fawn evening dress was accessorised with a Judith Leiber elephant clutch bag – in tribute to the elephant on which Russell had intended to propose until the fireworks intervened.

She and Russell were seated with Katy's friend Rihanna. While Russell drank tea, the girls were sipping cocktails and began to wind up Russell. Katy, a dab hand at napkin origami – particularly at turning them into rude things – transformed her dinner napkin into a pair of boobs. In response, Russell's simple creation rose out of his lap, as if hiding something very tall and erect underneath, while he wore a look of stupefied pleasure.

It wasn't big – well, not that big – and it wasn't clever. But it was funny. Rihanna was trying not to grin, to keep looking demure, but Katy was not bothered. She was killing herself laughing.

A week or so later, the trailer for *Get Him to the Greek* – Russell's big movie of 2010 – was released. That was funny too, and the movie, to be released in the US in early June, promises to be one of the comedy hit movies of the summer, if not the year. The question is: will Russell and Katy be married by then?

Don't be too surprised if at least one MTV awards show in 2010 is hosted by Russell and Katy – together.